PRELUDE TO WORLD POWER

HISTORY OF AMERICAN FOREIGN POLICY SERIES

GENERAL EDITOR: *Armin Rappaport*

Foster Rhea Dulles

PRELUDE TO
WORLD POWER

American Diplomatic History, 1860-1900

THE MACMILLAN COMPANY, NEW YORK
COLLIER-MACMILLAN LIMITED, LONDON

Table of Contents

Preface

This book covers the history of American foreign policy from the outbreak of the Civil War until the opening of the twentieth century. It is a time which may perhaps be divided into three major periods.

The first involves the active diplomacy which sought to forestall possible European intervention in the Civil War, helped repulse Louis Napoleon's aggressive designs on Mexico, and consummated the purchase of Alaska from Czarist Russia. A second period, extending through the 1870's and 1880's, found interest in foreign affairs at the lowest ebb in all American history, with the public almost totally absorbed in the overriding domestic problems arising from industrial expansion and the final settlement of the West. And then, as the century drew to a close against the background of a revived nationalism, the United States went to war with Spain to free Cuba, acquired an overseas empire, and importantly intervened in the affairs of eastern Asia. It had not abandoned its historic isolationist policy in that it continued to maintain its own freedom of action and still foreswore all entangling alliances. But, in the popular phrase of the day, it had emerged on the world scene as a great power.

Two major aspects of the history of these days may be singled out. The United States enjoyed what has been called a "free security." At no time from the Civil War to the end of the 1890's was its national safety ever threatened as it would be in the twentieth century. It could consequently afford, on many occasions, to allow foreign policy to become little more than an irresponsible instrument of political partisanship. At the same time, even during the quiescent years which marked the nadir of American diplomacy, the forces were at work which inevitably led to the attainment of its all-important world position and to the recognition of its new-found power both at home and abroad. The unfolding pattern of the future may be discerned in the developing need during these years to expand and safeguard foreign trade, in the slowly mounting interest of the American people in the world around them, and in a new sense of mission in the exercise of national power which would briefly spill over into the imperialism of 1898.

The foreign policies which the United States pursued in the latter half of the nineteenth century marked a transitional stage in the evolution of the nation from a continental to a world power. They were laying the foundation for the greatly expanded role America was to play in the global politics of the succeeding century.

In writing the account of these years I have had assistance from many quarters, but I should like especially to express my appreciation to Armin Rappaport, editor of the series of which this book is one, and to Herbert C. Cohen, of The Macmillan Company, for their helpful reading of the entire manuscript.

PRELUDE TO WORLD POWER

CHAPTER I

The Diplomacy of the Civil War

On April 1, 1861—less than a month after he assumed office—President Lincoln received a most remarkable document. He had been struggling with the harrowing domestic crisis precipitated by the secession of the southern states and pondering the grave decision that had to be reached on the possible provisioning of Fort Sumter. As his major cabinet appointee, Secretary of State William H. Seward became more and more exasperated by what he felt to be the weakness and indecision of the brooding President. He had been Lincoln's rival for Republican leadership; he considered himself the dominant figure in the new Administration, whoever might actually sit in the White House. Impetuous and self-willed, unable to brook further delay in meeting the critical situation the country faced, Seward had submitted, with arrogant self-assurance, "Some Thoughts for the President's Consideration."

The Administration was still without a policy, he admonished Lincoln, and immediate action was essential on both the domestic and foreign fronts if there were to be any chance whatsoever of averting the threatened civil war. He counseled caution at home. The paramount need, he suggested, was to emphasize in every possible way that the issue before the country was maintenance of the Union rather than the abolition of slavery. But in foreign affairs he called for a militant, challenging policy which he believed would create a belligerent nationalism and reforge the nation's shattered unity. Against the background of threatened intervention by the European powers in the affairs of the New World (Spain had designs on Santo Domingo and Louis Napoleon ambitions in Mexico), Seward saw the opportunity for decisive action: he would categorically demand explanations from Spain and France as to their policies, call upon Great Britain and Russia to declare their intentions, and send American agents into Canada, Mexico, and Central America to arouse a new spirit of continental independence. Should satisfactory explanations not be received from Spain and France, he went on to say, he would convene Congress and declare war against them. "It is not my special province," Seward concluded, in discussing how these proposals might be implemented. "But I neither seek to evade nor assume responsibility."

Lincoln quietly pocketed this stupefying document. A lesser man might have taken Seward to task for his immense assumptions as to his role in the government and for the irresponsible recklessness of his proposals, but the new President realized that he would have to work with his politically powerful Secretary of State. Tactfully avoiding anything like a direct clash, he quietly let it be known that he fully intended to be President in fact as well as in name and that his was the final responsibility in making policy both at home and abroad. Nothing further would be heard of the "wrap-the-world-in-fire" policy as a desperate means of trying to save the Union.

Moreover, as time went on and the Civil War followed its unhappy course, Lincoln and Seward were to work together in close harmony. Lincoln revealed in foreign as in domestic affairs his innate wisdom and continuing patience; Seward substituted for his early belligerency (especially noted in his attitude toward Great Britain) a surprising moderation. The two men, however different in background and temperament, came to recognize fully each other's abilities, and they developed a mutual trust in their common devotion to the single, overwhelming task of preserving the Union.

The diplomatic phase of this task remained throughout the war the necessity of forestalling any action on the part of the European powers that might strengthen the South or weaken the North. Both the British and the French Governments, at the beginning of hostilities, believed that the Confederate States would succeed in winning their independence. And it was an eventuality that they foresaw with anything but alarm or distaste. The breakup of the Union would weaken a dangerous commerical and political rival in the calculations of British power, while in the case of France it would remove the principal obstacle to the schemes Louis Napoleon was hatching in Mexico. Moreover, the conservative forces in political control throughout Europe felt a natural sympathy for the Confederacy. It exemplified the ordered, aristocratic principles supporting their own authoritative regimes.

"An involuntary instinct, all powerful and unconquerable," a French observer stated, "at once arrayed on the side of the pro-slavery people all the open or secret partisans of the fanaticism and absolutism of Europe."

While there was consequently no question that the dominant governing class in Europe would have liked to see the United States fall to pieces, the more liberal elements both in England and on the Continent felt quite differently about the outcome of the struggle in America in that they feared just what the conservatives so hopefully anticipated. They not only had a deep antipathy for slavery, which in itself was enough to turn them against the South, but they also sensed that defeat of the North and disruption of the Union would be a harsh blow to the democratic cause in every land and to all their own hopes for political and social reform. The common people throughout Europe, so far as they knew of what was taking place on the other side of the Atlantic, were also generally convinced that the North stood for principles and ideals in whose support they were struggling in their own countries against all the forces of entrenched privilege.

Neither the liberals nor the common people, however, were making policy in England and France during these days, let alone in the other countries of Europe. Both Lincoln and Seward knew that it was important to build up popular sympathy for the North and they encouraged Americans going abroad to do everything they could to bolster the Union cause. But more immediately they had to deal with existing governments. It was those who sat in the seats of power who had to be convinced, without provocation but with unalterable firmness, that the United States would not under any circumstances brook interference in what was a wholly domestic conflict.

England held the key to European policy. Whatever Louis Napoleon might want to do in pursuit of his own restless ambitions, he fully realized that France would have to follow the lead of Great Britain. The dangers in his own position in the complicated maze of European power politics would not allow him to offer any encouragement to the Confederacy except in partnership with the British Government. He could propose mediation or recognition of the independence of the Confederacy, as he was prepared to do, but he dared not act alone. The recurrent crises in foreign relations during the war years might find France hovering in the wings, but they centered on what England might or might not do.

Fortunately for the United States, it had in the person of its minister at the Court of St. James's a diplomat whose consummate skill fortified the policies followed by Lincoln and Seward. Through background, experience, and personal traits, through the confidence he inspired among Englishmen of all persuasions, in and out of government, Charles Francis Adams was admirably suited to represent his country in England during these perilous days. Combining the utmost tact with unswerving insistence upon American rights, capable of toning down Seward's sometimes overly brusque dispatches without any surrender of principle, Adams played a major role in preventing the recurrently strained crises between Great Britain and the United States from breaking down into open conflict.

A first crisis in Civil War diplomacy grew out of a series of events initiated by the South. On April 17, 1861—five days after the firing on Fort Sumter—Jefferson Davis, President of the Confederate States, offered letters of marque commissioning southern privateers to prey upon northern commerce. President Lincoln promptly countered by stating that privateers molesting United States ships would be treated as pirates and declaring a blockade of the entire southern coast line. These moves were necessary to sustain the Union cause, but they at once brought into question the right of the United States to enforce a blockade. Under the rules of international law foreign ships could not be legally stopped, should they attempt to run a blockade, except in case of war. If the powers were to honor the Union blockade it could only be on the basis that the Confederacy was a responsible government engaged in a recognized war and entitled to the rights of a belligerent.

Lincoln in theory considered the people of the South to be citizens in open rebellion against their government and on this basis the seceding states were not entitled to belligerent rights. But in declaring the blockade he bowed to realities to enable the United States Navy to lawfully exercise the wartime rights of search and seizure in seeking to prevent any foreign vessels from carrying military supplies or other contraband to southern ports. He tacitly acknowledged the belligerency of the Confederate States the better to ensure their ultimate defeat.

In immediate reaction to these moves Great Britain, closely followed by the other European powers, declared its official neutrality in the American struggle and thereby itself acknowledged the belligerent status of the Confederacy. Nothing could have been more logical, but the haste with which Great Britain took this step nevertheless came as a dismaying shock to the northern government and the northern public. It was interpreted as reflecting a hostile attitude toward the Union and aroused a widespread fear that the British Government might soon recognize the Confederacy as an independent state. Nothing would have more depressed the North or encouraged the South. It could have had incalculable consequences in the struggle to preserve the Union.

Arriving in London the very day—May 13, 1861—that the British Government issued its official neutrality proclamation, Charles Francis Adams found himself facing what he believed to be an imminent challenge to the northern cause. On instructions from Secretary Seward he was prepared to do everything possible to forestall any further moves toward recognition of the Confederacy, and he promptly informed the British Government that the United States would consider it an unfriendly act.

The South was in the meantime doing everything it could to advance its own interests and had dispatched special agents to London and the major continental capitals to plead its cause. Jefferson Davis was highly confident these agents would be successful. "England will recognize us," he declared optimistically, "and a glorious future is before us." Nor did his hopeful expectations appear for a time to be wholly unreasonable. Although he did not officially receive the envoys sent to London, Lord John Russell, the British Foreign Secretary, twice talked with them informally, and there were other indications of a sympathetic British attitude toward the Confederacy.

Washington became more than ever alarmed. On May 21 Secretary Seward, taking an even sterner stand than in his earlier notes to London, instructed Adams to desist from all contacts whatsoever with the British Government should it "continue intercourse of either kind [official or unofficial] with the domestic enemies of this country." Confronted by such an unequivocal assertion of the attitude of the United States, Lord John Russell did not again see the Confederate envoys and the immediate crisis died down.

Apart from these alarms and the foreshadowing of possible future dangers in Anglo-American relations, Great Britain's neutrality proclamation was actually serving the interests of the North in that it constituted acknowledgment of the Union's right to establish a blockade of southern ports. And even though this blockade could not always be made effective along the 3,500 miles of coast line stretching from Alexandria, Virginia, to New Orleans and the Mexican border, the British continued to accept its legality. Moreover they did not contest American enforcement of the historic doctrine of "continuous voyage" whereby the Union navy intercepted neutral vessels and searched them for contraband even though they were bound for European possessions off the Atlantic coast line rather than Confederate ports. The United States was thus able to prevent military supplies from reaching such intermediate ports where they could have been reshipped on Confederate vessels designed to run the Union blockade.

The British Government adopted this seemingly complaisant attitude toward the blockade for very practical reasons rather than out of any consideration for the North. It felt that in any future war in which England might become engaged the broadest possible interpretation of the legality of a blockade (applying, for example, to European continental ports) and acceptance of the doctrine of continuous voyage would redound greatly to its benefit. There was something ironical in this whole situation in the light of Anglo-American disputes over neutral rights during the Napoleonic Wars, but the British were ready to seize upon the immediate difficulties of the Union to provide the precedents which would help safeguard England's security should it again be a belligerent and the United States a neutral. And in fact these precedents established in the 1860's were to prove of immense value to Great Britain in 1914.

In spite of its official neutrality, sustained by refusal to receive the Confederate envoys as well as acceptance of the expansive scope of the Union blockade, Great Britain's general attitude continued to be anything but friendly to the northern cause. The failure of the Union armies immediately to subdue the rebels strengthened the widespread conviction that a separation of North and South was inevitable, and British leaders including Prime Minister Palmerston and Lord John Russell, scarcely concealed their welcome anticipation of a Confederate victory as furthering British interests.

The London *Times* significantly reflected this hostile feeling. It chose to believe that the American contest was in essence one for empire on the part of the North and for independence on that of the South, drawing a happy analogy between the American colonies and the England of George III in 1776. "These opinions may be wrong," it stated magisterially, "but they are the general opinions of the British nation."

However, what still most importantly influenced the attitude of British conservatives (as well as those on the Continent) was their interpretation of the Civil War as a contest between democracy and aristocracy. Firm in their belief that the Confederacy's triumph would strengthen the established order to which they were themselves committed, they cheerfully foresaw in the expected dissolution of the Union the final collapse of whatever dangers a republican America might once have represented for a monarchial Europe.

Surveying the English scene from his post in London, hearing so much criticism of the North and such praise for the South, Charles Francis Adams remained very worried. It seemed almost certain that in spite of present hesitancies, this widespread sympathy for the Confederacy would sooner or later lead to official recognition.

At this uncertain juncture of affairs—in November, 1861—there took place the most sensational and potentially dangerous incident affecting Anglo-American relations of the entire war period. For a time actual hostilities appeared to be imminent. The United States was prepared to accept them if necessary; the British Government made clear its resolve by dispatching a first contingent of eight thousand special troops to Canada. The inci-

dent causing this warlike excitement on either side of the Atlantic was the famous *Trent* affair.

Cruising in the South Atlantic, Captain Charles Wilkes, a
naval officer already well known for his exploratory ventures
and at this time in command of the U.S.S. *San Jacinto,* learned
that two newly appointed and important southern commissioners, James M. Mason and John Slidell, were aboard the
Trent, a British mail steamer, bound for London. Acting entirely
on his own initiative, Captain Wilkes overhauled the *Trent,* fired
two shots across her bow, and sent a landing party aboard her
with orders to seize her passengers. He then allowed the mail
steamer to proceed on its course and took the two Confederates
to Boston, where they were imprisoned.

The news of his startling deed was a bombshell, creating
immense excitement—from quite different points of view—in
both America and England. Smarting under the impact of the
military defeats sustained in the first phase of the war and ir-
ritated by British sympathy for the southern cause, the entire
North went wild. Here was a twofold victory: the Confederacy
had been humiliated by the capture of its commissioners and
England had been shown that the United States could act decisively in safeguarding its interests. That Captain Wilkes had
acted highhandedly with complete disregard for international
law mattered not at all. He overnight became a national hero.
The Secretary of the Navy gave emphatic approval to his exploit
and the House of Representatives promptly voted him a gold
medal. Typical of the reaction of the northern press was an
editorial of *The New York Times:*

There is no drawback to our jubilation. The Universal Yankee Nation
is getting decidedly awake. . . . As for Commodore Wilkes and his
command, let the handsome thing be done. Consecrate another
Fourth of July to him. Load him down with services of plate and
swords of the cunningest and costliest art. Let us encourage the happy
inspiration that achieved such a victory.

The popular commotion in England was no less intense. The
upstart Yankees had insulted the British flag, perpetrated a

"ruffianly outrage," and deserved immediate chastisement. The general feeling was reflected in government circles, which assumed that Captain Wilkes had acted under official orders. "You may stand for this," Prime Minister Palmerston was reported to have told his cabinet, "but damned if I will." Under his direction Lord John Russell drafted a note to Washington which demanded the immediate release of the southern commissioners and an apology for the affront to national honor in taking them off a British steamer by force of arms.

The harsh tone of this dispatch as originally written was somewhat toned down on the express wish of Queen Victoria's consort, Prince Albert, who was then lying on his deathbed. Nonetheless it still amounted to a virtual ultimatum with the firm statement that unless a suitable reply was promptly received, the British Government would have no alternative to severing diplomatic relations. "This nation," wrote a youthful Henry Adams, serving as his father's secretary in the American legation in London, "means to make war."

The Lincoln Administration found itself caught in an acute dilemma. Captain Wilkes' action was legally unjustifiable, and every dictate of common sense argued for the prompt release of Mason and Slidell. In the prevailing state of public opinion, however, acceptance of the British ultimatum threatened to create such a popular storm as seriously to weaken the Administration and therefore the entire war effort. Could Lincoln run the risk of possible hostilities with Great Britain? "One war at a time," he reputedly told Seward, but still he hesitated to give in to British demands. Finally, at a meeting on Christmas Day, 1861, his entire cabinet agreed that there was actually no choice but to liberate the Confederate commissioners.

Seward nevertheless worded the note announcing this decision so skillfully that he succeeded in allaying the popular clamor that the Administration had feared in giving way to the British demands. Captain Wilkes had been justified in seizing Mason and Slidell, the Secretary of State declared, because "persons as well as property may become contraband," but he had been at fault in forcibly removing them from a neutral vessel instead of bringing the ship—and her passengers—into port as a prize of war. Seward then continued, for obvious home consumption, to draw an analogy between the seizure of Mason and Slidell and British impressment of American sailors against which the United States had so strongly protested in 1812. "We are asked to do to the British nation," he self-justifiedly wrote in respect to the release of the Confederate envoys, "just what we have always insisted all nations ought to do to us . . . they will be cheerfully liberated." The reasoning may have been specious, but it turned the trick so far as the American public was concerned. In its eyes there had been no surrender. "Seward is not only right," wrote Richard H. Dana, "but sublime."

The sharp, sudden storm died down as quickly as it had arisen. The excitement in the North cooled off; the British were appeased. Charles Francis Adams was soon able to report that the incident had remarkably cleared the air. "The current which ran against us with such extreme violence six weeks ago," he wrote on January 10, 1862, "now seems to be going with equal fury in our favor." There were to be further critical periods in the relations between the United States and Great Britain before the Civil War came to an end—the settlement of this crisis had not resolved the basic problems created by the British attitude toward the Confederacy—but this threat of actual war was happily averted.

Throughout the rest of 1862 the possibility was always present that Great Britain and France might still decide to recognize the Confederacy as an independent state or otherwise seek to encourage the separation of North and South. Various economic factors have been advanced as influencing their policy, both in support of and in opposition to such possible intervention in American affairs. The efforts of historians to analyze the international situation from this point of view, however, have tended to obscure rather than clarify a most confused set of circumstances. It would seem safer to suggest that while economic factors may have affected the views of various segments of public opinion both in Great Britain and on the Continent, they never importantly affected the determination of national policy.

At the outset of the war, the Confederacy had expansive hopes of European intervention in its behalf because of what was believed to be the dependence of both England and France on continued supplies of cotton for their important textile industries. The leaders of the South were fully convinced that since these two countries drew some 80 per cent of their cotton from the southern states, they would face economic collapse unless they forcefully challenged the Union blockade. "The cards are in our hands," one southern newspaper wrote exultingly, "and we intend to play them out to the bankruptcy of every cotton factory in Great Britain and France or the acknowledgement of our independence." In their unalterable belief that "cotton was king," assuring their ultimate victory, the southerners went so far as to supplement the Union blockade of their commerce by themselves burning some 2,500,000 bales of cotton in the hope of forcing the issue of European intervention as quickly as possible.

What the Confederate leaders failed to realize was that in 1861 there was actually an oversupply of cotton in Europe as a result of the South's bumper crops the previous year. The warehouses of textile mills in England and France were bulging with such large excess stocks that a cessation of imports proved to be a benefit rather than a disaster for the cotton manufacturers. They profited handsomely from the higher prices induced by the curtailment of imports, and instead of facing depression, the European textile industry enjoyed a wartime boom. Moreover, by the time the surplus stocks on hand in 1861 had been exhausted, the manufacturers had successfully found new sources of supply in Egypt and India which largely freed them from their former dependence on the southern states.

For a time production was cut down as available stocks began to dwindle and the new sources of supply were not yet fully developed. Even though this did not too seriously affect the cotton manufacturers, it did lead to widespread unemployment among the mill operatives in England and France and acute distress for their families. But even had they so desired, these factory workers were in no position to bring pressure to bear upon their governments to break the Union blockade or support the Confederacy. They were politically helpless. However, as a matter of record, they did not favor such action. As already suggested, the sympathies of the working class were with the North rather than with the South. The English mill hands realized that whatever their immediate hardship, their long-term interests were closely identified with the northern cause.

Such a rational approach to the possible repercussions of the Civil War's outcome was not necessarily instinctive with the depressed workers in England. It resulted from the persistent agitation of British liberals who were fighting for reform at home and more clearly understood what a serious setback the triumph of the South would represent for the democratic movement throughout Europe. They engineered the mass meetings which were to adopt resolutions emphasizing the moral issue at stake in the abolition of slavery and expressing the workers' sympathy for the Union. And with the aid of contributions from American philanthropists, the British liberals also did everything possible to alleviate the distress of the unemployed and make them feel that there was an identity of interest between the progressive forces in America and the proponents of social reform in Great Britain.

A supposed reliance on cotton consequently had little or no effect in determining British policy. While the manufacturing interest was actually profiting rather than suffering from the curtailment of imports from the South, the textile workers themselves, even though they were the victims of the unemployment resulting from the blockade, continued to maintain their sympathy for the Union. The Confederacy had made a vast miscalculation in believing that cotton was so important as to encourage any foreign intervention in support of the southern cause.

It has also been suggested that economic interests may actually have encouraged a friendly attitude toward the North rather than toward the South. Just as England and France were freeing themselves from any dependence on southern cotton, a series of short wheat harvests was forcing greatly increased grain imports from the United States. "Old King Cotton's dead and buried," a happy Union poet sang in the *Continental Monthly:* "brave young Corn is King." Economic historians have argued that in such circumstances neither England nor France would have wanted to risk an anti-Union policy that might have endangered the continued flow of such essential supplies. Nevertheless there is no more conclusive evidence in the case of grain than in the case of cotton that the need for American imports played any part in the formulation of the European nations' foreign policies during Civil War days.

Other economic factors in the situation were the wartime profits that British manufacturers were making and the benefits accruing to British trading interests from the heavy losses that American shipping suffered at the hands of Confederate commerce raiders. But while it was possibly to the advantage of such groups that the war continue (as opposed to a quick peace secured through European mediation), it has never been shown that they exercised any influence on government policy.

What remained far more important in its effect on the British outlook on the Civil War than the contradictory interplay of economic factors—whether wheat, cotton, or commercial wartime profits—was the deep conviction that the future of democracy greatly depended on the preservation of the Union. While the British liberals, as conspicuously represented by such leaders as John Bright and Richard Cobden, continued on this basis to sympathize strongly with the North, the conservative, aristocratic-minded elements controlling the government continued by the same reasoning to favor the South. Whenever the course of the war appeared to make such a step feasible, the latter were ready to propose mediation in the hope that it would result in a permanent separation of the states.

As Seward had fully realized when the possibility of British recognition of the Confederacy first suggested the dangers to the North in European sympathy for the South, any such intervention might well be disastrous for the Union cause. He repeatedly let it be known that the United States could never accept foreign mediation in what remained a domestic conflict. Should Great Britain or any other European country persist on a course seeking to force mediation on the United States, the Secretary of State declared, it would only provoke war, and, he added emphatically, "we shall not shrink from it."

The gravest danger of foreign intervention developed in September, 1862. Convinced that the Union cause had become hopeless as a result of northern defeat in the battle of Bull Run, Prime Minister Palmerston suggested to Lord John Russell that the time had come for England and France to propose joint mediation looking toward "an arrangement upon the basis of separation." Three days later Russell replied, not only agreeing with this proposal but going further in stating that should it fail "we ought ourselves to recognize the Southern States as an independent state." There was no question of France's willingness to participate in any such program. Louis Napoleon had been talking of intervention ever since the Civil War started, and on one occasion had specifically suggested to the British Foreign Secretary—who then rejected the idea—that England and France should act together to break the northern blockade of southern ports.

How strongly official circles in England supported the southern cause was further reflected in a speech made by the Chancellor of the Exchequer, William Gladstone, while a final decision on mediation still hung in the balance. Speaking to an enthusiastic audience at Newcastle, he said:

There is no doubt that Jefferson Davis and other leaders of the South have made an army; they are making, it appears, a navy; and they have made what is more than either—they have made a nation. . . . We may anticipate with certainty the success of the Southern States so far as regards their separation from the North.

What stopped this possible move toward Anglo-French intervention was the North's repulse of General Lee's invasion of

Maryland at the Battle of Antietam on September 17. If this victory was hardly a decisive one in military terms, it had a vital effect on Europe's attitude toward the war. It caused an immediate pause in the plans of both England and France. When news of the battle was received in England, Palmerston at once told Lord John Russell that their common project would have to be held in abeyance—"we must continue merely to be lookers-on till the war shall have taken a more decided turn." The cabinet thereupon rejected the idea of mediation altogether.

Louis Napoleon was not quite so easily persuaded that something might not still be done to aid the Confederacy. Following the collapse of the joint mediation scheme in October, he suggested that France, Great Britain, and Russia might together propose a six-months armistice to the contending forces in America. He got no support whatsoever and reluctantly abandoned this plan. Then in January, 1863, he went so far as directly to offer mediation himself, proposing to both North and South that their representatives meet on neutral grounds to discuss possible peace terms. Seward naturally rejected the proposal out-of-hand, and an angry Congress passed a joint resolution reiterating that any attempted foreign interference in the domestic affairs of the United States would be considered an unfriendly act.

The reluctance of Great Britain to be drawn into any quarrel with the Union now that the tide of battle appeared to have turned was the decisive influence in determining what was to become Europe's general hands-off policy for the remainder of the war. But the attitude of Russia was also an important factor in the situation. The Czar's Government, unlike those of Great Britain and France, favored the northern cause. It had no sympathy with the democracy which the Union symbolized, but a strong, united America was as much in Russia's interest as a divided one appeared to be in the interests of England and France. It was a foil to what the Czar's ministers were convinced were the aggressive and hostile ambitions of Great Britain in the interplay of European power politics.

Russia's desire above everything else, its foreign minister told the American chargé in St. Petersburg, was "the mainte-nance of the American Union, as one indivisible nation." More-over, he made his country's position very clear to both the British and French Governments. Lord John Russell had worried over this in considering the proposed mediation in September, 1862, and on one occasion expressed very grave doubts as to whether "we and France should stir if Russia holds back." When the French Foreign Minister later sounded out the attitude of St. Petersburg on possible cooperative action, he reported that his suggestions had been met "by an almost scornful refusal."

The American people knew of Russian sympathy for the Union, and, without attempting to analyze why so autocratic a monarchy should support a democratic republic, they rejoiced in this one display of friendship among the European nations. Their sense of gratitude was further enhanced when in October, 1863, a fleet of Russian warships visited New York and shortly afterwards another squadron called at San Francisco. These visits were actually due to a desire on the part of the Russian Govern-ment, fearful that autumn of possible war with Great Britain, to base its naval forces in a neutral harbor to prevent their being bottled up in the Black Sea. The American public knew nothing of this, however, and "a thrill of joy" swept through the country at what was interpreted as a symbolic gesture of Russian good will. The nation generally echoed Secretary of the Navy Welles' heartfelt "God bless the Russians," and the national sentiment of the day was later reflected in a poem by Oliver Wendell Holmes:

> Bleak are our shores with the blasts of December
> Fettered and chilled is the rivulet's flow;
> Throbbing and warm are the hearts that remember
> Who was our friend when the world was our foe.

In his continuing battle to win the sympathy of Europe—or more accurately, perhaps, to ward off any move in favor of the Confederacy—Lincoln realized that the slavery issue was of the utmost importance. The liberals and the working classes, both in

England and on the Continent, were in part drawn to the North, as we have seen, because they were convinced that victory for the Union meant liberation of the slaves. Even some conservatives were greatly troubled over the moral dilemma they faced in supporting the slave-holding South. It was obvious that any move the President could make to clarify his determination to free the slaves would aid the northern cause.

The needs of foreign policy, however, warred in this instance against the imperatives of domestic policy. Lincoln dared not act decisively until he was sure that anything he might do would not alienate the loyal slave-holding states. It was not until September, 1862—following that same battle of Antietam which had dissuaded the British Government from proposing mediation—that he felt his hands were free. He was then confident enough to issue his preliminary Emancipation Proclamation, and finally on January 1, 1863, gave it its final definitive form in declaring that all slaves in the areas in rebellion against the United States Government would be "forever free."

The Emancipation Proclamation had its obvious limitations, applying only to the states which had seceded, but it nonetheless could be interpreted as demonstrating that Lincoln's ultimate purpose, once the rebellion had been suppressed, was to do away with slavery altogether. Whatever its domestic implications, the proclamation was consequently a highly significant stroke in the field of diplomacy. The South was now placed in a morally indefensible position, and whatever lingering sympathy for its cause still existed among Europeans was almost wholly dissipated. "The Emancipation Proclamation," Henry Adams reported from England, "has done more for us than all our former victories and all our diplomacy. It is creating an almost convulsive reaction in our favor all over this country."

Yet Adams was exaggerating. The Emancipation Proclamation undoubtedly had a tremendous influence on public opinion in England and on the Continent, but what had done most for the Union cause was its victories on the field of battle. It was these indications of an ultimate victory for the North that had really dissuaded England and France from pursuing the idea of mediation. They knew that to persevere on such a course risked a war, a war which in the case of Great Britain would leave Canada an almost helpless hostage in American hands. That any sort of intervention would be regarded as an unfriendly act had been made clear so repeatedly—by Congress, by the Secretary of State, by the American Minister in London—that no doubts of the Union reaction could remain. What the Emancipation Proclamation did was to give a final moral endorsement to policies which the European powers had already adopted out of the practical exigencies of the day.

Although President Lincoln was now freed of the haunting fear of possible foreign intervention, another crisis of quite a different order in relations with Great Britain was not far distant. The Confederate envoys in Europe had nowhere won official recognition, but they had nevertheless succeeded in placing substantial private orders for military supplies and for shipbuilding. Some of these supplies had been run through the Union blockade, and a number of warships built for the Confederacy in Great Britain had been duly delivered and were taking a heavy toll of northern shipping.

The construction of such warships for a belligerent could hardly be reconciled with the spirit of neutrality, and it was also contrary to the provisions of a British domestic statute. Shipbuilders, however, sought to avoid all possible legal restraints by not actually arming the ships they were building until after they had put out to sea. In these circumstances they were freed to become commerce raiders, and it would be later estimated that they destroyed some 250 American merchantmen and whaling ships during their marauding careers.

Charles Francis Adams exhausted every possible resource to prevent these vessels from leaving England. He collected masses of incontrovertible evidence showing that they were being built as warships for the Confederacy, declared that their construction was contrary to the British neutrality act, and insisted that the Government seize the vessels before they left port.

The most conspicuous among such ships was one originally designated *Number 290* but later known as the *Alabama*. Adams discovered in July, 1862, that she was about to put to sea, and passed this information on to the British officials. They were reluctant to seize her until they had indubitable proof of their legal right to do so. The evidence had to be examined and the seizure order passed upon by the Queen's Advocate. For five days the essential papers lay on this official's desk and nothing happened: the Queen's Advocate had at this highly critical juncture of affairs somewhat inopportunely gone insane!

The five days before this unfortunate occurrence was discovered proved to be a fateful lapse. The firm building the *Alabama*—the Laird Brothers of Birkenhead—had somehow got wind of their vessel's possible seizure and, under pretense of a trial run, took her down the Mersey with a party of sight-seers. At the river's mouth they put the visitors aboard a tug and sent their ship to sea. After rendezvousing in the Azores with two ships carrying arms and equipment, the *Alabama* then set out on a course that was to bring flaming destruction to scores of Yankee merchantmen. The British authorities had in the meantime telegraphed her builders to hold her in port, but they were obviously a little late.

The American public was incensed on learning of the *Alabama*'s escape and then more and more angered on word of her widespread depredations on the high seas. Anti-British feeling flared up dangerously, and Congress passed a bill authorizing the construction of American privateers which could only be interpreted as aimed at possible future trouble with England, since the South had no merchantmen on which privateers could prey. In the spring of 1863 the British Minister in Washington reported that the state of Anglo-American relations appeared to him "more alarming than it has been since the *Trent* affair."

And over the horizon was another graver crisis. The Confederate agents in England had also contracted with the Laird

Brothers for the construction of two armored warships, which constituted a far more formidable threat to the Union than the *Alabama* or any other commerce raider. For these vessels were to be equipped not only with nine-inch guns but also with iron rams that were designed to pierce any wooden ship. They were known to be nearing completion in the late summer of 1863, and even though it was announced that they were being built for the Egyptian Government, the subterfuge fooled no one.

Should these vessels be allowed to put to sea, Union officials realized that the northern navy would be completely at their mercy and even northern ports would be subject to possible attack. "We have no defense against them," Secretary of the Navy Welles warned. "It is a matter of life and death." Charles Francis Adams had perhaps no greater cause for anxiety at any time during all his worrisome days in London, and he insistently demanded that the British Government at once take the necessary steps to prevent the Laird rams, as they came to be called, from escaping as had the *Alabama*. Finally on September 5, 1863, in the belief that nothing was being done, he delivered a memorable note to the Foreign Office. After expressing his profound regret at the British Government's apparent decision to take no action, he stated solemnly, "It would be superfluous in me to point out to your Lordship that this is war."

Fortunately, unknown to Adams, Lord John Russell had already become convinced that, regardless of legal niceties, he would have to act. Two days earlier he had given orders for seizure of the rams. Adams' statement had not been an idle threat. The United States could not have afforded, whatever the risk, to allow the Confederacy to procure in England the weapons that might have encompassed its own destruction. Only the British Government's timely recognition of the vital importance of preventing a recurrence of the *Alabama* incident had saved the day.

The danger of any breakdown in the relations between the United States and England came to an end with the resolution of the crisis over the Laird rams. And even though the Civil War was to drag on for another eighteen months, there would be no more talk of mediation or possible recognition of the Confederacy. Such sympathy as had once existed for the South continued to dwindle throughout all Europe. With clarification of the moral issue centering on slavery, a despairing Confederacy recognized its tragic dilemma by offering to free its own slaves in return for foreign recognition. But it was much too late. Moreover, the troubled state of Europe's own political relations began more and more to absorb the attention of its statesmen. As 1863 gave way to 1864, the Civil War still raging in America seemed to be almost forgotten.

"Our affairs," Henry Adams noted with sharp relief after the troubled events of the previous year, "are quite in the background, thank the Lord."

Perhaps Great Britain, with its public opinion always divided and the economic and other motives underlying national policy so generally confused, would not in any circumstances have gone so far as to challenge the Union by any overt act in these years of America's distress. Nevertheless, the succession of crises created by the *Trent* affair, possible recognition of the Confederacy in 1862, the escape of the *Alabama,* and the business of the Laird rams found the United States and Great Britain dangerously skirting the brink of war. The resolute and yet restrained policies that the Government at Washington so persistently pursued were highly successful in at once safeguarding the national interest and preventing possible hostilities.

The whole approach to foreign issues during the war years could hardly have differed more sharply from the belligerent and irresponsible tone of those "Thoughts for the President's Consideration" which Seward had so arrogantly submitted on April 1, 1861. In keeping with his grave responsibilities in foreign and in domestic affairs, Lincoln always acted with the broad vision that served his country so well. Seward learned to conduct his negotiations with a skill that places him high among the nation's secretaries of state. And Charles Francis Adams never faltered in his more immediate relations with the British Government—and the British people—when a single misstep might have been fraught with disaster. In spite of dangerous pressures building up at home as well as arising from abroad, the situation was kept under control. The diplomacy of the Civil War had its highly important part in making possible the preservation of the Union in its hour of most dire peril.

CHAPTER II

Mexico, the Monroe Doctrine, and Latin America

When the prolonged agony of the Civil War at last came to an end, the United States took up some unfinished business in the field of foreign policy which it had been too preoccupied to handle effectively while hostilities were still in progress. The possible ambitions of the European nations in the Western Hemisphere, which had given Seward the excuse for his wild proposals in 1861 for declaring a foreign war, did in fact constitute a challenge to the basic principles of the Monroe Doctrine to which the United States could not remain indifferent. There was in the first instance the attempt on the part of Spain to reassert its former control over Santo Domingo, and far more important were the intrigue and scheming whereby Louis Napoleon was seeking to establish an empire in Mexico.

The threat to the interests of the United States in the latter instance was direct and dangerous. In meeting it with a forthright and determined defense, as he so notably did once his hands were freed, Secretary Seward gave to the Monroe Doctrine a new strength and vitality. Even though he never mentioned it specifically in his diplomatic correspondence with France, he never left any doubt as to how firmly the United States stood by its principles. His policy marked what the Monroe Doctrine's foremost historian, Dexter Perkins, has termed a decisive stage in its evolution. "No informed publicist, no responsible statesman," he has written, "could henceforward ignore the existence of a powerful prejudice among the American people against the intervention of Old World states in the affairs of the New."

Moreover, subsequent developments in this post-Civil War period were to expand still further the American interpretation of the Monroe Doctrine and thereby win increasing recognition from the powers of Europe that they had to respect the determination of the United States to safeguard its sister republics in the Western Hemisphere from any foreign interference. The public may have had little concern with Latin American affairs in general during the latter half of the nineteenth century, but it was always ready to rally to the defense of the Monroe Doctrine.

The situation that developed in Santo Domingo during the 1860's ultimately resolved itself. At the request of the Dominican president then in power, who was fearful of possible attack by Haiti, the Spanish Government had formally reannexed the troubled little country in May, 1861 and firmly established military control over its affairs. The Dominican people were not happy over this turn of events, however, and revolt soon flared up against the imposition of foreign rule. The Spanish troops were unable to maintain order, yellow fever began to take a frightful toll among the occupying forces, and conditions steadily deteriorated. Spain maintained its tenuous hold on the island throughout the period of the Civil War but by 1864 had decided to give up what had proved to be an impossible task. A year later it withdrew its army in complete abandonment of the annexation program, and Santo Domingo resumed an independent course.

Seward had protested vehemently against Spain's policy, and in this instance, most notably in a belligerent note in June, 1861, directly reaffirmed the principles underlying the Monroe Doctrine:

It is the moral and political significance of the act of Spain which gives it importance, and because this is the first instance since the foreign policy of the U. S. was announced to the Allied Powers of Europe in 1823, that any nation has failed to see its own clear interests in the maintenance of that policy . . . the undersigned has now to fulfill the duty imposed upon him by the President, and in the name of the government of the U. S. of America solemnly protests against the assumption or exercise of Spanish authority in the island of San Domingo; and this protest the U. S. in every case will expect to maintain.

In the summer of 1861, however, the United States was in no position to back up its protest. Seward was bluffing, and the Spanish Government well knew it. It paid no attention whatsoever to the Secretary of State, and in the circumstances he had no alternative than to retreat ingloriously from a position he could not sustain. He was saved from a worse defeat for his over-zealous diplomacy in this early stage of his career (before he had learned the lessons of moderation taught by the Civil War) only by Spain's mounting troubles in Santo Domingo and its ultimate decision to give up the whole idea of the little republic's annexation.

In the meantime the far more serious developments in Mexico were running their unhappy course, and here Seward showed a deliberate restraint so long as he was unable to support his words with possible action. Only after the conclusion of the Civil War did he begin to exert the unyielding diplomatic pressure that became an important factor—though not the only one—in causing France to withdraw from Mexico as Spain had already retreated from Santo Domingo.

It was the chaotic conditions prevailing in Mexico at the opening of the 1860's that provided Louis Napoleon with the pretext and the opportunity to develop his imperial program. After a period of embittered civil strife, the country's more liberal, republican elements, under the leadership of Benito Juárez, a Zapotec Indian, had overcome its conservative forces, primarily composed of the landlords and Catholic clerics, and succeeded in setting up a new republican regime. President Juárez was faced with the most difficult, if not insoluble, economic and financial problems, however, and he consequently suspended all payments on Mexico's large foreign debts. In conjunction with England and Spain, France launched a joint expeditionary force (the United States was originally asked to participate but declined) to collect what was due to the foreign powers by force of arms. After reaching an agreement which specifically declared that there would be no interference with Mexico's internal affairs, troops from the three countries occupied Vera Cruz in January, 1862.

The joint intervention, however, only masked the scheme that Louis Napoleon had plotted to build up French power through establishment of a puppet empire in Mexico with the Archduke Maximilian of Austria, brother of the Emperor Francis Joseph, on the throne. Considering himself the great protector of Catholicism, which was being assailed by the revolutionary and anticlerical forces in Mexico, and also persuaded by reactionary exiles in Paris that the Mexican people would welcome the creation of a monarchy, Louis Napoleon may have convinced himself that his goals were noble and high-minded. "I seek nothing but good," he wrote his minister in London on one occasion, "convinced that to try to make people prosperous is to work effectively for the prosperity of all." But the fanciful dreaming and inordinate ambitions that underlay his grand design are revealed in another letter, addressed to Marshal Forey, the commander of the French troops in Mexico, which defined the goal of intervention as seeking to block the possible predominance of the United States in Mexico and forward the interests of France.

Should the United States succeed in dominating Mexico, consequently securing control of Central America and the isthmian passage between the Atlantic and the Pacific, wrote the French Emperor, it would become the only power in all America. However, if Mexico was able with the support of French arms to sustain its territorial integrity and support a stable government,

the day would be saved for the political and commercial interests of France. "We shall have imposed an insuperable barrier
to the encroachments of the United States," Louis Napoleon
concluded in elaborating on his program for setting up a
French-controlled Mexican empire, ". . . and this influence will
radiate northward as well as southward, will create markets for
our commerce, and will procure the materials indispensable for
our industry."

A few months after the initiation of the allied enterprise
nominally set in motion for no other purpose than the collection
of debts, both England and Spain recalled their military forces.
Having learned something of Louis Napoleon's broader schemes,
they completely rejected them. Undaunted, the French Emperor
pressed ahead with his own plans which now called for the occupation of all Mexico, convocation of a Council of Notables that
would invite the Archduke Maximilian to become Mexico's ruler,
and then establishment of the puppet empire. The French forces
were soon on the march for Mexico City.

They met stiff resistance. Harassed by the guerrilla forces
of President Juárez all along their difficult route, they were for a
time checked in their efforts to capture the important town of
Puebla, and only after the replacement of Marshal Forey by
Marshal Bazaine and the arrival of 30,000 additional troops was
the French army able to subdue the republican forces. After
wintering over at Orizaba, it then resumed its advance and
finally in June, 1863, triumphantly entered Mexico City.

Marshal Bazaine promptly summoned the Council of Notables, and according to the prearranged plan it dutifully extended a formal invitation to the Archduke Maximilian to ascend
the Mexican throne. Eager as he was to assume his imperial role,
Maximilian hesitated for a time, undecided whether the Council
really spoke for the country. After a supposed popular plebiscite,
carefully rigged by the landowning and clerical elements in
league with the French military, appeared to promise popular
support for the empire, he waived all further doubts and agreed
to accept the proffered crown. Together with his wife, Carlota,

daughter of Leopold I, King of the Belgians, he then set off for Mexico in April, 1864.

The dominant figure in this whole affair was that personage of such great importance in his own estimation, that man of so many illusions—the Emperor Louis Napoleon. The roles played by Maximilian and Carlota, however, have always clothed the Mexican adventure in a shimmering cloak of romance and tragedy. The scion of the House of Hapsburg was a fair-haired, handsome, and very likable young man; Carlota was beautiful and glamorous. They were both extremely ambitious, completely beguiled by the glittering prospects of empire, and incredibly naïve.

From the outset their families and other counselors had urged them not to be drawn into Louis Napoleon's imperialistic schemes. "What a lot of cannon-shots it will take to set up an emperor in Mexico," the Austrian minister in Paris exclaimed, "and what a lot to maintain him there." But knowing nothing whatsoever of Mexico or of the temper of the people, Maximilian and Carlota easily allowed themselves to be persuaded—the wish was clearly father to the thought—that the Mexicans would welcome them with warmth and enthusiasm. They fancifully dreamed that once their empire was firmly established in Mexico, they might extend their domain still farther, perhaps bringing all Central America under their benign and liberal rule.

They also accepted without hesitation the promised support of Louis Napoleon in their great adventure. He had agreed in the Convention of Miramar, concluded just before Maximilian and Carlota sailed for Mexico, that in return for the new regime's assumption of the debt Mexico owed France and payment of the costs of the French expeditionary force, France would continue military support for at least three years. Moreover, in looking to the longer future, Louis Napoleon categorically assured his protegés that the "assistance of France shall never fail the new Empire."

Things did not work out quite as Maximilian and Carlota (let alone Louis Napoleon) had so blithely assumed they would.

The Council of Notables that had elected Maximilian emperor did not at all represent public opinion. With the backing of only the reactionaries, the empire faced the mounting resentment of the Mexican people who had had nothing to do with its establishment. Juárez was irreconcilable. The imperial couple lived luxuriously amid all the trappings of royalty at Chapultepec Castle, in Mexico City, or in their palace at Cuernavaca, with its lovely gardens and impressive mountain scenery, but they had little direct contact with the real Mexico. In many ways weak and irresolute, but also blindly stubborn in holding to any course on which he had embarked, Maximilian sat uneasily on his artificially contrived throne while about him swirled the intractable forces of popular discontent.

Louis Napoleon, finding that his Mexican adventure was costing far more than he had anticipated and that the whole business was very unpopular in France, soon began to waver in his support of such a dubious undertaking. He did not want to withdraw the French troops who alone sustained his faltering overseas empire—there were, after all, the pledges he had made in the Convention of Miramar and his own unwillingness to admit a mistake—but before the year 1864 had run its course, he was already covertly seeking some way to separate France from the whole affair.

The United States had watched these developments in Mexico with the gravest misgivings, but torn and distracted by the Civil War, it could do nothing about them. It dared not risk any action that might alienate France and possibly lead that country to throw its support behind the Confederacy. Nevertheless, Secretary Seward sought to keep the record clear. He had not protested the original joint intervention of France, England, and Spain, but when Louis Napoleon's monarchial plot began to unfold early in 1862, he set forth the American position in a letter of instructions to William L. Dayton, the American Minister in Paris, which was designed for the ears of French officialdom. After unobtrusively suggesting that no monarchial government supported by foreign bayonets could hope to survive in Mexico and that its position would be still further weakened by placing a European prince on the throne, Seward warned that the sympathies of the United States would always be with the American republics. He then concluded:

It is not intended on this occasion to predict the course of events which might happen as a consequence of the proceeding contemplated, either on this continent or in Europe. It is sufficient to say that, in the President's opinion, the emancipation of this continent from European control has been the principal feature of its history during the last half century.

At the time this mild—but pointed—remonstrance was as far as Seward felt able to go. He somewhat later wrote Dayton, "we are too intent on putting down our insurrection, and avoiding complications that might embarrass us, to seek for occasion of dispute with any foreign power." The United States nonetheless continued to recognize the Juárez government, although most of the European powers recognized that of Maximilian, and as military victories began to strengthen the Union's prospects Seward's correspondence took on an increasingly firmer tone. It left little doubt, as Louis Napoleon could hardly fail to realize, that once the United States was free to do so, it would assuredly take more active measures directed against both French intervention in Mexico and Maximilian's shadowy empire.

Well before this, popular sentiment in the Union had become a good deal less restrained in its reaction to the situation than had the Secretary of State. Partly as a consequence of the incessant prompting of the able Mexican Minister in Washington, who played up on every possible occasion the threat to American interests in the establishment of a French-controlled Mexican empire, newspapers throughout the country began to attack Louis Napoleon and strongly protest French policy. Finally, on April 4, 1864—on the eve of Maximilian's final decision to accept the Mexican crown—the House of Representatives unanimously adopted a significant resolution. After reference to "the deplorable events" taking place in Mexico, it expressly stated that it was not in accord with the policy of the United States "to acknowledge any monarchial government erected on the ruins of any republican government in America under the auspices of any European Power."

On learning of the adoption of this resolution, the French Minister of Foreign Affairs asked the American Minister in Paris at their next meeting, "Do you bring us peace or war?" But still moving cautiously, Seward instructed Dayton to give the French Government assurances that Congress did not determine foreign policy and that the opinions the House had expressed were "not in harmony with the policy of neutrality, forbearance, and consideration which the President has so faithfully pursued."

As the Civil War drew to an end in the United States, the popular pressure for a firmer stand in support of the Monroe Doctrine continued to mount, with various proposals advanced for immediate military measures to drive the French out of Mexico altgether. Shortly after Appomattox, General Grant himself urged such a course with a plan for General John M. Schofield to lead an army to Mexico City. A number of cabinet members were also convinced that the time for temporizing was over and that Louis Napoleon should be confronted with a show of force.

There were warnings against any such precipitate action from the American legation in Paris, where John Bigelow had now replaced William Dayton as Minister. "I doubt if there is a power in Europe," Bigelow reported, "that would formally sustain our pretensions under what is called 'the Monroe Doctrine,' while England, France, Spain, Denmark, Austria and Brazil would lend their moral support and some of them probably material support to any sovereign that would resist them. . . . In a war to redress the wrongs of Mexico, or to propagate republicanism by the sword we should, in my opinion, be likely to fail."

President Johnson was nevertheless strongly to affirm the American position, both reflecting and intensifying the prevalent anti-French feeling, in his annual message to Congress in December, 1865. He frankly stated that the United States would regard any European challenge to the right of the American people to defend republicanism against foreign interference as a great calamity to the cause of good government and to the peace of the world. Since this was exactly what France appeared to be doing, the import of his statement could hardly have been more clear.

Secretary Seward, to whom the President left the actual negotiations with France, was in the meantime continuing to move with calculated caution. While he did not waver in his resolution to force Louis Napoleon out of Mexico, he hoped to be able to do so by steadily increasing the diplomatic pressure rather than by threatening war. In a firm note to Paris in July, 1865, he had explicitly stated that the sympathies of the American people were wholly on the side of the republicans in Mexico and gravely warned that his countrymen were "disposed to regard with impatience the continued intervention of France in that country."

Louis Napoleon's mounting desire to free himself of the incubus of his puppet empire was in these circumstances reinforced. While the French reply to Seward's *démarche* was that France would not be swayed by "haughty injunctions or threatening insinuations," it also indicated that the government had under consideration the gradual withdrawal of French troops. Moreover, the Emperor had another suggestion: he would be all the more ready to evacuate his forces from Mexico if the United States would undertake to recognize Maximilian.

Seward spurned any such bargain, but Louis Napoleon's proposal encouraged him to believe that he was winning the fight on his own grounds. In early November he dispatched the strongest note he had yet penned: the policy that France was following in Mexico was "disallowable and impractical," the United States had no intention of recognizing Maximilian, and he regretted that he had not yet received any firm commitment from the French Government that seemed to justify the United States in believing that it was prepared to remove "the cause of our deep concern for the harmony of the two nations." The next move was clearly up to France.

Louis Napoleon now prepared to throw in his hand altogether. The complex political situation in Europe, the ever-increasing expenses that his operations in Mexico entailed, and further evidence of the opposition of the French people to the whole mad escapade undoubtedly influenced his final decision. The stiffening attitude of the United States, however, forced the issue. It was the last straw. Even as the official reply to this latest American note was being considered, Louis Napoleon secretly gave orders to Marshal Bazaine to prepare for the evacuation of the French army from Mexico.

Seward maintained the pressure. He told the French Minister in Washington that the traditional friendship between the United States and France would be brought into "immediate jeopardy" unless intervention was not only publicly disavowed but speedily terminated. Louis Napoleon thereupon assured Minister Bigelow in Paris, in a talk on Christmas Eve, that he planned to withdraw all French troops by the following autumn. While the issue now appeared to be wholly settled, Seward still wanted more precise and official confirmation of what was in effect the Emperor's surrender. On February 12, 1866, he categorically demanded definitive information as to "when French operations may be expected to cease."

Compelled to answer this very specific question, the French Government stated, some two months later, that its troops would be withdrawn in three stages, beginning in the autumn, and that they would all be out of Mexico in another year. Ignoring the pledges that he had made in the Convention of Miramar and all his fine words about France never failing the Mexican Empire, Louis Napoleon had taken the final step in abandoning Maximilian to his fate.

Deserted though he was by his protector, the Austrian Archduke clung stubbornly to his doomed throne. Even after the final evacuation of the French troops in the spring of 1867 (Louis Napoleon had actually speeded up the original schedule for their withdrawal), he refused the pleas of his friends that he leave the country. His cause was completely hopeless without the support of foreign bayonets. Juárez had never given up his savage guerrilla warfare against the imperial regime, and now the whole country rose in outraged revolt. But the young Emperor, perhaps vain and foolhardy rather than rationally courageous, held out against impossible odds until on May 15 he was taken prisoner at Querétaro by the republican forces. He had saved only his honor in the crumbling ruins of empire.

The last chapter in the story is unrelieved tragedy. In spite of pleas from every foreign quarter, including the vigorous interposition of the American Secretary of State, Juárez was determined that Maximilian should die for his crimes against Mexico. After a hurried court-martial, the former Archduke of Austria and Emperor of Mexico met his death, with fortitude and dignity, at the hands of a military firing squad on June 19, 1867. In the meantime, the Empress Carlota had gone to Europe to seek help, first pleading desperately with Louis Napoleon to abide by his pledges of assistance, and failing there, making a last frantic appeal to the Pope. Her mission was completely fruitless, and in her gathering despair Carlota went insane. She was to live on, a sad reminder of the whole misguided adventure, well into the twentieth century, and died only in 1927, sixty years after the final climax of the tortuous events in which she had played such a conspicuous role.

Seward's policy in upholding the basic principles of the Monroe Doctrine and yet avoiding a direct clash with France had proved to be successful. Even though historians may continue to debate as to whether domestic difficulties at home or pressure from the United States was the more important factor in forcing Louis Napoleon's withdrawal from Mexico, the Secretary of State had won an impressive victory. Moreover, in giving a fresh vitality to the Monroe Doctrine, he had helped to make it an unquestioned article of faith in the minds of the American people.

Soon afterwards its scope was to be further broadened. As an offshoot of a futile and misguided effort to promote the

American annexation of Santo Domingo in 1870, President Grant developed the thesis that over and beyond opposing further foreign colonization, as set forth by President Monroe, the United States could not countenance any shifts in territorial control which might benefit a European power. To the involved circumstances that led to the Santo Domingo annexation fiasco and the domestic controversy it engendered we shall return, but its relation to the Monroe Doctrine may be most usefully noted at this point.

In defending his annexation policy, President Grant argued that unless the United States moved to take over control of the always troubled little republic, Santo Domingo might again offer itself to some European power as it had offered itself to Spain in the early 1860's. Therefore, it was the responsibility of the United States, by this reasoning, to annex Santo Domingo as the only way of preventing another power from doing so. Such action would then constitute no more than "an adherence to the Monroe Doctrine."

To make what he had in mind entirely clear, regardless of what might happen in the immediate instance affecting Santo Domingo, Grant then further declared, on May 31, 1870, that the concepts originally embraced in the Monroe Doctrine of 1823 had to be expanded to meet new contingencies. "I now deem it proper to assert," he said, after outlining President Monroe's original message, "the equally important principle that hereafter no territory on this continent shall be regarded as subject to transfer to a European power."

This elaboration of the Monroe Doctrine did not have any significant impact in the immediate post-Civil War period; the European powers paid little if any attention to President Grant's new dictum. The nontransfer principle nevertheless became a part of the American credo, and it was to be repeatedly reaffirmed in the later statements of both presidents and secretaries of state. Several times, when there were rumors in these years of possible territorial shifts, although none of them materialized, the occasion was seized to emphasize this new corollary to the Monroe Doctrine in order that there might not be any doubt, as one official pronouncement phrased it, "with regard to the attitude of the United States upon these important topics." The basis was thereby securely laid for a policy which became of far greater importance when in the twentieth century there appeared to be a very real danger that by acquiring the colonies of other powers (the Danish West Indies in 1917, the Dutch West Indies and the French Caribbean islands in 1940), Germany might obtain a foothold on the American continent.

Still another new interpretation of the Monroe Doctrine was an outgrowth of mounting concern over possible European control of an interocean canal. Although it was not until 1904 that the construction of such a canal actually commenced, it had been contemplated and talked about for more than half a century. The international aspects of the problem had not originally worried the United States. In concluding in 1850 the famous Clayton-Bulwer Treaty with Great Britain, it had indeed agreed upon a cooperative canal project and bound itself not to seek exclusive control over any future waterway. But the aroused interest in a canal after the Civil War was attended by a strong popular conviction that its construction and operation should be a wholly American undertaking. Europe could no more be allowed any rights in such a matter than in any other question involving territory in the Western Hemisphere.

Secretary Seward made a number of moves seeking to safeguard the American interest in an isthmian canal, including abortive treaties with both Nicaragua and Colombia, but it was not until the close of the 1870's that the issue became of real importance. A private French company, under the imaginative leadership of Ferdinand de Lesseps, the great engineer who built the Suez Canal, obtained a concession from the Colombian Government for construction of a canal across the isthmus of Panama, at this time a part of Colombia. American public opinion became greatly concerned and various newspapers asserted that such a venture, under the auspices of a foreign power, could not be reconciled with the Monroe Doctrine. Responding to such pressures President Hayes vigorously asserted the paramountcy of American rights in the construction of any possible canal in Panama and in 1880 declared that the United States could not "consent to the surrender of this control to any European power or combination of powers." Affirming that an isthmian waterway would essentially change the geographic relationship between the Atlantic and Pacific Oceans, he then further stated that it would become "virtually a part of the coastline of the United States."

A year later, when Colombia broached the idea of an international treaty guaranteeing the neutrality of a future canal, Secretary of State James G. Blaine spoke up even more sharply in behalf of the new Administration of President Garfield. After reiterating that any such canal would be an extension of the country's coast line, he strongly emphasized the long settled American conviction that any extension of Europe's political system to the Western Hemisphere, in whatever guise, would endanger the peace and safety of the United States. He was ready to brush aside the Clayton-Bulwer Treaty. As he even more explicitly—and belligerently—said on another occasion, the United States "will not consent to perpetuate any treaty that impeaches our rightful and long established claims to priority on the American continent."

Blaine's brusque diplomacy did not win friends in Europe, particularly exasperating Great Britain through its repudiation of the joint canal policy agreed upon in 1850. A realistic editorial, however, appeared in the London *Times*:

The United States are indisputably the chief Power in the New World. . . . The United States coast-line may come by and by to extend in reality to the full limits which Mr. Blaine fancifully or prophetically assigns to it. Manifest Destiny is on one side. The Clayton-Bulwer Treaty is on the other.

The European governments may have scorned the new pretensions of the United States and certainly they were not willing to acknowledge Blaine's thesis in regard to its priority on the entire continent. The American people, however, accepted these broader implications of the Monroe Doctrine without question. When Blaine was succeeded at the State Department by Frederick T. Frelinghuysen, a treaty was negotiated with Nicaragua which in open violation of the provisions of the Clayton-Bulwer Treaty provided that the United States should have the exclusive right to build a canal on the sole condition that it guaranteed Nicaragua's territorial integrity. The Senate did not approve this treaty, but it nevertheless pointed up what would henceforth be undeviating national policy on this aspect of the canal issue.

Soon after this, in 1887, a private American corporation, the Maritime Canal Company, entered the canal construction field in Nicaragua in competition with de Lesseps' French company in Panama. Unable to obtain funds and facing imminent bankruptcy, both companies were soon forced to abandon their projects. It was clearly apparent that the job was much too big for private enterprise and would depend on government support. The American advocates of a canal, whether in Nicaragua or Panama, continued to press their cause, but popular interest subsided. It was not until the close of the century that the matter again became important. Nevertheless, the association built up in the public mind during these earlier years between the control of any such canal and national rights under the Monroe Doctrine was to bear unperishable fruit. The American people were henceforth emphatically to insist that the construction of any interocean waterway was exclusively "an American question."

Throughout the 1860's and the 1870's, opposition to any European encroachments in the Western Hemisphere, as set forth in an unwavering defense of the Monroe Doctrine, constituted the sum and total of popular interest in the countries lying south of the Rio Grande. National policy in the Western Hemisphere was anti-European rather than in any significant sense pro-Latin American. When Blaine was Secretary of State in 1881, however, he not only staunchly asserted the priority of the United States in the American continents, but also sought to develop a more affirmative Latin American policy bringing the republics of the New World more closely together, both politically and economically.

President Garfield had appointed Blaine, who was without diplomatic experience of any kind, to head the State Department for wholly political reasons. He was the bright, shining star of the Republican party; a man of commanding presence, great oratorical gifts, and magnetic charm. In the light of his tremendous popular following, Garfield could not ignore him, and in his turn Blaine was convinced (as Seward had been twenty years earlier) that he rather than the President was destined to dominate the administration in which he served. Moreover, with his eyes always fixed on his own expansive ambitions, Blaine hoped to develop a spirited foreign policy that would help to smooth his own path to the White House at the next presidential election. Looking about, he chose Latin America as the field in which he thought he could play the most conspicuous and profitable role.

Even though Blaine's motives may have been primarily political, his over-all design was nevertheless broad-minded and imaginative. He hoped to make the United States the guardian of peace throughout the Western Hemisphere, ultimately developing a new system of international arbitration, and he also sought to promote more integrated commercial relationships benefiting all the American republics. However, in the first phase of this task he rushed precipitately into situations about which he really knew very little, and far from strengthening the forces of hemispheric peace, did little more than create ill will.

He rather summarily intervened in a threatening quarrel between Mexico and Guatemala, and then singlehandedly attempted to mediate a far more important territorial dispute in which Bolivia and Peru were arrayed against Chile in the War of the Pacific. Although he repeatedly affirmed that his single goal was "to be the impartial friend of each and all," Blaine could not have blundered more egregiously in his self-assumed role of peacemaker. His interventionist policy settled no disputes and served only to arouse the deep mistrust of each of the nations concerned. He weakened rather than strengthened existing relations between the United States and its sister republics. His domestic political foes with considerable warrant condemned his policy as one of "meddling and muddling," and the peoples of Latin America saw in it no more than a new manifestation of Yankee imperialism.

Undeterred by such reactions to his diplomatic maneuvers, Blaine all the more resolutely tried to implement his commercial program. Latin American trade was based on an exchange of manufactured products for raw materials, and the United States was annually confronted by an adverse balance of something like $100 million in its international payments. The Secretary of State hoped to convince the Latin American governments that they should turn more to this country than to Europe for their foreign imports and thereby encourage a more extensive hemispheric commerce. To this end he persuaded President Garfield, in July, 1881, to summon an inter-American conference in Washington to explore the whole question.

This project suffered an abrupt setback, however, when as a consequence of President Garfield's assassination and the succession to the Presidency of Chester A. Arthur, Blaine found himself in a position where he could no longer control foreign policy. In the embittered infighting of the Republican party in the 1880's the new President and the Secretary of State were in opposing camps. While Blaine succeeded in persuading a reluctant Arthur to send out the invitations for his inter-American conference, the situation between the two men became so difficult that within a few weeks Blaine felt compelled to resign. One of the first moves of his successor, Frederick T. Frelinghuysen, was to cancel the inter-American meeting. Politics clearly led to this sharp reversal of policy, but the new Administration sought to justify it on the ground that, because of existing circumstances, the proposed conference would simply create jealousy and ill will rather than encourage either peace or trade.

The idea implicit in these first unsuccessful moves toward Pan-Americanism did not die. Seven years later, Congress itself called upon the President, who was now Grover Cleveland, to renew the call for an inter-American conference, and once again invitations went out to the governments concerned to send representatives to Washington. Yet still another change of administration took place before his meeting was actually held, and then by a curious quirk of fate it was James G. Blaine, once again made Secretary of State by President Harrison, who in October, 1889, officially received the delegates of the seventeen Latin American republics and served as the conference chairman. He was to have the chance that he had missed in 1881 to promote more directly hemispheric solidarity.

On their first arrival in Washington, Blaine extended an invitation to the visting delegates to make a nationwide tour of the country, and before settling down to any formal business, they traveled the length and breadth of the land in a special railroad train placed at their disposal. It was a most imposing junket. Citizens' committees at countless towns and cities met the sometimes bewildered Latin Americans with brass bands, entertained them royally, and took them on intensive sightseeing tours of industrial plants, banks and stores, government buildings and other local sights. From all accounts they returned to Washington completely exhausted, but the tour was judged a great success. It had provided the conference delegates a unique opportunity to learn something of the United States and had for a time focused the public's attention on Latin America as never before.

The meetings in Washington lasted five months, but they did not prove to be as productive as Blaine had hoped. He worked incessantly in support of two specific projects which reflected the ideas he had first tentatively advanced in 1881: the establishment of a system of arbitration that might strengthen peace throughout the Western Hemisphere, and the formation of a custom union for the further promotion of inter-American trade and commerce. In spite of all his urging, the conference rejected both of these projects. Its one concrete achievement—whatever may have been the intangible value of bringing representatives of Latin America and of the United States together around a conference table—was the formation of an International Bureau of American Republics, later to become the Pan-American Union.

Blaine was ahead of the times in attempting to create closer political and economic ties with the countries south of the Rio Grande, and his vision of hemispheric unity remained an unrealized dream. But he laid the groundwork for future developments in the next century that were to mark greater progress toward his ambitious goal. Even then—in spite of reciprocal trade agreements, mutual security pacts, and foreign aid—Latin American relations were to remain for the United States a constant and seemingly intractable problem.

The one clear, consistent, and successful aspect of Latin American policy throughout the latter half of the nineteenth century remained the determined defense of the principles underlying the Monroe Doctrine. Seward had greatly invigorated them in forcing France out of Mexico; Blaine had given them a new importance in later negotiations, and in the 1890's (as we shall subsequently see), Cleveland was to uphold them with exceptional vigor and force. Monroe might not have always recognized the doctrine that bore his name, but it had become the unassailable core of national policy in the Western Hemisphere.

CHAPTER III

Postwar Expansion

The spirited defense of the Monroe Doctrine first undertaken at the close of the Civil War was not the only sign at that time of a quickened interest in foreign affairs on the part of policy makers in Washington. Once freed of the burdens of internal strife, they sought to revive the expansionist sentiment that had been so widespread in the 1850's and to seek out for the United States new territories in both the Caribbean and the Pacific. There was even talk of the possible annexation of Canada. If the proponents of such ambitious ideas were notably unsuccessful in arousing popular support, it was not for want of trying.

"Comprehensive national policy," President Johnson stated in his annual message to Congress in 1868, "would seem to sanction the acquisition and incorporation in our Federal Union of the several adjacent continental and insular communities as speedily as can be done peacefully, lawfully, and without any violation of national justice, faith or honor."

The real driving force behind administration policy in the pursuit of such expansive goals, however, was the Secretary of State rather than the President himself. Johnson left Seward almost entirely in charge of foreign affairs; it was his sentiments that were expressed in the Presidential message in 1868. Seward never contemplated abandoning the basic isolationist policy that remained the unquestioned heritage of Washington and Jefferson. He was fully convinced that the geographical position of the United States, its territory and its resources, made it "singularly independent of the varying policy of foreign powers and protect us against every temptation to 'entangling alliances.'" Nevertheless, he did believe strongly in territorial expansion and never considered it as in any sense violating isolationist principles.

Seward would have liked to annex Santo Domingo and purchase the Danish West Indies, or Virgin Islands; he favored the possible acquisition of the Hawaiian Islands, and he even considered the possibility of securing some sort of foothold in China. He jumped at the opportunity to purchase Alaska from Russia. Always an imperialist at heart, he thought in terms of naval bases, dominion over the western ocean, and geopolitical strategy. In a much-quoted speech when he was a member of the Senate before the Civil War, he had stated that the Pacific was destined to become "the chief theater of events in the world's great hereafter," and enthusiastically declared that the United States "must command the empire of the seas which alone is real empire."

These grandiose dreams had not dimmed with the passage of time, and he not only looked to further extension of American territory overseas but envisioned continental sovereignty. "I know that Nature," he said in a speech in Boston in 1867, "designs that this whole continent, not merely these thirty-six states, shall be, sooner or later, within the magic circle of the American Union." His overpowering faith in America's imperial destiny foreshadowed the hold such ambitions won over the imagination of the expansionists of the 1890's.

In January, 1866, the Secretary of State undertook a cruise through the Caribbean, announced as "for his health," which took him to the Virgin Islands, Santo Domingo, Haiti, and Cuba. Almost immediately afterwards he opened negotiations with Denmark for the purchase of its island possessions and commenced talks over the possible annexation of Santo Domingo. The first step in his expansionist program was a faltering attempt to acquire the naval bases that would assure complete American control of the Caribbean and extend national influence into Central America.

The negotiations over the Virgin Islands were to drag on rather slowly, but Denmark was really anxious to sell them and in July, 1867, a treaty was concluded wherein the Danish Government agreed to their cession to the United States, subject to a plebiscite among their inhabitants, for $7,500,000. Even before any action was taken on this pact by the Senate, however, it became apparent that Seward's plans commanded little public support. The country was in no mood to acquire further territory at this time, and a devastating hurricane that inopportunely swept over the Virgin Islands made them seem especially unlikely additions to the national domain. Although the Danish Minister in Washington did everything possible to encourage approval of the treaty during extensive public hearings, the Senate Foreign Relations Committee unanimously tabled it.

There the matter rested for two years. It was brought up again when General Grant entered the White House in 1869, but the new President gave the treaty no support whatsoever. "That is entirely Seward's plan," he stated, "with which I desire absolutely nothing to do." The Senate committee thereupon reported adversely on the treaty, and the project died. The purchase of the Virgin Islands was deferred for nearly half a century, until the United States gladly paid $25,000,000 for them in 1916 to prevent their possibly falling into Germany's hands during the First World War.

In the meantime, Seward had been no more successful in regard to Santo Domingo. Even though that unhappy little island republic had succeeded in freeing itself from Spanish domination during the Civil War years, it was again fearful of the designs of its stronger neighbor Haiti, and also in dire financial straits. Its shaky government would have been glad to bail itself out in these circumstances, either by ceding a naval base at Samaná

Bay to the United States or by placing Santo Domingo entirely under American protection. Seward was more than willing to consider such proposals, but he could awaken no more popular support for them than for the purchase of the Virgin Islands. His ambitions were in this instance blocked short of the treaty he would have liked to negotiate by the prompt action of Congress in overwhelmingly rejecting a test resolution calling for Santo Domingo's annexation.

How far Seward might have liked to go in promoting a territorial acquisition nearer home—that of Canada—is more problematic than his clearly defined ambitions in the Caribbean. Indeed, he made no effort to avail himself of one possible opportunity for action that developed in the late 1860's. Seeking to embroil the United States and Great Britain in controversy as a means of promoting the cause of Irish independence, the Fenians, a secret society of radical Irish-Americans, organized a number of raids on Canadian territory. One of them assumed considerable proportions when an invading force of eight hundred men, most of them Civil War veterans, captured the village of Fort Erie and were driven back by the Canadians only after a bloody pitched battle. It was charged that the Secretary of State had been somewhat lax in seeking enforcement of the neutrality laws, so clearly violated by the Fenians, but Seward soon made it clear that he had little sympathy for such aggressive activities. Nor did he support the agitation for Canada's possible annexation that the Fenians tried to stir up. There is only the evidence of his Boston speech that he ever considered very seriously Canada's actual union with the United States.

This whole idea was in fact visionary. While it was for a time thought that the Canadians themselves might favor union, the noisy propaganda in this country, and especially the Fenian raids, served to strengthen Canadian nationalism. Moreover, such feeling was further reinforced at this very time, for Great Britain finally granted Canada dominion status through the passage of the British North America Act of 1867.

It was in the unexpected area of the most northerly section

of the continent that Seward achieved his one success in expanding the national domain. He was singlehandedly responsible for the purchase of Alaska from Russia. Even as he was failing to attain his goals in the Caribbean or in the Pacific, here he succeeded in the face of widespread public apathy and lively political opposition. And except for the casual annexation of little Midway Island, almost lost in the vast reaches of the Pacific, this would prove to be the only new accession of territory by the United States in the half century between the expansion of the 1840's and the imperialism of the 1890's. In the light of future circumstances, the purchase of Alaska was to have momentous consequences hardly foreseen in 1867. It is hard to imagine in just what ways—but obviously ways of great importance—the course of history might have been changed had Russia still held this territory on the North American continent during the twentieth century.

The idea of the possible transfer of what was then called Russian America had first arisen in the late 1850's. The experience of the Crimean War (even though Alaska had been neutralized during that European conflict) had convinced many Russian leaders that in the event of another war with Great Britain, it would be extremely difficult, if not impossible, for Russia to hold such a distant territory. The Grand Duke Constantine, strongly supported by the Russian Minister in Washington, Baron de Stoeckl, consequently recommended that Russia let it go. Better sell Alaska to a friendly United States, ran his straightforward thesis, than leave it as an indefensible hostage at the mercy of British power in North America.

Stoeckl opened informal conversations on the question in 1860, not with Secretary of State Cass but with Senator William M. Gwin of California and Assistant Secretary of State John Appleton, and he shortly reported to his government that the Buchanan Administration appeared to be favorably inclined toward the proposed transfer. A price of $5 million was mentioned. However, neither Russia nor the United States was yet ready to commit itself definitely, and while the project still hung fire, the shadow of the impending Civil War fell over America and the negotiations came to an end.

In the mid-1860's Russia was more than ever anxious to sell Alaska. Apart from its being so completely at the mercy of Great Britain in the event of war, the Russian-American Company, which controlled its affairs, was now facing bankruptcy, and the Czarist Government was finding the territory an increasing economic burden as well as a political liability. Moreover, its potentially rich resources—the Russian authorities already knew of its gold deposits—had further convinced Baron de Stoeckl that sooner or later Americans on the Pacific coast would begin to covet its hidden wealth. Believing that it would be impossible to resist their encroachments, he persuasively argued on a visit to St. Petersburg in the autumn of 1866 that it would now be doubly wise to sell Alaska before it was too late.

His ideas completely won over his government. A few of the more conservative officials in St. Petersburg expressed their opposition, declaring that Russia should never surrender any territory and particularly hold on to "every clod of earth" on the shores of such an important ocean as the Pacific. However, a majority of the Czar's counselors fully agreed with Stoeckl's thesis that the practical difficulties in defending Alaska against possible aggression, whether on the part of Great Britain or that of the United States, would be insurmountable. After a meeting of the Council of Ministers in December, Stoeckl was instructed to return to Washington and negotiate the sale of Alaska as his judgment dictated. The minimum price for the proposed deal was set at the tentative figure discussed six years earlier—$5 million.

The Russian Minister was both shrewd and realistic; he was not the man to put Alaska on the auction block without carefully preparing his sales campaign. But he need not have worried. Secretary Seward was so anxious to purchase the territory that he played directly into Stoeckl's hands.

Two very slender ties linked the United States with Alaska at this time. One was a possible concession for a projected telegraph line to Europe by way of North America and Siberia; the other was the concern of Pacific coast fishermen over free entry to Alaskan ports. Beyond these very minor matters, there was no interest whatsoever in the Russian territory outside the fertile and imaginative mind of the Secretary of State. Moreover, the telegraph project fell through with the successful laying of the Atlantic cable in 1866, and only a handful of people in the northwest really cared a whit about the Alaskan fishing grounds.

Seward nevertheless seized upon a convenient memorial from the Washington territorial legislature in March, 1867, to open conversations with Stoeckl about Alaska's future. The astute Russian Minister had probably hinted indirectly that something was in the wind, but it was the American Secretary of State who was taking the initiative and making the formal overtures in these first negotiations. He proposed that the American and Russian Governments consider "the importance of some early and comprehensive arrangement between the two countries to prevent the growth of difficulties arising out of the fisheries in the Russian possessions."

A delighted Stoeckl listened calmly to Seward's suggestions, which soon took shape and form as a direct offer to purchase Alaska, and without revealing that he was definitely instructed to sell the territory, quietly suggested that Russia might consider a reasonable offer. Two more willing partners to a prospective transfer of real estate could hardly be imagined. Their negotiations proceeded with speed and in complete secrecy.

Seward offered $5 million as a purchase price; Stoeckl countered with the figure of $7 million. A compromise was clearly in order, but Seward was such an eager buyer that Stoeckl saw no need to lower his price. After some halfhearted haggling, agreement was reached on the original Russian figure of $7 million. Moreover, when some question arose over various concessions and franchises that the Russian-American Company had made to private corporations, the Secretary of State offered to throw in another $200,000 if Alaska came to the United States free of all encumbrances. Stoeckl thereupon asked official authorization from his government to complete the deal, using the new Atlantic cable, and Seward sought out the approval of a surprised and somewhat skeptical President Johnson.

The Secretary of State's son has recorded the next step in this interesting transaction:

On Friday evening March 29, Seward was playing whist in his parlor with some of his family, when the Russian minister was announced.

"I have a dispatch, Mr. Seward, from my Government by cable. The Emperor gives his consent to the cession. Tomorrow if you like, I will come to the department, and we can enter upon the treaty."

Seward, with a smile of satisfaction at the news, pushed away the whist table, saying:

"Why wait till tomorrow, Mr. Stoeckl? Let us make the treaty tonight."

The Secretary of State routed out the departmental secretaries, summoned Charles Sumner, the redoubtable chairman of the Senate Foreign Relations Committee, and promptly repaired with the Russian minister to his State Department office. Far into the night and the following morning lights burned in the otherwise deserted building as Seward and Stoeckl hammered out the actual terms of the treaty. They completed their task at four in the morning. In those few brief hours they had arranged —at the purchase price of $7,200,000—for Russia's transfer to the United States of a vast territory totaling some 591,000 square miles, an area twice the size of Texas and equal to nearly one-fifth of the continental United States. And later this same day President Johnson sent a special message to the Senate in which he laconically presented for its approval "a treaty for the cession of Russian America."

Only a handful of people in Washington had any inkling of what Seward had been about, and the announcement of his dramatic coup was first greeted with stunned surprise. Newspaper editors hurried to their encyclopedias to discover what they could about this almost totally unknown territory he proposed to buy from Russia. Surprise was quickly succeeded by indignation. For the most part editors could see no point whatsoever in spending what was then the huge sum of $7,200,000 for a great hunk of land that was said to be frozen throughout the year to a depth of six feet, whose streams were all glaciers, and whose only products appeared to be icebergs and polar bears. The editorials greeting announcement of the proposition hooted at the Secretary of State with scorn and derision.

The embittered political opposition to President Johnson on the part of the Radical Republicans, who were soon to impeach him for his defiance of their policies on reconstruction, heightened the criticism of his Secretary of State's treaty along partisan lines. Nevertheless, the newspapers' initial reaction (it would later become more favorable) generally reflected the public's sense of outraged bewilderment over what the United States could possibly want with "Johnson's Polar Bear Garden" and "Seward's Icebox." The New York *Herald* was later to support the treaty, but in its first comment sarcastically advised Seward to purchase Patagonia as well in order "to make both ends meet" and gleefully published the advertisment:

CASH! CASH! CASH!—Cash paid for cast-off territory. Best price given for old colonies, North or South. Any impoverished monarchs retiring from the colonization business may find a good purchaser by addressing W.H.S., Post Office, Washington, D.C.

So violent was the outburst in some quarters against this "dark deed done in the night," that Senator Sumner went so far as to advise Baron de Stoeckl to seek withdrawal of the treaty to avoid its being summarily rejected by the Senate. But Seward himself was undismayed. He promptly launched a nationwide campaign to convince the country—and Congress—that Alaska was worth far more to the United States than the $7,200,000 he had pledged for its purchase. In the literature sent to newspapers throughout the land, he compared the new territory with Louisiana, declaring opposition to its purchase was as provincial and shortsighted as had been that to Jefferson's purchase in 1803. He expatiated enthusiastically on Alaska's potential wealth in fish, furs, and lumber, and even more strongly stressed its great commercial and strategic importance in relation to the position of the United States in the Pacific. He also argued that the United States owed Russia a great debt for its sympathetic attitude during the Civil War, and could not in good conscience rebuff its friendly overtures in being willing to sell Alaska.

Seward's first important victory was in winning the support of such an outspoken foe of the Johnson Administration as Senator Sumner. The latter's own expansionist ideas led him to uphold Seward's hand on this project, even though he later admitted that "the Russian treaty tried me severely," and he was also greatly influenced by the argument that the United States should not reject such a cordial offer from the Czarist Government. He set forth his views in a memorable speech before the Senate that had a perhaps decisive influence in winning that august body's support.

Sumner made three major points. If the United States did not carry through the proposed territorial transfer, Alaska would some day fall into the hands of Great Britain: the United States should consequently seize the opportunity immediately presented to acquire the territory and assure American control of the Pacific. Secondly, with the Aleutian Islands "extending a friendly hand to Asia," their possession would be of immense value in the development of trade with both Japan and China. And finally, after recalling the circumstances of the Civil War, Sumner emphatically stated that it was difficult to see "how we can refuse to complete the purchase without putting to hazard the friendly relations which happily subsist between the United States and Russia."

On April 9, 1867—only ten days after the treaty's signature—the Senate conquered its scruples and gave its approval to Seward's bold move to add Alaska to the United States. The majority was 27 to 12. Moreover, when it was then proposed to make the vote unanimous as a gesture of cordiality toward "the

old and faithful friend of the United States," the opposition fell
to only two votes.

Yet this is not the end of the story of Alaska's purchase.
Senatorial approval was one thing; it was still necessary to secure
the consent of the House to the required $7,200,000 appropria-
tion. It was for long in doubt. The impeachment proceedings
against Johnson absorbed the public attention and the ill feeling
they engendered appeared for a time to make it unlikely that
Congress would ever approve anything attributed to his Administration. Baron de Stoeckl became so discouraged that at one
point he proposed to his government that it attempt to shame
Congress into taking some action by offering to forgo payment
for Alaska's transfer. The Russian Foreign Minister, perhaps fearful that Congress would take advantage of such an offer, did not
approve the suggestion.

A new complication also developed in the course of the
Congressional debate in respect to certain private claims brought
against the Russian Government and the insistence of a number
of congressmen that they be settled preliminary to any American
payment for Alaska's transfer. When it was revealed that these
claims were probably fraudulent, an atmosphere of possible cor-
ruption began to shadow the whole Alaskan transaction, and it
was widely rumored that bribery was being used to win the support of wavering representatives for the appropriation bill.

These charges were never conclusively proved, Seward indeed officially stating that "no engagement was ever made with
anybody for any part of the purchase-money, or any other fund,"
but the suspicion still lingers that the line between legitimate
propaganda activities and buying votes was not always too carefully drawn. The Russian Minister later reported to his government that the greater part of the $200,000 added to the original
purchase price for Alaska had been used for "secret expenses."
Among President Johnson's papers there was found a memorandum quoting Seward as having said that very considerable
sums had been paid a number of leading members of the House
of Representatives in return for their votes. Hearsay evidence

perhaps, but the taint of bribery remained. Once the whole business was completed, in any event, Baron de Stoeckl asked his government to transfer him to another post where he could "breathe an atmosphere purer than that of Washington."

The discussion in the House, whatever the facts in regard to money expended in influencing votes, followed very much the lines already laid down in critical newspaper editorials. "Alaska, with the Aleutian Islands," Representative Ferris of New York declared, "is an inhospitable, wretched, and God-forsaken region, worth nothing, but a positive injury and encumbrance as a colony of the United States." Washburn of Wisconsin suggested that if the United States was determined upon acquiring a white elephant, it could get a much superior one "in Siam or Bombay for one-hundredth part of the money, with not a ten thousandth part of the expense incurred in keeping the animal in proper condition." And Representative Williams of Pennsylvania in asking "have the people desired it?" answered emphatically: "Not a sensible man among them ever suggested it. The whole country exclaimed at once, when it was made known to them, against the ineffable folly, if not the wanton profligacy, of the whole transaction."

Although political bias rather than calm evaluation of the potential worth of Alaska obviously inspired many of these caustic comments, the haste and secrecy with which Seward had conducted his negotiations provided some basis for the charges brought against the Administration of trying to put something over on a completely uninformed public. Congressional resentment at being faced with the *fait accompli* represented by the treaty itself was moreover heightened by the fact that without waiting for appropriation of the necessary funds, Seward—on October 18, 1867—had ordered the American flag to be raised over Sitka. Congress felt it was being dragooned into paying out an immense sum for a very questionable acquisition without ever being allowed to consider the issue on its real merits. When one congressman patriotically declared that once the flag had been raised, "Palsied be the hand that should dare to remove it!" the opponents of Alaska's purchase bitterly realized that the ground had been swept from under them.

Still, there were spokesmen in the House with a broader vision than the treaty's foes who at least realized Alaska's strategic value. Representative Maynard of Tennessee argued that its possession would give the United States commercial and naval supremacy throughout the Pacific. It would be as complete, he declared, as "Great Britain has for two centuries enjoyed on the Atlantic Ocean." William Mungen of Ohio carried this idea even further in stating that Alaska's purchase would "cage the British lion on the Pacific coast," and with the consequent decline in England's power, the day would come when "the two great Powers on earth will be Russia and the United States." Nathaniel P. Banks, chairman of the House Foreign Relations Committee (he was said to have received appropriate encouragement from the Russian Minister), even more directly echoed Seward's views as to the future of the Pacific:

That ocean will be the theatre of the triumphs of civilization in the future. It is on that line that are to be fought the great battles of the hereafter. It is there that the institutions of the world will be fashioned and its destinies decided. If this transfer is successful, it will no longer be an European civilization or an European destiny that controls us. It will be a higher civilization and a nobler destiny. It may be an American civilization, an American destiny of six hundred million souls.

The extreme positions taken by the foes and friends of Alaska's cession—the territory was either completely worthless or a guarantee of American supremacy throughout the whole Pacific region—reflected the air of unreality marking the entire debate. Seward had indeed presented Congress with a *fait accompli;* the Congressional speechmaking was only for the record. It came to an end on June 23, 1868. The House then appropriated the necessary funds by the clear-cut majority of 113 to 43, and with the Senate quickly concurring, the measure went to the President. Upon his signature the commitment that

Seward had made some sixteen months earlier was at last officially confirmed and Alaska became a part of the United States.

It is hardly necessary to add that the purchase soon proved its value many times over in every way. Within a few years the profits derived from the Alaskan fishing and sealing industries exceeded the $7,200,000 paid for the territory, and even before the famous Klondike Rush in 1896, gold production had at least equalled what had seemed in 1867 such a high purchase price. From the point of view of military and naval strategy, Alaska's importance has of course long since been conclusively proved. First organized as a territory, it became in 1958 the forty-ninth state, and its continued economic and commercial development has still further confirmed Seward's prophecies of almost a century earlier.

The purchase of Alaska was the only concrete result of Seward's plans for acquiring new territory. The Grant Administration, coming into office in 1869, did not harbor his imperialist ambitions, and the new Secretary of State, Hamilton Fish, was far more conservative in his outlook than his predecessor. As already noted in discussing the Monroe Doctrine, however, President Grant himself became deeply involved in a highly complicated, rather unsavory, and completely unsuccessful attempt to annex Santo Domingo in 1870.

A group of American speculators seeking to protect certain land and mineral concessions which they had obtained from the Dominican Government first interested Grant in the possible acquisition of this territory, and once the idea had taken hold, he clung to it with the tenacity that had marked his operations in the rather higher cause of preserving the Union. While, as we have seen, he would have none of Seward's plan to purchase the Virgin Islands, he committed himself, wholeheartedly and stubbornly, to obtaining Santo Domingo.

His first step in seeking to carry out this program, completely bypassing the State Department, was to send his military secretary, General Orville E. Babcock, to Santo Domingo to explore the possibilities of annexation. After a brief visit in the summer of 1869, this personal emissary returned with two agreements, later incorporated in draft treaties. The first provided for Santo Domingo's annexation, with a pledge of ultimate statehood, and the second was limited to a long-term lease of Samaná Bay with the right to purchase it at any time for $2 million. Everything about the negotiation of these treaties was highly irregular. The influence of the American land speculators gave the whole business a very questionable aspect, and the transaction was further muddied by a personal agreement concluded by General Babcock which stated that the President was prepared to use his personal authority in support of one or the other treaty.

Grant accepted the annexation treaty and lobbied aggressively for it, exerting all his influence on individual senators to win their votes. But neither the country nor Congress showed any real interest, and the frustrated President found he could make little headway. When the issue came to a head in June, 1870, the senatorial vote on the treaty was 28 to 28, far short of the two-thirds majority necessary for approval. In spite of this defeat, Grant continued to seek other ways to secure his goal and ill-advisedly suggested a possible joint resolution for Santo Domingo's annexation. It was not until October, 1871, that he finally gave the matter up. Secretary Fish, who had never approved the project, happily noted in his diary that "a troublesome, vexatious, and unnecessary question is, as I trust, finally got rid of."

This last episode in the post-Civil War expansionist movement did not redound to the credit of anyone involved in it, but over and beyond the immediate opposition to the annexation of Santo Domingo itself, it was highly revealing of the popular attitude toward possible acquisition of new territory. Whatever the dreams of Secretary Seward—and, in this instance, the ambitions of President Grant—the public could not have been more indifferent to the call of imperialism. It had accepted the pur-

chase of Alaska only grudgingly, and Congress had then made
known its unequivocal opposition to any further accessions. Nowhere was there any real popular support for overseas dominion.
The American people remained far too absorbed in the problems
of postwar economic recovery, currency inflation, agrarian unrest, and southern reconstruction.

A deeply disappointed Seward had soon come to realize how
completely public attention was centered on domestic matters.
"The public mind refuses to dismiss these questions," he wrote
somewhat ruefully, "even so far as to entertain the higher but
more remote questions of national extension and aggrandizement." It was his sad conclusion that the leaders of both parties
shrank from any suggestion involving a new national enterprise
because "we have come to value dollars more and dominion less."

There was no question that he was right in this analysis of
the popular temper. "The true interests of the American people,"
the Philadelphia *Press* declared, "will be better served at this
important period of our national history by a thorough and complete development of the immense resources of our existing
territory than by any rash attempt to increase it." The *Nation*
even went so far as to say that if the national future was in any
way imperiled, "it is not for want of territory but from excess
of it."

In many quarters it was also maintained—foreshadowing the
arguments of the anti-imperialists of the 1890's—that even if a
case could be made out for the value of overseas naval bases
(such as Santo Domingo or Haiti, or even the Hawaiian Islands),
a republic could not morally acquire them. "We cannot have
colonies, dependencies, subjects," the New York *Tribune* stated
(this would not be its attitude in 1898), "without renouncing the
essential conception of democratic institutions." Such ideas were
also vigorously expressed in Congress during the debate on the
possible annexation of Santo Domingo. Senator Thomas F.
Bayard of Delaware gravely warned of the dangers to a republican system of government should the United States embark
"upon the vast and trackless sea of imperialism," and Carl Schurz

of Missouri, answering the statements already being made that overseas expansion was the nation's manifest destiny, stated glumly that if such a course were to be followed, either acquiring tropical islands as "satrapies" or admitting them to the Union as states, he would be seriously tempted to call it "manifest doom."

Everything militated against overseas expansion in these years, and it was only natural that the American people, rarely looking beyond their own borders, should become increasingly absorbed in domestic affairs. The Civil War had released their energies to carry through the two great tasks of building up the country's industries and settling the West. The vast prairie lands that had once been called the Great American Desert—the area lying between the Missouri and the Rocky Mountains—were still to be freed of the Indian menace, carved into homesteads, and planted to wheat and corn. Here was more than enough to keep Americans busy at home. Not until the close of the century would the imperialistic spirit that Seward had vainly hoped to stimulate undergo the revival that led to the overseas dominion of which he dreamed.

CHAPTER IV

Relations with Great Britain

For all its absorption in primarily domestic problems, there was one country with which the United States, through its very close associations, was unable to avoid repeated and sometimes acrimonious controversy in the latter half of the nineteenth century. This was of course Great Britain. There was still a residue of distrust and suspicion arising from the historic conflicts of the past, but over and beyond memories of the Revolution and the War of 1812, other disputes continued to give an often precarious cast to Anglo-American relations.

The attitude of the English during the Civil War had not proved to be very endearing, and Americans continued to resent the British Government's laxity in allowing the escape of the *Alabama* and other British-built Confederate raiders. Its policy in postwar years in respect to the Monroe Doctrine, especially in matters relating to a possible isthmian canal, was also highly suspect. And then there was Canada. Even when the popular agitation over possible annexation died down, quarrels were almost inevitable with this northern neighbor—boundaries, fishing rights, and rival claims to sealing grounds. The confrontation between the United States and Great Britain over such issues, however relatively unimportant in themselves, invariably inflamed national passions on either side of the Atlantic, and on occasion the most trivial incidents were artificially built up into what momentarily seemed to be dangerous crises.

The first serious dispute arose over the American demand for compensation for the damage inflicted by the Confederate commerce raiders. Americans generally felt that the British Government's failure to prevent the escape of these vessels during the Civil War had not only cost the United States a great sum in the loss of the shipping they had destroyed, but had so prolonged hostilities as to have been responsible for a further immense toll in both lives and property. Great Britain should be made to pay both the direct and indirect costs attributed to her laxity. For their part, the British believed they had done everything possible to uphold their neutrality, and while willing to make some compensation for actual losses resulting from the destruction of American vessels by the commerce raiders, the popular and official feeling was that any additional American demands were extravagant and unjustified. What became known as the *Alabama* claims issue was to arouse deep emotions in both countries.

Secretary Seward, engrossed as he was with his own expansionist ambitions, was not carried away by the anti-British feeling of the day, and he was hopeful of concluding an Anglo-American convention that would provide for the equitable settlement of all outstanding disputes. So too a new British Government, under the leadership of Prime Minister Gladstone, felt that every effort should be made to avoid further controversy. On the *Alabama* claims issue, Great Britain also had a very practical reason for trying to reach an accommodation with the United States. Congress was threatening, in retaliation for British laxity in enforcing its Civil War neutrality, to adopt the position that a neutral national could legally sell warships to a belligerent. In any future war this policy could gravely endanger British interests.

The consequence of this mutual willingness in both American and British official circles to settle the *Alabama* controversy was the conclusion, in January, 1869, of the so-called Johnson-Clarendon Convention. It was, however, doomed from the start. For while it provided for the settlement of individual claims arising from the depredations of the Confederate cruisers built in Great Britain, it fell far short of satisfying popular demands in the United States. It made no apology for allowing the *Alabama* to escape, upon which all patriotic Americans insisted, and it ignored the indirect claims to which this country considered itself entitled because of the effect of British policy in prolonging the war. Rising in its wrath, the Senate rejected the Johnson-Clarendon Convention out of hand by the overwhelming vote of 54 to 1.

Quite as significant as this decisive defeat for the convention was a sensational, free-swinging speech that Charles Sumner, who remained one of the most powerful political figures in the country, delivered in the course of senatorial debate. Sumner flatly stated that the unneutral attitude of Great Britain during the course of the war had served to double the period of hostilities. Its government should consequently not only pay the claims growing out of the depredations of the *Alabama* and other commerce raiders, which he set at $15 million for ships actually sunk and $110 million for losses of revenue sustained by other merchantmen driven from the seas, but it should also meet all such further costs as could be attributed to the prolongation of the war. Placing the Union's over-all wartime expenses at $4 billion, he then left what Great Britain actually owed the United States for doubling the period of hostilities to the public's ready imagination—"everybody can make the calculation." There was also a clear implication in what Sumner said, though he made no specific mention of it, that Great Britain could only meet this impossible bill and satisfy the United States by agreeing to the cession of Canada.

The speech created intense excitement. Americans generally cheered to the echo its flamboyant exposition of the popular position on England's debt to the United States. Many of them welcomed the hint that only the transfer of Canada could clear the slate. On the other hand, the British were outrageously shocked by such extravagant and exorbitant demands. Their re- action clearly suggested that England would go to war rather than be dragooned into the surrender of Canada.

The new Administration of President Grant had come into office on the eve of the Senate's rejection of the Johnson-Claren- don Convention, and for a time its policy appeared to be in doubt. However, it had in Hamilton Fish, who was a wealthy New Yorker and one-time governor of his state, a Secretary of State of wide experience and sober judgment. Grant had ap- pointed him almost by accident, but he was to prove to be one of the most realistic-minded, far-seeing, and skillful diplomats ever to grace the State Department. No one realized more clearly the dangers inherent in the anti-British attitude which Sumner's bel- ligerent speech exemplified. As President Grant became absorbed in his Santo Domingo intrigues (and other members of the cabinet in even less exemplary activities), Fish set himself to the task of resolving the grave difficulties with Great Britain through patient, persistent, behind-the-scenes diplomacy.

The *Alabama* claims controversy was not the only disagree- ment disturbing Anglo-American relations at this time. Questions had also arisen over the northwest boundary between the United States and Canada, and over conflicting American and Canadian fishing rights in the northeastern coastal waters. Secretary Fish held a series of informal discussions over these matters, as well as the *Alabama* claims, with the Canadian Minister of Finance, Sir John Rose, and the two men agreed on the importance of a conciliatory approach to the whole complex of issues in dispute. On a visit to London, Sir John then sounded out the British Government as to its willingness to renew the formal negotiations which had been broken off after rejection of the Johnson- Clarendon Convention. The British Government's response to these indirect overtures was favorable, and it agreed to try once more for a general settlement whereby all questions at issue would be subjected to impartial arbitration. Early in 1871 the American and British Governments thereupon appointed a Joint

High Commission to conclude a new and comprehensive Anglo-American treaty.

The Commission held its meetings in Washington in an atmosphere of expansive cordiality, sedulously encouraged by a succession of banquets and other entertainments, that contrasted sharply with the popular storms of the preceding year. After several weeks of intense negotiations, full agreement was reached on the way the disputed issues should be handled, and on May 8 the Commission members signed the Treaty of Washington. It referred the northwest boundary dispute to the binding arbitration of the German Emperor; outlined a direct settlement of the fisheries controversy through a reallocation of territorial rights and American compensation to Canada for additional privileges granted American fishermen; established a mixed claims commission to handle a number of other minor matters, and, most importantly, provided for the submission of the *Alabama* claims to an arbitral tribunal whose five members would be individually named by the United States, Great Britain, Italy, Brazil, and the Swiss Confederation.

Great Britain expressed its regret in this document for the escape of the *Alabama* and the other Confederate cruisers, acknowledging that a neutral government was obligated to exercise "due diligence" in preventing any ship intended for a belligerent from leaving its ports. In respect to possible reparations, nothing was said about the so-called indirect claims growing out of the supposed prolongation of the war, and it was tacitly assumed by such an omission that the United States had agreed to waive them. Common sense appeared to have carried the day, and both nations—their governments and their people—fully approved the treaty. The British felt that a satisfactory formula had been found for placing Anglo-American relations on a reasonable basis; Americans were gratified that the settlement, whatever its monetary terms might prove to be, included a British apology for the *Alabama's* escape highly satisfying to national pride.

When the tribunal set up by the Washington Treaty met in

Geneva in December, 1871, its high hopes of being able to arrive at a speedy settlement on the actual amount of the *Alabama* claims were unexpectedly dashed. The United States revived its demand for compensation for the indirect losses suffered during the war. The British Government, incensed over what it regarded as Yankee perfidy in bringing this question up again, bluntly refused to allow its submission to the arbitrators. To do so, Gladstone told Queen Victoria, would be "wholly incompatible with national honour." Under heavy political pressure, Secretary Fish in turn felt compelled to fall back on this vague abstraction and defend the American position. It would be an impossible surrender, he asserted, for the United States to allow any other nation to dictate how it should present its case at Geneva. The two countries once again appeared to have reached a complete impasse.

There was irresponsible talk of possible war in both the United States and Great Britain. Prices fell sharply on their respective stock exchanges, and their business communities showed great alarm. But the absurdity of allowing domestic politics, beating the drums of nationalism, to block an agreement which both countries so strongly desired, was recognized on either side of the Altantic and a search made for some way out of the dilemma. The successful formula was found by Charles Francis Adams, who, after serving his country so admirably in London during the Civil War, was now the American member of the arbitral tribunal. To satisfy political expediency and the demands of national honor in the two countries, he persuaded his colleagues in Geneva to give an "extra-judicial opinion" on the indirect claims, thereby complying with British demands that they not be taken up by the tribunal and yet satisfying the American requirement that they should not be altogether dropped. The arbitrators then solemnly gave their informal advice that *if* the indirect claims were taken up, they would be dismissed as not allowable under international law. Both the American and British Governments were satisfied; the arbitrators got back to their real business.

The tribunal heard months of argumentation from the two sides before finally—on September 14, 1872—handing down its long-awaited award. It then held that Great Britain had indeed failed to exercise due diligence in the escape of the *Alabama* and the other Confederate commerce raiders and awarded the United States a total of $15,500,000 in damages for the losses suffered by American shipping. Even though its claims had been whittled down, the United States considered this decision satisfactory; Great Britain (though its representative on the tribunal angrily refused to sign it) also felt that in the circumstances the award was quite reasonable. "We simply wanted the judgment of five men of sense and honour," the London *Times* commented on the decision; "we cheerfully abide by it."

Wholly regardless of the actual terms of the agreement, the real triumph, as all the world realized, was for peace.

For all the success of the Washington Treaty in providing for the settlement of immediate Anglo-American disputes, no piece of parchment or tribunal award could entirely allay the anti-British feelings still lying so close beneath the surface in American life. They were to be stirred up once more, with deft prodding from Irish-Americans, when, fourteen years after the treaty's signature, the old fisheries dispute flared into new prominence. The issues at stake were hardly vital ones, but for a time jingoism and politics kept the pot boiling so furiously that there was again much silly talk of possible war before reason finally had its way.

American opinion had become convinced in the early 1880's that certain aspects of the fisheries settlement agreed upon in accordance with the Treaty of Washington were no longer applicable and should be modified. Responding primarily to political pressures from New England, Congress thereupon invaded the field of foreign policy and by a joint resolution, to become effective on July 1, 1885, arbitrarily terminated the privileges which had been granted the Canadians for fishing in American waters. Charging an inexcusable breach of faith, Canada retaliated by giving orders for the seizure of any American fishing schooners found in its waters. Not to be outdone, Congress then adopted a further measure in March, 1887, authorizing the President, in answer to the Canadian Government's move, to bar all Canadian ships from American ports and suspend their trading privileges in the United States.

Here was, indeed, a mixed-up situation. President Cleveland was in office when this controversy came to a head, and while he signed the Congressional bill authorizing him to penalize Canadian trade, he had no idea of enforcing it. He favored frank negotiation of the issue with Great Britain, representing Canada, and through his Secretary of State, former Senator Thomas F. Bayard, he proposed the establishment of another joint commission to study the whole problem and work out a fair solution safeguarding both American and Canadian interests.

Politics, however, now took over completely. Cleveland was a Democrat, coming up for possible re-election in 1888, and it was to the interest of the Republicans, so often accused, especially by the Irish, of being pro-British, to demonstrate that it was the Democrats who were ready to betray the national interest by truckling to Great Britain. The idea of negotiating the fisheries issues was attacked as abject surrender. "Why should the United States want a treaty?" one irate Republican senator demanded; "England has never kept a treaty; she has never made one that she did not violate." The President was fiercely attacked for his supposed British sympathies, and his able and conciliatory Secretary of State was caustically characterized as "the most popular Englishman ever born in the United States."

The Democratic newspapers upheld the President's moderate course, *The New York Times* declaring that foreign policy should not be pushed to the dangerous extremes a Republican-controlled Congress was seeking to drive it. The opposition press, however, called for direct action to defend the rights of American fishermen and, frantically waving the flag, once again stirred up talk of war. The New York *Tribune* heaped obloquy on the Democrats' "craven and pusillanimous policy" in the face of the Canadian

Government's seizure of American vessels. In some quarters, the possibility of British hostilities encouraged the old idea of the United States taking over Canada. If Great Britain did not back down in the fisheries dispute, the Columbus *Dispatch* declared, the opportunity should be seized to invade Canada and "the continent will be ours." Following the same line, the Detroit *News* gloated over what "elegant states" the Canadian provinces would make, and printed the popular verse:

> *We do not want to fight,*
> *But by jingo, if we do,*
> *We'll scoop in all the fishing grounds*
> *And the whole Dominion, too.*

Undismayed by the storm raging around them (perhaps encouraged by such comments as that of the Nashville *American*, which declared the country was not going to war "for the sake of a few hundred Yankee fishermen and a few stinking codfish"), Cleveland and Bayard continued on their conciliatory course, and in February, 1888, the negotiations they had instituted with Great Britain led to the conclusion of a mutually satisfactory treaty governing the respective rights of American and Canadian fishermen. But the exigencies of an election year continued to stand firmly in the path of any reasonable accommodation. When the fisheries treaty came before the Senate, it divided along strictly partisan lines without the slightest regard to the agreement's possible merits. The Democrats cast their twenty-seven ballots in favor of ratification; the Republicans threw their decisive thirty votes against it.

Cleveland, in his turn, now made a move that may have been designed to give him leverage in any further negotiations with Great Britain, but certainly had as well its partisan motivation. He proposed strict enforcement of the retaliatory measures against Canadian ships which he had opposed and refused to apply when a Republican Congress had first suggested them. By so doing he placed his political foes in a neat box. The economic consequences of cutting off such trade might well cost them

more votes, in an election year, than they had formerly hoped to
gain by charging Cleveland with truckling to Great Britain. The
same Congress that had rejected the treaty peacefully settling
the fisheries dispute because it entailed the surrender of American rights, now turned around to block the countermeasures the
President proposed for forcing Great Britain to acknowledge
those rights.

The Presidential campaign of 1888 was consequently fought
amid charges and countercharges of subserviency to British interests and irresponsible encouragement of war. Cleveland and
his Republican opponent, Benjamin Harrison, found themselves
vying for the popular vote, among other issues, as the more stal-
wart champion of national rights. Moreover, as the election drew
to a close, this rather absurd situation was further complicated
when the British Minister in Washington, Sir Lionel Sackville-
West, inadvertently added more fuel to the fires of partisanship
by allowing himself to be drawn into the controversy.

This bungling and most inept of diplomats fell into a trans-
parent political trap when he answered a letter, which he supposed to be genuine but which was actually written by a Republican party worker posing as a naturalized citizen born in
England, asking his advice about the election. The question was
whether Cleveland's proposals for stiff retaliatory action against
Canada in the fisheries dispute meant that the Democratic candidate had deserted the British cause. In his reply Sir Lionel
ingenuously expressed the view that once the election was over,
the Democrats would prove to be very friendly toward Great
Britain and that Cleveland had given every manifestation of "a
spirit of conciliation." The Republican high command gleefully
published this revealing letter as final and conclusive evidence of
Cleveland's weak-kneed attitude. Anti-British feeling was won-
derfully revived, and a sympathetic friend wrote Secretary Bayard
that "the effect on our Irish Democracy is such as to utterly
destroy all hope for us."

Cleveland was enraged by such stupid intervention in domestic politics on the part of a foreign diplomat and demanded

Sackville-West's immediate recall. When the British Foreign Office appeared to hesitate, he took matters in his own hands and summarily dismissed the offending envoy. This prompt action, greatly discomfiting the British, who refused to replace Sackville-West while Cleveland remained in office, may have won a few votes which might otherwise have been lost. It did not, however, save an election which the Republicans handily won, at least in part because of the popular outcry they had inspired against Cleveland for being "conspicuously unpatriotic" in his willingness even to consider negotiations with Great Britain.

The final outcome of all this furor, perhaps the most striking example in the 1880's of how frivolously the country treated matters of foreign policy, was very much of an anticlimax. The American and British commissions that had drawn up the treaty Cleveland had submitted and the Senate had rejected in 1888 had also concluded a *modus vivendi* governing American and Canadian fishing rights, which was to run for two years. When the treaty went down to defeat, this *modus vivendi* automatically came into force through an executive agreement which did not need senatorial approval. The dying down of popular excitement over the whole issue after the Presidential election and the inherent reasonableness of the terms of the *modus vivendi* then led to its being quietly renewed after the expiration of the two-year term by the new Republican President. What had been such an explosive issue under the pressure of domestic politics was soon almost completely forgotten. A good many years later the points still at issue were submitted to arbitration at The Hague, and a conclusive settlement of the historic fishing controversy was finally reached on a lasting basis.

Still, there was as yet no really satisfactory *rapprochement* in Anglo-American relations. Even as the fisheries dispute was subsiding after the election of 1888, another controversy had arisen between the United States and Canada. The incoming Harrison Administration found itself quarreling with the British Foreign Office over international sealing rights in the Bering Sea.

In an interesting reversal of what had happened in the fisheries controversy, the Canadians were in this instance encroaching on what were deemed to be American waters, and the United States had arbitrarily seized a number of their vessels. Needless to say, the Canadians were no more pleased over such seizures than the Americans had been happy when the Canadians had taken over their schooners in the northeastern fishing grounds. In support of Canada, the British Government entered a vigorous protest and challenged the whole American position in the Bering Sea.

The peculiar habits of the fur seal (an animal which the diplomatic historian, Samuel F. Bemis, has engagingly described as "ubiquitous and carnivorous, uniparous, gregarious and with all polygamous!") precipitated this minor but troublesome controversy. Great herds of this valuable fur-bearing mammal—numbering some four million—inhabited the Pribilof Islands, which the United States had acquired with the purchase of Alaska, and in their oceanic wanderings they did not always observe the territorial limits of American maritime jurisdiction. Canadian pelagic sealers—that is, sealers hunting in the open sea rather than on land—hovered just outside the three-mile limit to take a heavy toll of the seals from the Pribilof herd. The real trouble resulting from this practice was that the Canadians indiscriminately slaughtered both males and females, whereas in their land-hunting operations, the American sealers were careful to kill only the males. Pelagic sealing threatened the complete extinction of the seal population on the Pribilof Islands.

In justification of the seizure of the Canadian sealing vessels, the United States had first claimed that the Bering Sea was "a closed sea" and thereby under American jurisdiction without regard to the usual three-mile limit. Great Britain flatly denied any basis for such a broad claim. When James G. Blaine, serving his second term as Secretary of State under Harrison, found himself confronted with these issues, he shifted the grounds of the earlier debate. He maintained that since the basic issue was that pelagic sealing threatened to exterminate the Pribilof herd, the United

States had the prescriptive right—moral as well as legal—to protect the seals against indiscriminate slaughter. In objecting to this policy, he declared, Great Britain ignored the real basis for it. "One step beyond that which Her Majesty's Government has taken in this controversy," he belligerently concluded a spirited dispatch dated January 22, 1890, "and piracy finds its justification."

In answering the American note Lord Salisbury, the British Foreign Secretary, tore Blaine's arguments to pieces as being without any legal validity whatsoever. He based the British case, however, primarily on the ground that no nation, under any circumstances, had the right to seize the vessels of another in time of peace. "Her Majesty's Government," he firmly stated, "must hold the Government of the United States responsible for the consequences that may ensue from acts which are contrary to the established principles of international law."

The challenging nature of these diplomatic exchanges were hardly conducive to an easy solution of the sealing controversy. In the United States they fanned the smoldering embers of Anglophobia, and the old cry arose for teaching Great Britain a lesson. The dispute, however, appeared even less important to most people than that over the northeastern fisheries (although a vogue for sealskin coats and muffs was forcing up the price of the fur), and the public refused to become very excited over it. One newspaper suggested that the United States revenue cutters should shoot on sight at any Canadian sealing vessels daring to enter the Bering Sea, but the general opinion was perhaps more faithfully reflected by another journal which scoffed at any idea of inciting hostilities over "a few greasy, ill-smelling seal skins."

In any event, the rather bellicose tone of the diplomatic dispatches exchanged between Secretary Blaine and Lord Salisbury gradually gave way to a more reasoned approach to the problem, and in February, 1892, the two governments had reached a point where they were prepared to accept arbitration. The dispute had followed what seemed to be becoming an accepted pattern in Anglo-American relations: a sudden flare-up of controversy, political agitation, and patriotic exhortations never to surrender, the gradual moderation of popular sentiment, and final agreement on arbitration.

The tribunal that was set up to deal with the sealing issue and decide the conflicting claims of the United States and Great Britain in respect to jurisdiction in the Bering Sea rejected the American position altogether and awarded Great Britain $473,151 in damages for the illegal seizure of the Canadian vessels. In these circumstances pelagic sealing continued, but its serious consequences, not only for the herds on the Pribilof Islands but for those in other parts of the North Pacific, soon came to be more generally appreciated by all the nations concerned. Ultimately an agreement was reached among the United States, Great Britain, Russia, and Japan whereby pelagic sealing was outlawed throughout the entire North Pacific.

The way in which the disputes with Great Britain over the *Alabama* claims and over fishing and sealing rights were exacerbated by popular prejudice was typical of this period. But it did not very much matter. The country could still afford to treat foreign policy as a plaything of domestic politics rather than as a shield for national defense. The United States—though without either an army or a navy—continued to enjoy through its continental isolation that free security which would persist well into the twentieth century. In these circumstances both major parties felt they were justified in seeking such political advantage as they could in handling Anglo-American relations by appealing to the easily aroused anti-British sentiments of the public. Especially in an election year, there appeared to be no surer way to win popular support than to take a strong stand in defense of national honor against some real or fancied British insult.

How strongly this partisan approach governed Congressional attitudes on foreign affairs was strikingly revealed in the statement of one Republican senator during the struggle between Congress and President Cleveland over the retaliatory measures to be taken against Canadian trade in the course of the quarrel over fisheries. "We cannot allow the Democrats," he stated with singular candor, "to take credit for settling so important a dispute."

Nevertheless, in every instance of controversy during these years, after a reasonable period devoted to making political capital out of the ancient and honorable sport of twisting the British lion's tail, the forces of moderation had prevailed and the dispute was submitted to arbitration. Indeed, an underlying trend may be discerned, in spite of all the flare-ups of excitement so warmly encouraged by the Irish-Americans, toward a more friendly relationship between the two English-speaking nations. Their acceptance of arbitration where other countries might have resorted to war was highly significant; it helped pave the way to the cordial Anglo-American *rapprochement* at the century's close.

Before such harmony prevailed, there was, however, a final controversy, involving the boundary between British Guiana and Venezuela, which for a time in 1895–1896 threatened to get completely out of hand. An apparent British challenge to the principles of the Monroe Doctrine, looming much larger in the public mind than disputes over "stinking codfish" or "ill-smelling seal skins," seemed to have the most threatening implications. Moreover, the temper of the country had changed significantly in the intervening years: the United States was beginning to take a far greater interest in world affairs.

The consideration of the Venezuelan crisis and its aftermath may consequently be postponed in favor of those developments in the evolution of American foreign policy that were to create the new conditions of the 1890's.

CHAPTER V

American Interests in Eastern Asia

The affairs of Eastern Asia were of relatively little concern to the American people in the latter half of the nineteenth century as compared with their mounting and ultimately critical importance in the twentieth. China and Japan were very far away. The little that was known about them came largely from the China traders' stories of hong merchants and mandarins in Canton and Shanghai; from the accounts of American sailors who first met Japan's haughty samurai when Commodore Perry in midcentury sailed into the Bay of Yedo; and from the reports of missionaries seeking to bring the heathen Orientals into the Christian fold. Even though more substantial information was gradually becoming available, a hundred years ago an air of exotic unreality still clung to the mysterious East, and ignorance warred with fascination when Americans looked out across the Pacific to the distant shores of Asia.

Nevertheless, the gradual expansion of oriental trade—and even more, what was believed to be its immense potential for the future—combined with the zealous activity of the missionaries to build up a growing interest in China, Japan, and even Korea. Step by step the way was being prepared for the interventionist policy that the United States was to adopt at the turn of the century.

American interests in China, which had grown out of the trade with Canton initiated at the close of the eighteenth century, were safeguarded by the most-favored-nation principle incorporated in the first American-Chinese treaty concluded in 1844 and by the rights and privileges embodied fourteen years later in the Treaty of Tientsin. The United States never made war on China; it did not seek territorial concessions. Nevertheless, it did not hesitate to insist on its right to share whatever privileges England and France might wring from the impotent Chinese Empire by force of arms. Without itself following an imperialistic course, it was not averse to enjoying the fruits of European imperialism.

In spite of such seeming contradictions in its policy, the United States had nonetheless endeavored throughout the Civil War period to develop a cooperative approach on the part of the foreign powers that would protect China's sovereignty. While this friendly policy had the full support of Secretary of State Seward, it was more directly the creation of the American Minister in Peking, Anson Burlingame, a former Massachusetts congressman whose diplomatic skill and personal charm had quickly made him the leader among the foreign representatives at the Imperial Court. As set forth in a dispatch to Washington in June, 1863, his aim was to hold China to a strict compliance with all foreign treaty rights but to follow a course which would in no way interfere in its jurisdiction over its own people or "ever menace the territorial integrity of the Chinese Empire."

In pursuing this policy Burlingame constantly sought to restrain or moderate the more excessive demands the other foreign envoys so often made on the weak and vacillating Imperial Government, and his success in doing so won the appreciation of Chinese officialdom. Moreover, this sympathetic American Minister not only believed that everything possible should be done to preserve China's independence, but he was ready to extend generous aid in helping China's government in the immense task of adjusting itself to closer contacts with the Western world. Burlingame optimistically believed that if the powers followed the conciliatory and cooperative approach which he advocated, it would be entirely practical to "engraft western upon eastern civilization, without a disruption of the Chinese empire."

So completely did Burlingame win the confidence of the Chinese that when in the late 1860's the time approached for the possible revision of the existing treaty relations between China and the Western powers, the imperial authorities prevailed upon him to head a Chinese mission to America and Europe. The subsequent treaty concluded between China and the United States on the mission's visit to Washington was consequently rather unique in that it was negotiated by Secretary Seward and the former American Minister in Peking, now serving as a special envoy of the Chinese Government.

The general purport of this treaty, signed in July, 1868, as an amendment to the Treaty of Tientsin, was to reaffirm the traditional friendship between the United States and China, but it incorporated a new provision whose significance was hardly recognized at the time. The two countries agreed on the free immigration of each other's nationals. In the light of the intensive opposition to unrestricted Chinese immigration so soon to develop in the United States, this was an irreparable blunder by Washington. At the time, however, the major consequence of the treaty appeared to be a notable strengthening of the historic bonds between the American and Chinese people.

The imperial mission, which included two mandarins and some thirty other Chinese, was greeted enthusiastically throughout the United States. President Johnson welcomed the envoys to the White House, Congress held a special reception for them, and citizens' groups everywhere from San Francisco to New York staged public entertainments in their honor. Their progress across the country was a series of triumphs, and the Chinese made a very favorable impression. "Whether in the public assembly or the fashionable soirée or in the domestic circle," one contemporary wrote, "they were everywhere at their ease. Their gracefulness of manner, their unpretending and cordial politeness, their ready wit and pleasantry were subjects of general remark."

Burlingame acted as their official spokesman, and his public addresses reiterated the theme that China was making tremendous progress, was prepared to welcome foreigners, and wanted above all else to develop trade and friendly relations with the West. His plea to his own countrymen was to recognize the difficulties that China faced in adjusting itself to the ways of the Western world and to have confidence in its ability to work these problems out:

Let her alone; let her have independence; let her develop herself in her own time. She has no hostility to you. Let her do this and she will initiate a movement which will be felt in every workshop of the civilized world. . . . The imagination kindles at the future which may be, and will be, if you will be fair and just to China.

His eloquence—sustained by complete sincerity—reflected what has so often in the past been the romantic, sentimental view Americans have held toward China without any regard for either actual conditions in eastern Asia or the real attitude of the Chinese people. At the time Burlingame was so enthusiastically rhapsodizing about China's adaptation to new ways of life, this ancient empire was in fact economically stagnating, stubbornly resisting the broader impact of occidental civilization, and following policies anything but friendly to the West. While Burlingame spoke in the name of the Imperial Government, he was far from expressing the actual sentiments of the mandarinate at Peking.

China's ruler at this time, and for the greater part of the entire period until the century's close, was the imperious, strong-willed, and completely fascinating Empress Dowager Tzu Hsi. Whoever may have sat upon the Dragon Throne, it was she who held the reins of power and also the affection of her people. Throughout her long life, however, Tzu Hsi was arrogantly anti-foreign. Her feelings both reflected and perhaps served to intensify the contemptuous scorn that all Chinese officialdom had for westerners. She had approved the Burlingame mission not as an instrument for developing greater trade and more friendly relations with the outside world, as envisaged by its American leader, but as a device whereby China might ward off any further interference in its own affairs on the part of either the United States or Europe.

A number of secret memorials upon which Tzu Hsi approvingly cast "the Sacred Glance" reveal the attitude of the court at this time far more accurately than the glowing rhetoric of Anson Burlingame. One of them explicitly advanced the view that it would be disastrous for China to grant any further privileges or concessions to foreigners; another questioned whether China could gain any benefits at all from an extension of its commerce. The prevailing spirit in Peking was even more pointedly revealed in a controversy over whether the Empress should grant the foreign ministers an audience (even as her own envoys were being so cordially received abroad), and if so, how these importunate barbarians should be treated at court. One memorialist wrote:

They think only of profit, and with the meretricious hope of profit they beguile the Chinese people. These men know not even the meaning of duty and ceremony, wisdom and good faith, yet we profess, forsooth, to expect them to act as if they were endowed with the five cardinal virtues! . . . It seems to me that one might as well bring together dogs and horses, goats and pigs, in a public hall and compel these creatures to perform the evolutions of the dance!

Burlingame was not to have the opportunity—or have to face the impossible dilemma—of trying to reconcile his glowing promises of Chinese cooperation with the intransigeant policy the Empress Dowager was actually prepared to follow. Going on to Europe with the imperial mission, he died in St. Petersburg. His successor as American Minister in Peking, J. Ross Browne, was soon to report, however, that the bright expectations the mission had aroused were wholly illusory:

An impression seems to have obtained in the United States that the government of China is peculiarly friendly to our country and that great advantages to our commerce are about to accrue from this preference. . . . I need hardly say that these anticipations are without foundation. The government of China may have preferences; but it has no special regard for any foreign power. The dominant feeling is antipathy and distrust towards all who have come in to disturb the administration of its domestic affairs.

There were all too soon to be antiforeign outbreaks and other disturbances, presaging the Boxer Rebellion of 1900, which gave still more concrete evidence that the optimistic Burlingame had given a quite fanciful picture of China's real attitude toward the West.

In the meantime, developments affecting the free immigration clause in the treaty of 1868 began to place a strain on Chinese-American relations far outweighing the possible benefits to be derived from the treaty's fair words of friendship and cooperation. The United States found itself involved in a continuing controversy that was to counterbalance other more conciliatory aspects of its Far Eastern policy and create much ill will on both sides of the Pacific.

An original eagerness to welcome Chinese laborers, inspired by the great demand for their services in building the transcontinental railroads, rapidly gave way in the 1870's to fierce opposition to their continued presence in the country as a threat to the wage scales and the jobs of American-born workers. The Chinese were willing to work for incredibly low pay, and throughout the West, especially in California where they were most numerous, their industry and their extremely frugal manner of living appeared to menace the very basis of the American way of life. Economic rivalry then served to compound all the instinctive fears born of racial prejudice. The unsocial habits of the Chinese immigrants—their addiction to gambling, opium smoking, and prostitution—deepened economic resentments, while greatly exaggerated stories of their supposed barbaric customs still further intensified popular bigotry. All along the West Coast the cry rang out, "The Chinese must go."

In these circumstances memorials from various business and labor organizations began to flood Washington with demands for the restriction of further Chinese immigration. Political pressure, especially built up by outraged workers in California, forced some action and Congress replied by appointing an investigating commission. Its conclusions upheld the popular charges that the Chinese were threatening living standards and endangering public morality. Soberly reporting the imminent prospect of the Chinese population in California exceeding that of native-born whites (the actual number of Chinese in California in 1880 was about 75,000, or 9 per cent of the state's total population), the commission recommended revision of the Burlingame treaty to relieve the Pacific states of "the terrible scourge" from which they were suffering. An aroused Congress did not wait for treaty revision. As a measure that would effectively cut off immigration without openly doing so, it passed, in February, 1879, a bill that would have prohibited any ship from bringing more than fifteen Chinese passengers into the United States.

President Hayes vetoed this bill as a patent violation of the Burlingame treaty. He realized, however, that something had to be done in the face of rising anti-Chinese agitation on the West Coast, and dispatched a special mission to Peking, headed by President James B. Angell of the University of Michigan, to negotiate a new treaty that, without violating China's international rights, would restore to Congress its authority to legislate on immigration as a matter of domestic policy. The mission succeeded in concluding an agreement, signed on November 18, 1880, wherein the Chinese Government conceded that the United States might "regulate, limit, or suspend, but not absolutely prohibit" the further immigration of Chinese laborers. Any limitation, however, was to be "reasonable," and the rights of Chinese already in the country were to be safeguarded.

Congress thereupon proceeded to adopt a new bill suspending all Chinese immigration for twenty years. Chester A. Arthur was now in the White House. He was as sensitive as President Hayes had been of international responsibilities and vetoed this twenty-year suspension as going far beyond the provisions of the new treaty. His critics wrathfully declared that such action would "empty the teeming, seething slave pens of China upon the soil of California," but they could not command the votes to override his veto. Nevertheless, Congress soon passed another bill, in 1882, suspending immigration for ten years and providing that hereafter no Chinese could be admitted to American citizenship. Even though this measure still violated the spirit if not the letter of the Angell treaty, President Arthur felt constrained to accept it.

The new exclusion law cut off immigration, but it by no means allayed the agitation against the Chinese already living in the United States. Angry mobs in the West took to directly attacking them, driving them out of their homes, and beating them up unmercifully. It became a popular sport "to chase pigtails," and the inability of the Chinese to win any protection or redress for the injuries they suffered gave popular currency to the grim phrase, "not a Chinaman's chance." Such rowdyism and mob action reached a climax when in September, 1885, a white mob in Rock Springs, Wyoming, killed twenty-eight Chinese, severely injured fifteen, and burned the local Chinatown to the ground.

The Chinese Government immediately demanded redress for this outrage, and the whole immigration problem once again became a matter of national concern and political jockeying. The result was a new agreement, finally concluded in 1888, in which the United States undertook to pay an indemnity for the losses the Chinese in America had suffered through mob action while China accepted a provision for the exclusion over a twenty-year period of laborers seeking to enter the United States. While this treaty's ratification by the Imperial Government was still in question, an impatient Congress again took matters into its own hands. Ignoring both the Angell treaty of 1880 and current diplomatic negotiations, it responded to popular pressures from the

West Coast by itself arbitrarily adopting the treaty's exclusion provisions.

Upon President Cleveland's approval of this bill, the Chinese Government withheld its ratification of the pending treaty and bitterly protested the unilateral action taken by Congress as "a violation of every principle of justice, reason and fair-dealing between two friendly powers." The new legislation nevertheless remained the law of the land. Moreover, in further violation of existing treaty rights, Congress sought to make assurance double sure in 1892 by tightening earlier bans on the entry of laborers, and then ultimately went on to make the exclusion of Chinese from the United States a permanent feature of the nation's immigration policy.

Congress had the constitutional right to control immigration in any way it saw fit, and yet there was an ironic twist to its callous disregard of China's treaty rights. The United States was doing to China what it had so often charged the Imperial Government with doing in respect to the treaty rights of Americans in China. There was only this difference in the situation as it affected the two countries: when China failed to live up to its responsibilities toward the foreigners living within its borders, the Western powers had the gunboats to enforce compliance with their treaty rights; when the United States violated its treaty obligations, whether in respect to banning immigrants or failing to provide adequate protection for the Chinese already resident in the western states, the Imperial Government could only vainly protest. The inequities in this situation, however, made little difference when the basis for the American attitude, over and beyond any question of economic competition, was a universal belief in racial superiority which appeared to justify the exclusion of Chinese from the United States without regard to international law.

This unfortunate aspect of American-Chinese relations was never fairly resolved and encouraged bitter anti-American feeling in the Chinese treaty ports and repeated boycotts on the importation of American goods. Yet it remained true that in other respects the traditions of a long friendship were maintained. The United States was at least to stand apart from the scramble for territorial concessions in which the European powers were soon to engage. Apart from its Congress-inspired position on immigration, it continued to follow the principles laid down by Anson Burlingame in 1868. In the interest of its own trade and commerce, but also to the benefit of the Chinese people, it was prepared to respect the territorial integrity of the Chinese Empire.

As an offshoot of its relations with China, the United States also became interested in Korea and the possibility of opening up what was then called the Hermit Kingdom to international intercourse. Although dangerously situated between such powerful and rival neighbors as China and Japan, Korea was in theory an independent nation. Its status, however, was obscured by China's assertion of a shadowy sovereignty and the constant challenge to any such claims on the part of an ambitious Japan. The Koreans consequently found themselves helpless pawns in what was to prove a continuing power conflict, in which Czarist Russia soon joined, and they had no means to defend their independence no matter from what quarter it might be threatened.

The first contacts between Americans and Koreans occurred in 1866, when an American merchantman, the *General Sherman,* was wrecked off the Korean shore and natives murdered passengers and crew. Learning of this tragic incident through a French admiral seeking to visit Korea, Secretary Seward for a time considered joint American-French intervention to obtain redress. This idea was dropped, however, and not until 1871 did Korea again become of interest. The United States then dispatched a naval expedition of five ships, under the command of Commodore John Rodgers and also having aboard Frederick P. Low, the American Minister to China, to try to open up relations and secure guarantees from the Korean Government for the protection of American missionaries. While surveying the Han River before moving on to Seoul, the American ships were fired upon by the Korean shore forts. Countering this hostile action, Commodore Rodgers stormed the forts, totally destroying them and killing some two hundred Koreans. The American expedition, realizing that only further force could obtain its objectives, then withdrew without having made any contact with the Korean Government.

In reporting these unhappy developments to Congress, President Grant was to state that the action of Commodore Rodgers had "vindicated the honor of the flag," but it was all too clear that the expedition had been a total failure. Minister Low, declaring that it had now become the duty of all civilized nations to consider what policy should be followed toward Korea, favored further direct action. But again nothing more was done to persuade the recalcitrant Koreans to adopt a more friendly attitude toward the West.

Seven years later, in 1878, President Hayes decided to make a more sustained effort to open up Korea, and as a preliminary step instructed Commodore Robert W. Shufeldt, in command of the U.S.S. *Ticonderoga,* to explore with both the Japanese and Chinese governments the possibilities of their cooperation in initiating commercial intercourse between Korea and the outside world. The Japanese were anything but encouraging, according to the report Commodore Shufeldt made on returning to this country in 1880, but the Chinese promised their assistance.

As a consequence of these developments, James G. Blaine, as Secretary of State in the new Garfield Administration, instructed Shufeldt the next year to return to eastern Asia and take the matter up with China's powerful viceroy, Li Hung-chang. In late 1881, the American naval officer consequently proceeded to Tientsin.

He at first met only with evasion and delay in seeking the active aid of the Chinese. Their attitude convinced him, as he wrote home, "that deceit and untruthfulness pervade all intercourse with foreigners; that an ineradicable hatred exists, and that any special appeal across this barrier, either of sympathy or gratitude, is utterly idle." The current immigration controversy, hardly endearing the United States to the Chinese, undoubtedly affected Li Hung-chang's attitude. Nevertheless, after protracted negotiations he finally did agree to support a commercial treaty between Korea and the United States with explicit provision for tariff control and extraterritorial rights. Li Hung-chang also sought to have Commodore Shufeldt recognize Korea as a dependency of China, but while the American naval officer accepted a letter stating this relationship, he refused to incorporate any such provision in the Korean treaty.

Commodore Shufeldt went on to Seoul, and far from forcing Korea to come out of her shell at the cannon's mouth, as popular accounts have maintained, he now found conclusion of a treaty to be an easy and wholly ceremonious affair. The orders of Li Hung-chang had been all that were necessary to ensure Korea's compliance with the American request for trade. The officers of the *Ticonderoga* were politely wined and dined, and on May 22, 1882, an American-Korean treaty was formally signed with mutual expressions of friendship and good will.

The Korean Government cordially received an American Minister the next year and in its turn sent a mission to the United States. However, neither trade nor other intercourse flourished very notably. Some missionary activity was undertaken under the lead of Dr. Horace N. Allen, but relatively few Americans found their way to the one-time Hermit Kingdom. Torn by factional strife revolving around the rivalries of the Chinese and Japanese, unable to satisfy the competing demands of the European nations, especially Russia, Korea was to have an increasingly unhappy history. The United States sought in its relations to maintain the fiction that Korea really was an independent country, but in the tangled web of political intrigue that enmeshed Seoul, it could make little headway either in upholding its own position or helping the Koreans.

The United States had broken down the barriers of Korean seclusion and succeeded in negotiating the first treaty Korea had ever concluded with a Western power. It was prepared to exercise its good offices in seeking to help Korea preserve its independence. Nevertheless, there was nothing in this relationship, really of such slight concern to the American people, remotely to suggest the role that the United States was to play some seventy years later when it championed Korea's independence under the wholly unforeseeable circumstances of the mid-twentieth century.

The relations of the United States with Japan, the third of the countries of eastern Asia, followed a quite different—and happier—course during these years. That island empire had been opened up to the Western world by Commodore Perry's famous expedition in 1853–1854, and the friendly intercourse established at that time and strengthened four years later by a treaty of commerce and amity negotiated by Townsend Harris continued without break or conflict until the century's close. The United States viewed Japan almost as a ward in the world of international affairs, and Japan looked upon the United States as its most sympathetic friend among all the Western powers.

During the Civil War Secretary Seward was prepared to follow a cooperative policy with the other powers toward Japan, as he had in the case of China, and to preserve this united front he was even willing to participate on one occasion in a naval demonstration to enforce Japanese compliance with foreign rights. This temporary resort to force was, however, entirely out of keeping with the conciliatory attitude the United States more generally maintained. Seward was undoubtedly influenced in this instance by the need to preserve the closest possible accord with England and France as a part of his Civil War diplomacy rather than by any desire to humiliate Japan. In any event, once the pressures of wartime were removed, the United States reverted to its independent policy. Its basic goal, sustained by its own interest in a growing trade, was to help Japan in every possible way to adjust to its new position in the world. Seward once spoke of American "tutelage" as the most effective means whereby this newcomer on the international stage could strengthen its own freedom and avert any possible foreign intervention in its domestic affairs.

After the restoration of the Emperor in 1868, marking the end of civil war and the final overthrow of the power of the Tokugawa Shogunate, Japan's approach to the problems arising from its new contacts with the West could hardly have differed more sharply from that of China. Where the Empress Dowager Tzu Hsi stubbornly continued to resist all foreign influence, the Meiji Emperor warmly welcomed aid from every quarter. In his charter oath this enlightened ruler had declared that "knowledge shall be sought for all over the world." The samurai leaders engaged in making over feudal Japan into a modern state were open-minded, liberal, and progressive as compared with the obscurantism governing the attitude of the mandarinate in Peking. Having accepted the inevitable in opening Japan's doors to trade and commerce, they quickly shed the self-centered prejudices and deep-seated scorn for westerners that had characterized their views during the long years of national isolation.

The United States had cordially welcomed a Japanese embassy that toured the country in 1860 (even before the visits of the Chinese and Korean missions), and it responded generously to the requests of the Meiji government for aid and assistance in its program for Japan's modernization. The original treaties between the two nations included the special tariff provisions and extraterritorial rights incorporated in all Japan's foreign treaties. Recognizing that they constituted an infringement on Japanese sovereignty, the United States was nevertheless prepared to surrender such privileges once Japan had put its own house in order and revised its judicial system along lines promising protection for the foreigners' legitimate rights. It did make the abandonment of extraterritoriality dependent on comparable action by the other powers, however, and consequently it was not until the 1890's, when Great Britain finally swung into line, that Japan finally secured the treaty revision that fully established its international equality. Throughout these years, the Japanese Government appreciated the part the United States had played in supporting its claims for treaty revision and welcomed, too, its generally friendly attitude. Moreover, the Japanese people themselves came to feel that they owed a special debt to America for its consistently sympathetic attitude.

"When we remember," wrote one of Japan's foremost educators, Fukuzawa Yukichi, in 1886, "that it is to the United States that we owe our success and our advancement to our present proud position, we cannot help entertaining for them sentiments of peculiarly deep respect and esteem."

Unlike the situation that developed in the relations between the United States and China, no diplomatic problems whatsoever marred the smooth course of Japanese-American relations in the 1880's and 1890's. Japanese laborers were not yet seeking to emigrate to the United States and consequently there were in this period no controversies over immigration. The American missionaries who began to go to Japan almost immediately after the country was opened up met with a generally friendly reception and never provoked the fierce antiforeign feeling that in China was to culminate in the Boxer Rebellion. However resistant they might be to Christian proselytizing, the Japanese valued the educational and medical services that the missionaries so freely offered them.

Apart from such aid, there were many other instances where Americans directly helped the Meiji government in reforming the ancient institutions of Japan. David Murray, a professor from Rutgers University, was for a time in charge of administration in the Ministry of Education and became primarily responsible for establishing an elementary school system largely based on American models. Other educators played an important part in developing and staffing the new Japanese universities. After a time, American influence was to be supplanted by that of France and Germany, but in the early years of Meiji, it was a dominant force in the dramatic transformation of Japan's whole educational system. Individual Americans also served in advisory capacities in the Foreign Office, in the establishment of a modern banking and fiscal system, in the determination of economic policy, and in many other phases of Japan's modernization.

One unique instance of American aid to Japan, foreshadowing in some respects the technological assistance afforded underdeveloped countries under the Point Four program in the mid-twentieth century, resulted from the Japanese Government's employment of agricultural and other technical experts in the economic development of the northern island of Hokkaido. General Horace Capron, who had been President Grant's Commissioner of Agriculture, headed a mission in the early 1870's which introduced modern methods of farming, mining, and industrial enterprise. The evidence of American influence in Hokkaido may still be seen in the large farms, barns, and silos which give a midwestern air to the countryside, and in the grid pattern of city planning that was adopted for the island's capital at Sapporo.

Still another source of American influence was the training received by the many young Japanese (at least 300 between 1865 and 1885) who entered American schools and colleges. "We come to study your strength," one of them, a future Prime Minister, wrote at the time, "that, by adapting wisely your better ways, we may hereafter be stronger ourselves." In this early period these young men, for the most part the sons of samurai, were a dedicated group who, after learning all they could of science and engineering, law and medicine, returned to their own country to introduce the knowledge of the West and better enable Japan to meet the world on equal terms.

In the treaty which Townsend Harris negotiated with the representatives of the Shogunate in 1858, the United States pledged its good offices in any dispute between Japan and a foreign power. A first opportunity for offering such assistance—on an unofficial basis—arose when former President Grant visited Japan in the course of a round-the-world tour in 1879. Japan was currently involved in a serious dispute with China over ownership of the Lew Chew or Ryukyu Islands—those same islands where, ironically enough, the United States was to establish its great air and sea base at Okinawa after the Second World War —and there was a very real danger of a Sino-Japanese war. Grant offered his friendly counsels in helping to avert hostilities and particularly warned the Japanese against creating a situation which might lead to foreign interference. He said:

In your discussion with China on Lew Chew, and on all matters at issue, do not invite or permit, so far as you can avoid it, the intervention of a foreign power. European powers have no interest in Asia, so far as I can judge from their diplomacy, that do not involve the humiliation and subjugation of the Asiatic people. Their diplomacy is always selfish, and a quarrel between China and Japan would be regarded by them as a quarrel that might ensue to their own advantage.

This visit to Japan of the former President had further consequences in promoting American-Japanese goodwill. Shattering all precedent, the Emperor Meiji not only received General Grant in official audience but at a series of informal and personal meetings as well. The constant refrain of the American's advice, as reported in the Japanese transcripts of these unusual conversations, was that Japan should continually strive to maintain its complete freedom, standing foursquare against any foreign meddling in the conduct of either its foreign or domestic policies.

Fifteen years later Japan and China became involved in the war which Grant had helped to avert in 1879. The status of Korea rather than that of the Ryukyu Islands was the cause of this conflict, however, and it marked the first stage in the development of what was to become Japan's consuming ambition to extend its power to the Asiatic mainland. The United States was again ready to extend its friendly services in the cause of peace, but it did not try to exert any pressure on either belligerent and maintained throughout the war a strict neutrality.

Its sympathies in 1894 were nevertheless with Japan rather than with China. It flatly rejected an English proposal that in conjunction with the other Western powers, the United States should support a plan that would have led to foreign intervention in the war and placed Korea under international control. It was the American view, as expressed by Secretary of State Walter Q. Gresham, that "the deplorable war between Japan and China endangers no policy of the United States in Asia." However, when Japan's unexpected and dramatic victories over its larger foe gave rise to reports that the European powers might intervene to rob it of the fruits of victory, Gresham conveyed a friendly warning to the Japanese that, if they pushed matters too far, the powers might demand a settlement of the war "not favorable to Japan's future security."

Germany, France, and Russia did in fact insist after the conclusion of hostilities that Japan moderate its peace terms and withdraw its demands on China for the cession of territory in Manchuria. The Tokyo Government had no alternative than to acquiesce, however reluctantly, to such pressure. But the United States did not join the European powers in this move, and Japan remained deeply appreciative of an attitude more sympathetic toward its interests than that displayed by any other foreign nation. The Emperor Meiji wrote President Cleveland that the position maintained by the United States during the war had "served to draw still closer the bonds of friendship and good brotherhood which happily unite our two countries."

The imperialistic impulses already at work beneath the surface of Japanese life, so highly dramatized in the war with China, awoke some forebodings among Americans living in Japan. The writer Lafcadio Hearn, who had fallen deeply in love with the old Japan, sensed the changing atmosphere and began to feel that "we are secretly despised or hated or both. This by the new Japan, of course." After the Sino-Japanese war he wrote of his fears that there would be a renewal of the strong antiforeign sentiments of an earlier day, and that they would be directed against America as well as against the European powers in spite of the two countries' traditional friendship. "The nation will show its ugly side to us," he said, "after a manner unexpected but irresistible." Still, such forebodings were shared by few of his countrymen. With little realization of impending political rivalry, or of the impact of what was to become an embittered controversy over immigration, Americans and Japanese continued as the century drew to a close to enjoy a mutual good will as Pacific neighbors.

Even though this good will was to be so tragically shattered forty-odd years later, it was again to have a revived influence. The memory of a day when America and Japan experienced a close and cordial association helped to encourage the renewal of their early friendship after the cruel interruption of the Pacific war. It provided a foundation on which peace could be more securely re-established in the mid-twentieth century.

In the most general terms, the basic aims of American Far Eastern policy in the latter half of the nineteenth century were the cultivation of friendly relations and the promotion of foreign trade. Unlike the European powers, the United States had no territorial ambitions and sought no more than the most-favored-nation treatment in matters of commerce as incorporated in its treaties with both China and Japan. In spite of the ill feeling engendered by the immigration laws, where Congress had adopted a policy that ran directly counter to such major policy objectives, the course it followed was to give the United States a strong position throughout all eastern Asia.

Even though this may have been of relatively slight concern to the American people as a whole, the relationship built up with both China and Japan was nevertheless in some ways closer than that maintained with the countries of continental Europe. The interest in eastern Asia's potential trade, where Americans felt they had greater opportunities than in any other part of the world, partly accounted for this, and also highly important were the associations growing out of the widespread activities of American missionaries. Their influence in teaching the peoples of Asia about the United States and those of America about the

Far East was highly significant. Letters from the men and women in the mission field and their writing and talking while on home leave built up an interest in Asia which spread deeply into the hinterland from which so many of the missionaries themselves originally came.

There was a consequent widespread belief that the United States had a very special mission in Asia. Over and beyond the possibilities so optimistically accepted in missionary circles for the conversion of China and Japan to Christianity ("the evangelization of the world in this generation" was the slogan of the 1890's), many people felt that the Far East was a part of the world where it might be possible to plant the seeds of democracy. America would lead the way in making over the ancient institutions of Asia, and as opposed to the more conservative and monarchial influence of Europe, encourage the growth of a progressively liberal—and American—way of life.

In these circumstances the United States was not only ready to encourage and safeguard trade and commerce with eastern Asia but prepared to give all possible support to the missionaries as they developed their program ever more widely in Japan and sought to penetrate deeper into the vast interior of China. Even before the more dramatic events of the century's close, America became very much involved in Far Eastern affairs, and the isolationism that so strongly featured its over-all foreign policy was far less pronounced in Asia than in Europe.

The growth of these Asiatic interests had a significance hardly appreciated at the time. It was not only that Asia was already beckoning when the accident of Spain's possession of the Philippine Islands opened up the opportunity for territorial advance across the Pacific in 1898. Even before the outburst of imperialism that year, the American commitment in eastern Asia gave rise to the compelling idea—it had been the prophetic conviction of Commodore Perry and Secretary of State Seward—that the United States should control the sea routes across the Pacific. There could be no question of letting Great Britain or any other power establish naval supremacy over this great ocean.

In spite of the post-Civil War apathy toward overseas expansion, there was consequently during these same years a number of hesitant, probing moves toward acquiring those commercial outposts or naval bases that might safeguard the road to Asia.

CHAPTER VI

Hawaii and Samoa

The two islands, or island groups, in which the United States first developed an active interest as Pacific outposts were Hawaii and Samoa.

The former, even though some two thousand miles off the country's western coast line, had been tenuously linked to the mainland since early in the nineteenth century through the visits of New England whalers and the local settlement of both traders and missionaries. The status of Hawaii was already of such concern in the 1840's that Daniel Webster, as Secretary of State in the Administration of John Tyler, explicitly stated that the United States would oppose its being subjected to the control of any foreign power. Moreover, in 1854, a treaty of annexation was tentatively concluded with the native Hawaiian king. The Senate would have none of it, largely because it provided for the islands' admission to the Union as a state, but the ties between the United States and Hawaii would nonetheless be drawn steadily tighter every ensuing year.

The far more distant Samoa had no such close associations before the Civil War. This island group was visited in 1839 by Commodore Charles Wilkes (who was later to take Mason and

Slidell off the *Trent*), and the United States soon afterwards appointed a local consul to aid the casual Yankee traders or visiting whalers who found their way to the South Seas. But that was all. It was not until the 1870's that any further contacts were made with Samoa, and even then they developed slowly.

In both cases the commercial interests of the American residents on the islands had an important part in the growth of their associations with the United States. However, the availability as potential naval bases of Pearl Harbor in the Hawaiian Islands and of Pago Pago in the Samoan Islands—two of the best natural harbors in all the Pacific—played a far greater role in the steps that ultimately led to annexation.

The original link in the chain of events that was directly to involve the United States in Samoan affairs—to consider first the less important of the two annexationist movements—was an undertaking in 1871 on the part of a New York shipbuilder, W. H. Webb, to discover a suitable coaling station for a projected steamship line running between San Francisco and Australia. He sent an agent to Samoa, who promptly forwarded a glowing report. The islands, where both English and German traders had already established themselves, were a marvelous garden spot, this agent wrote, and more important, the harbor of Pago Pago on Tutuila was "the most perfectly landlocked harbor that exists in the Pacific Ocean." His report also hinted that foreign influences were building up throughout the South Pacific and that both Great Britain and Germany appeared to be maneuvering for Samoa's annexation.

Webb forwarded copies of this interesting dispatch to both the Secretary of the Navy and Rear Admiral John A. Winslow, in charge of the American squadron on the Pacific station. The latter promptly instructed Commander Richard W. Meade to visit Samoa and try to secure from the local chiefs an agreement granting the United States a coaling depot at Pago Pago before foreign intrigue pre-empted the field. Commander Meade carried out this assignment with dispatch and efficiency. Having suc-

ceeded in persuading the chief of Pago Pago of the unique advantages of assuring himself American friendship and protection,
Meade signed a formal treaty with him on February 17, 1872, in
which the Samoan ceded exclusive control of the bay and harbor
of Pago Pago to the United States.

Although Commander Meade had signed this treaty without
any authorization from the State Department, President Grant
submitted it to the Senate. He moved somewhat cautiously. His
difficulties with his own scheme to annex Santo Domingo made
him extremely wary of proposing any other territorial acquisition.
Nevertheless, he emphasized in his message the benefits the
United States would secure from a naval outpost in the South
Pacific, and concluded that "with some modification of the
obligation of protection which the agreement imports, it is recommended to the favorable consideration of the Senate."

Both the anti-expansionist sentiment of the country at this
time and the existing political situation militated strongly against
the treaty's approval. The Senate would have none of it. Neither
the President nor Secretary of State Fish was prepared to drop
the matter altogether, however, and it was decided to send a
special agent to Samoa, Colonel Albert B. Steinberger, to investigate further current conditions on the islands. "It is not unlikely
that perhaps in the not distant future," Fish instructed Steinberger, "the interests of the United States may require not only a
naval station in the Samoan group, but a harbor where their
steam and other vessels may freely and securely frequent." The
cautious "not unlikely" and "perhaps" suggest that the Secretary
of State was not very strongly committed to such an unprecedented
venture. Nevertheless, his instructions to Steinberger underscore
the persistence of the idea, which William Seward had so vigorously tried to implement, of the importance to the United States
of obtaining the naval bases and commercial depots which it
needed for the protection of its commercial interests both in the
Pacific and the Far East.

On his arrival in Samoa, Colonel Steinberger talked with the
local chiefs and apparently inspired them to ask for Samoa's un-

conditional annexation by the United States. Returning to Washington with an official letter making such a request, he urged Fish to give it all possible consideration. Again the Secretary of State took a somewhat ambiguous position. He rejected the idea of annexation, warning that a measure so contrary to American tradition "probably would not receive such a sanction as would be likely to secure its success," but he nevertheless sent Steinberger back to Samoa as a special commissioner. He returned bearing gifts—guns and ammunition, a hundred sailors' suits, and three American flags.

The situation in Samoa now became—and would long remain—highly confused, a hotbed of native and international intrigue. The foreigners on the islands—Americans, British, and Germans—were for the most part engaged in the lucrative copra trade, but among them were also a number of land speculators looking to an even more prosperous Samoan future. These rival groups were constantly intriguing with the native chiefs for further privileges and a position of greater influence in Samoan affairs, and were zealously supported by their respective national consuls. Each of these officials, moreover, had become convinced that the only way things could really be brought under control was for his own government to establish a Samoan protectorate.

Colonel Steinberger plunged into this political whirlpool with zest. Disregarding the warnings of Secretary Fish, he began to agitate vigorously in favor of an American protectorate and so ingratiated himself with the native chiefs that they appointed him "premier" of the Samoan Government. He then suddenly abandoned the American cause, having at least the grace to resign his post as a special commissioner, and threw in his lot with the islands' German traders. Steinberger's shift did not, however, prevent the other Americans on the islands from continuing to work for a protectorate in growing rivalry with the comparable ambitions of the British and Germans. Finally, the Americans once again prevailed upon the local chiefs to seek annexation, and in 1877 they sent a native envoy to Washington with another official request that the United States take over the entire Samoan archipelago.

On reaching Washington, this envoy, M. K. Le Mamea, was first received by Undersecretary of State Frederick W. Seward, the son of William H. Seward, and then by both Secretary of State William M. Evarts and President Hayes. His proposal for Samoa's annexation was discussed and taken up at a cabinet meeting. Frederick Seward was to write that the Administration favored obtaining a territorial outpost in the Pacific—it believed, he wrote, that "my father's policy in this regard had been wise and judicious"—but, recognizing the popular opposition to any such move, felt compelled to turn down the Samoan chiefs' offer.

Mamea was not sent home empty-handed, however. Secretary Evarts concluded a treaty with him—in January, 1878—wherein Samoa agreed to establishment of a naval station at Pago Pago and granted full trading privileges and extraterritorial rights to American residents, while the United States undertook to offer its good offices to the Samoan Government in the event that it became involved in a dispute with any other foreign power. The Senate approved this treaty—it contained no suggestion of a protectorate, let alone annexation—and although no funds were appropriated for a naval station, its action marked a new and significant extension of American influence in the South Pacific.

The public was largely indifferent to these developments, but in Navy circles they were linked with other steps the United States had recently taken as a portent of the future. "The acquisition of Alaska and the Aleutians, the treaties with Japan, the Sandwich [Hawaiian] Islands and Samoa," wrote Commodore Robert W. Shufeldt, who was himself to open up Korea only two years later, "are only corollaries to the proposition that the Pacific Ocean is to become at no distant day the commercial domain of America." The Navy at least would never lose sight of Samoa.

Great Britain and Germany soon concluded treaties with Samoa which gave their nationals very much the same privileges as those extended to Americans, and the rivalry and intrigue among the foreign residents became more active than ever. Samoa had not secured the protection of a single power in the conclusion of its new treaties, but the protection of three mutually suspicious commercial rivals. Their respective consuls thereupon became engaged in a dangerous game. To safeguard their national interests, they threw their support behind first one and then another of the native chiefs who were constantly intriguing for the position of paramount Samoan "king," and each on his own responsibility renewed his earlier efforts to secure exclusive economic privileges.

The Germans were the most aggressive in this mounting rivalry. Their consul clearly appeared to be maneuvering to set up a protectorate that would give Germany a dominant position in Samoa, and in 1884 his intrigues created something of a local crisis. Upon the accession of a new native king, he forced upon him an agreement providing for establishment of a Samoan-German council of state, and when this chieftain refused to carry out its terms, the determined consul proceeded to raise the German flag over the government buildings and fomented a revolt to place a more compliant native leader on the Samoan throne. The Americans and British were incensed. Their prompt reaction was to reaffirm their support of the king who had defied German influence and, in a further challenge to German pretensions, the American consul in turn took steps toward setting up a protectorate.

When news of these developments reached the home governments of the contending consuls, the local situation in Samoa became a matter of international concern. The cable wires between Washington and Berlin were soon humming with mutual charges and countercharges over the threatening actions taken by the American and German consuls.

President Cleveland was in office when this flare-up of excitement took place in distant Samoa. While he was later to prove to be adamantly opposed to any idea of American overseas expansion, he was nonetheless alert to the broader commercial and strategic interests of the United States in the Pacific. He instructed his Secretary of State, Thomas F. Bayard, to disavow the embarrassing actions of the American consul but to protest vigorously against the moves made by the German consul in seeking to place his own candidate on the Samoan throne and raising the German flag. While the United States was not itself ready to move toward any sort of protectorate, it was sufficiently involved in Samoa to oppose the efforts of any other country to do so.

"The moral interests of the United States with respect to the islands of the Pacific, necessarily dependent in greater or lesser degree on our own American system of commonwealths," Secretary Bayard instructed the American consul in Samoa, "would counsel us to look with concern on any movement by which the independence of those Pacific nationalities might be extinguished by their passage under the domination of a foreign sovereign."

In the face of the strong protests from the United States, Germany made no attempt to force the issue. Chancellor Bismarck was at this time officially soft-pedalling any idea of embarking upon a colonial program, whatever may have been his secret ambitions. He denied any ulterior purposes in German policy in Samoa and categorically disavowed the actions of the German consul as having been taken without any authorization from Berlin.

Secretary Bayard seized upon the opportunity presented by these conciliatory messages to propose a new approach to a problem which seemed to be so constantly getting out of hand when left to the local consuls. He invited Germany and Great Britain to a conference at Washington to consider the possibilities of some sort of tripartite foreign control which would at once assure order in the islands and yet preserve Samoa's independence. Representatives of the three nations met in the summer of 1887. They found it impossible to agree on any plan, and the conference adjourned without taking any action.

Still another crisis was building up in Samoa as these events took place in Washington. The local Germans continued to support their candidate for the kingship, in opposition to the chieftain whose cause was upheld by both the Americans and the British, and the islands were torn by renewed civil strife. What made this all the more dangerous was that by this time each of the foreign powers had naval vessels in the islands to safeguard its interests, and any spark could set off an international clash which might easily get out of hand. The Germans did indeed land a force from their ships which engaged in open hostilities with the existing Samoan Government, but fortunately the Americans and British limited their counteraction to vigorous protests against such wanton interference in Samoa's internal affairs. The two consuls were nevertheless convinced, as they informed their governments, that this time the Germans were ready, if necessary by force of arms, to set up the protectorate they had formerly disavowed.

As reports of this inflammatory state of affairs reached Washington and Berlin (more deeply involved than London), official protests once again flew back and forth between the two capitals. Germany took the position that the overzealous activities of the American consul in Samoa were responsible for all the trouble; the United States countered that Germany's course in the whole affair had hardly been marked by the consideration which the ancient friendship between the two countries led it to expect.

When the American public learned of these untoward developments in Samoa, it promptly became concerned over what was widely interpreted as a direct German challenge to national interests in the South Pacific. Exaggerated and alarmist newspaper reports telling of the landing of German forces in Samoa and of their arrogant flouting of the rights of American residents led to a popular demand for a more vigorous policy in opposition to such aggressive tactics. An aroused Congress took up the matter and, in order to uphold the Administration's diplomatic protests, appropriated $500,000 for the protection of American lives and property in Samoa and earmarked an additional $100,000 for the long-delayed development of Pago Pago as a naval station.

There was some opposition to any further involvement in

such a remote quarrel. The *Nation* wrote caustically of "running this wild goose chase," and other papers felt Samoa to be much too far away to be of any real importance. The press more generally, however, called up President Cleveland to assert American rights in such a way that there could be no mistake about his policy. One belligerent newspaper dramatically insisted that the United States should uphold its position in Samoa "even if we have to do it at the cannon's mouth."

In the light of both the official Washington protests and such evidence of the strong anti-German feelings prevalent in the United States, Bismarck once again decided upon a conciliatory course. He now proposed that the United States, Great Britain, and Germany resume the negotiations that had been broken off in Washington in 1887, and once more try to work out a form of international control to restore order in Samoa. President Cleveland promptly accepted this proposal and, with Great Britain also approving, the plans were made for another conference which would this time meet in Berlin.

The powers were moving toward a negotiated settlement but in Samoa their representatives were still at swords' point. In the little harbor of the principal seaport at Apia, three German, three American, and one British warship, decks cleared for action, tossed restlessly at their anchors. Anything could happen in the tense atmosphere that had been created by Samoan strife, and far away from any effective control by their home governments, the American and German consuls were jealously determined to defend their interests. And then "in what seemed the very article of war," as Robert Louis Stevenson was to say, in a vivid account of the dramatic climax to the situation in Samoa itself, "the sword-arm of each of the two angry powers was broken."

It was the morning of March 16, 1889. A sudden, fierce hurricane had struck Samoa the previous night, overwhelming Apia, and as it gradually subsided, the little seaport's awestruck residents realized that the harbor had been swept clear of the foreign gunboats. The three American and three German vessels, suffering a tragic loss of life, had either been sunk in the raging storm or piled up on the harbor's reefs. Only the British ship had succeeded in getting safely to sea; otherwise not a sail was still afloat.

A sad quiet descended over Samoa, and as accounts of the disaster reached the outside world, all talk of possible hostilities died away. "Men and nations," wrote the New York *World*, "must bow before the decrees of nature." Nothing could have had a more sobering effect on the delegates to the conference at Berlin. They now met with a new resolve to work out the problems that had led to such dangerous rivalry in Samoa and indirectly caused such a heavy toll of life among the seamen of the foreign gunboats.

In six weeks of strenuous negotiations, they finally succeeded in hammering out a scheme for a tripartite Samoan protectorate very much along the lines that the United States had suggested two years earlier. The Berlin General Act, as this final agreement was called, guaranteed the independence and neutrality of the Samoan Islands, restored to power the local chieftain whom the United States and Great Britain had supported as the lawful king, and provided that appointees of the three powers would constitute a new supreme court which would have inclusive jurisdiction over Samoan laws and foreign disputes and also take over the municipal administration at Apia.

The participation of the United States in the arrangements embodied in the Berlin General Act constituted an unprecedented international involvement which ran counter to every tradition of the nation's wholly independent action in foreign affairs. The Senate nevertheless approved what President Harrison called "an honorable, just and equal settlement" by a majority of 38 to 12. The national interest in preventing Samoa from falling into German hands had broken down one of the major tenets of American policy. The Berlin General Act may not have been an entangling alliance in the usual meaning of the term but it did mean an entanglement in Samoan affairs from which the United States would not be able to extricate itself.

The conclusion of the tripartite treaty and establishment of the powers' joint control over the islands were not, of course, the last word in the history of Samoa. The protectorate did not work out very well; it led to new rivalries and new threats of internal strife. When Cleveland returned to office in 1893, he vigorously criticized it both for its impracticality and for its departure from established American policy. The Berlin General Act had led to an international involvement, he stated, which defied "the conservative teachings and warnings of the wise and patriotic men who laid the foundations of our free institutions." He continued to regret that the United States had ever let itself be committed to such an unwarranted responsibility.

Such criticism and the continued difficulties in Samoa were gradually to encourage the idea that not a joint protectorate but a division of the islands into separate spheres of influence might well represent the most viable solution to the whole problem. The final settlement that was to follow along these lines would not be reached, however, until the imperialistic fever born of the Spanish-American War changed popular attitudes toward the acquisition of overseas territory. Only then did the United States, after a division of the islands, annex American Samoa—the island of Tutuila with its wonderful harbor of Pago Pago.

During these same years, developments in Hawaii followed a quite different course but were similar in bringing a new territorial acquisition by the United States steadily closer. There was in the case of Hawaii—unlike Samoa—never any idea of accepting international control. Daniel Webster had settled that issue long since. But whether the United States should annex the islands or continue to support the independence of the native kingdom was an insistently plaguing issue, eventually becoming deeply involved in both Hawaiian and American politics.

Secretary Seward would have liked to annex Hawaii immediately after the Civil War, as we have already seen, in fulfillment of his imaginative dreams of the further expansion of American power in the Pacific. In his mind such a step was a logical corollary to the purchase of Alaska, and in reply to a query from the American Minister in Honolulu, he gave him secret permission to take the annexation question up with the Hawaiian Government.

"You are at liberty," Seward wrote, "to sound out the proper authorities on the large subject mentioned in your note." And later he supplemented these instructions—again confidentially—by stating "that a lawful and peaceful annexation of the islands to the United States, with the consent of the people . . . is deemed desirable by this Government."

Yet once again the ambitious Secretary of State had to accept the realities of popular opposition to territorial acquisitions. In spite of his private correspondence with the American Minister, he did not seek to conclude an annexation treaty which he knew the country would disapprove. He contented himself with negotiating an agreement for trade reciprocity. On even so limited a venture, however, Seward was still ahead of the times. The Senate rejected his commercial treaty out of hand and would continue to maintain its strong opposition to any such accord for nearly a decade. It was not until 1875, during the Grant Administration, that it shifted its position. It then accepted a reciprocity treaty whose provisions for the free entry of Hawaiian sugar made the islands economically dependent on the United States even though they retained political freedom.

By this time circumstances both in this country and in Hawaii had brought about a highly complex situation in regard to the underlying question, which could never be ignored, of the islands' possible annexation. The Americans in Hawaii, in many cases the sons of the earlier missionaries, had become engaged in trade and sugar production. They favored the closest possible ties with the United States, and their ultimate goal was annexation. Some of them consequently tended to question the wisdom of the reciprocity treaty, in spite of its immediate benefits, for fear that by assuring a duty-free market for sugar, it would postpone the fulfillment of their real ambition to see Hawaii become American territory.

So too there was a divided opinion in the United States over this new development. The proponents of annexation were still very much in a minority, but such popular interest as Hawaii commanded arose not so much from commercial considerations as from the islands' strategic position. There was consequently little interest in reciprocity. In approving the treaty of 1875, the Senate demonstrated what it felt to be really important by insisting on the incorporation in the pact of a clause wherein the Hawaiian Government agreed that it would neither lease nor otherwise dispose of any port, harbor, or other portion of its territory to any other power.

When the reciprocity treaty came up for renewal in 1884, its commercial aspects were even more significantly subordinated to strategic considerations. The Senate long delayed taking any action whatsoever. Under strong pressure from the Navy, which had consistently emphasized the importance of Hawaii as the key to naval control of the Pacific, it then predicated continuance of tariff reciprocity on Hawaii's grant to the United States of exclusive control over Pearl Harbor as a naval base. Only after the treaty had in 1887 been amended along such lines did the Senate finally agree to it.

Reciprocity had made Hawaii economically dependent on the United States; the grant of a naval base gave the United States an important strategic interest in Hawaii. Even though political union was still in the future, the relationship between the two countries was very close. When Great Britain and France, protesting the cession of Pearl Harbor, proposed a joint guarantee of Hawaii's independence and neutrality, the United States made it entirely clear that it would accept no foreign restraint whatsoever on its own policy.

This was the same year in which Secretary of State Bayard had first advanced the idea of some sort of international guarantee for Samoa's independence, but as already suggested, Hawaii was viewed in a quite different light. President Cleveland had no idea of letting either Great Britain or France restrict American freedom of action. He demonstrated his opposition to actual territorial expansion by refusing to ask Congress for any funds for the development of Pago Pago as a naval base, but he nevertheless expressed "his unhesitating conviction that the intimacy of our relations with Hawaii should be emphasized."

Developments in the islands themselves were by this time following a course that brought more and more into question whether Hawaii was really capable of independent self-government. The indigenous population was rapidly dwindling (it fell from 130,000 in 1832 to 34,000 in 1890 largely as a consequence of diseases introduced by the white man), and the proprietors of the sugar plantations were recruiting a labor force from Oriental immigrants, first from China and then from Japan. The political and economic power in the islands was centered in the hands of the American residents whose closest associations were with the mainland. Together with some few Europeans, they dominated the local scene. They owned the sugar plantations, generally monopolized foreign trade, and controlled the local legislature.

Moreover, the old royal family, which once had considerable stature, was itself dying out. A succession of short-lived native rulers, whose courts were corrupt and licentious, sat briefly on the Hawaiian throne. There was little prospect that the ancient dynasty would ever again make any real contribution to the country or be able to promote effectively either social or economic progress. A native Hawaiian kingdom seemed to be an anachronism.

Added to these political problems, an unexpected occurrence in 1890 brought about a sharp economic depression which was even more immediately threatening for Hawaii's future. Passage of the McKinley tariff removed the general duty on sugar imports into the United States and granted a bounty to American producers, thereby sweeping away all the special advantages that Hawaiian sugar had enjoyed under the terms of the reciprocity treaty. With economic distress added to political uncertainties, the American residents grew increasingly alarmed over how these unhappy developments might affect their extensive property holdings and other investments. Their fears were by no means allayed by the mounting disaffection of the natives in these days of depression and the growth of a threatening "Hawaii for the Hawaiians" movement.

This situation approached a climax when in January, 1891, a new Hawaiian sovereign, Queen Liliuokalani, came to the throne. Although she was later to be depicted in the American press as a vicious, depraved, untutored savage, the new Queen was actually a woman of superior culture (she wrote the popular Hawaiian song "Aloha Oe"), highly sophisticated, and possessed of an innate dignity. She had gone to England for Queen Victoria's Jubilee, when she was described as being "quite stylish, and dressed according to the latest Parisian mode," and on her way home briefly visited Washington. Nevertheless Queen Liliuokalani was outspokenly anti-American (she had opposed the cession of Pearl Harbor), very much of a reactionary in her political views, and both strong-willed and imperious. Egged on by a group of unprincipled and unscrupulous adventurers who for their own purposes were encouraging her to defy the American-controlled legislature, she was determined to halt the drift toward foreign domination of Hawaiian affairs and assert the ancient powers of the throne.

Sensing the need for vigorous action to protect their interests, the American residents began to consider plans to overthrow Queen Liliuokalani's reactionary regime, establish an American-controlled Provisional Government in its place, and formally seek annexation to the United States. They felt no time was to be lost. Immediate measures were necessary in the interests of both economic and political stability.

The pro-annexationists had the full sympathy and tacit support of the American Minister in Honolulu, John L. Stevens, an appointee of Secretary of State Blaine. He was an eager and ambitious proponent of "an avowedly American solution" of the Hawaiian problem. Soon after assuming his post in 1891, Stevens had reported on the serious conditions prevailing in the islands and the possibility that the resident foreigners might stage a revolt against Queen Liliuokalani's arbitrary rule. He pointed out the consequent danger that some other power might seek to in-

tervene in Hawaii's affairs unless the United States was prepared
to act promptly and energetically. "Annexation must be the future
remedy," he wrote emphatically on February 8, 1892; and then,
seeking instructions from his government nine months later, he
further disclosed his own views: "the golden hour is near at
hand."

Stevens was quite right. At the opening of 1893, relations
between the Queen and the American residents had reached the
breaking point. Liliuokalani had decided to proclaim a new constitution which would totally abolish the power of the legislature
and restore the throne's monarchial prerogatives. Even her own
ministers grew alarmed over such hasty action and persuaded
her to postpone her plan. But the Americans could hardly fail to
read the handwriting on the wall. They promptly organized a
Committee of Public Safety to carry through their program looking toward annexation, and on January 16 held a mass meeting
of all foreign residents. It demanded the Queen's abdication and
also called on the American Minister for assistance.

"We are unable to protect ourselves without aid," their
appeal stated, "and, therefore, pray for the protection of the
United States forces."

Stevens was more than willing to comply with this request
and was in a position to extend protection through the providential presence in Honolulu Bay of the U.S.S. *Boston.* He immediately ordered the landing of a force of marines to preserve
law and order, stationed these troops in positions best calculated
to intimidate the Queen, and raised the American flag over the
government buildings. Under such a broad protective umbrella,
the Committee of Public Safety (which had no native representatives) the next day issued a proclamation abolishing the
Hawaiian monarchy and setting up a Provisional Government "to
exist until terms of union with the United States have been
negotiated and agreed upon." The American Minister immediately recognized this Provisional Government, even though its
inability to protect itself without aid had been the excuse just
thirty hours earlier for landing the American marines, and the

next day gave his blessing to the special commission it dispatched to negotiate a treaty of annexation in Washington.

The unfortunate Liliuokalani had been completely powerless in the face of this fast-moving sequence of events. Whatever support she might have been able to command among her own people was hardly adequate to withstand the foreign rebels against her authority who were backed by American cannon. Under strong protest, she agreed to relinquish the throne and accept the revolution. In stepping down, however, the Queen made her position very clear. She had yielded, she stated with regal dignity, "to the superior force of the United States of America, whose plenipotentiary, John L. Stevens, has caused American troops to be landed at Honolulu and declared he would support the said Provisional Government."

The Harrison Administration, in which John W. Foster had the year before replaced Blaine as Secretary of State, was ready to act upon the Hawaiian annexation offer almost as speedily as the Provisional Government had moved in drawing it up. Foster instructed Stevens to continue his support of the new regime (although he did disavow his action in raising the American flag), and he cordially received the Hawaiian commissioners on their arrival in Washington. On February 14, less than a month after the outbreak of the revolution, the proposed treaty incorporating Hawaii as a territory of the United States had been duly signed and submitted to the Senate.

The report accompanying the treaty maintained that the United States had actually had no hand in the precipitate course of events in Hawaii and declared that under the circumstances there appeared to be no alternative to acceptance of the Provisional Government's offer of annexation. To do so conformed to the interests of both the United States and Hawaii, President Harrison declared, and then broad-mindedly added that these interests were not however wholly selfish since the possession of Hawaii by any other power "would not consist with our safety and the peace of the world."

The American public had not closely followed the developments that led up to the crisis in Hawaiian affairs, and, suddenly confronted with the proposal for the islands' annexation, hardly knew where the national interest really lay. Since a Republican Administration had negotiated the annexation treaty, Republicans tended to favor it, and from an equally logical political point of view, the Democrats more generally opposed it. But the situation was highly complex. The Republicans, defeated in the Presidential election of the previous year, were on the eve of handing over power to the incoming Democrats. A question arose in many quarters as to whether the Administration was justified in its apparent intent—to push through this important matter with such indecent haste. The matter could at least wait a couple of weeks, protested *The New York Times,* "without injury to anybody except the schemers who have precipitated it."

Even though the Republicans were in control, the Senate consequently hesitated to act before the new Administration took office on March 4. Nothing had therefore been done when Grover Cleveland returned to the White House as the leader of a triumphant Democracy. The new President promptly withdrew the Hawaiian treaty.

Cleveland was obeying his own anti-expansionist instincts in taking this action and also accepting the advice of his Secretary of State, Walter Q. Gresham. A man of idealistic and humanitarian principle, Gresham was not only an avowed anti-imperialist but in this instance felt a special sense of outrage because of what he considered "a great wrong done to a feeble but independent state by an abuse of the authority of the United States." The least that he felt should be done was to open up the whole Hawaiian question for further investigation and more reasoned consideration. Cleveland fully accepted this thesis, and therefore the new Administration's next move was to send to Hawaii a special commissioner, James H. Blount, a former chairman of the House Committee on Foreign Affairs, with instructions to conduct a thorough investigation and take such measures as seemed to be appropriate to meet the existing situation.

On arriving in Honolulu, Blount immediately ordered the

lowering of the American flag (still flying over government buildings) and the return to their ship of the sailors and marines whom Stevens had sent ashore for the ostensible purpose of maintaining order. It was clear that American policy was changing. Moreover, Blount's report to Washington could hardly have called into greater question the validity of the moves made by Stevens in support of the revolution. It embodied two definite conclusions: there had been direct collusion between the revolutionary leaders and the American Minister, and the sentiment of the Hawaiian people themselves was in favor of Queen Liliuokalani and against both the Provisional Government and American annexation.

Cleveland and Gresham accepted the implications of this report without hesitation, but there remained the complex question of how redress could be made for the injury done the Queen. At a cabinet meeting, the Secretary of State recommended the unconditional restoration of the monarchy, but Attorney General Richard Olney pointed out that the United States also had a certain responsibility to the Provisional Government which had assumed power—rightly or wrongly—under the protection of American armed forces. Taking the latter view into consideration, it was decided to send a new minister to Hawaii, Albert S. Willis, to try to work out a solution which would provide for re-establishment of the old government and yet safeguard the members of the revolutionary party. Willis was secretly instructed to secure from Queen Liliuokalani a complete amnesty for the rebels, and then having obtained such assurances, to inform the Provisional Government that it was expected "to promptly relinquish to her her constitutional authority."

Washington apparently believed that this further—and perhaps equally highhanded—interference in Hawaiian affairs would work out rather easily. Willis did not find this to be the case. In his first encounter with the Queen, she haughtily rejected any idea of an amnesty. "There are certain laws of my government," Willis reported her as saying with stubborn authority, "by which I shall abide. My decision would be, as the law directs, that such persons should be beheaded and their property confiscated to the Government." The American Minister was somewhat taken aback, as well he might have been, but for several weeks Liliuokalani clung to this harsh and obviously unacceptable decision. Only after the strongest pressure had been brought to bear by her own advisers did she finally relent and agree that on her restoration to her throne she would grant the desired amnesty.

Having at last succeeded in the first phase of his task, Willis took up his second objective and urged the President of the Provisional Government, Sanford B. Dole, the son of a missionary and a former judge of the Hawaiian Supreme Court, to agree to relinquish his authority to the Queen. Dole reserved a decision for three days but then gave the American Minister a decisive, unequivocal answer. The Provisional Government, he soberly stated, "respectfully but unhesitatingly declines to entertain the proposition."

Cleveland had already begun to despair of finding any way to reconcile the positions of the Queen and the Provisional Government. Indeed, even before he received the official report on Dole's answer to the proposal advanced by Willis, he was ready to toss the whole issue into the lap of Congress. His own program had admittedly failed. But while the President told Congress in a special message on December 18 that after a careful survey of what had happened in Hawaii he did not feel the duty of the United States could be fulfilled simply by refusing "to consummate this questionable transaction," he gave no hint of what he thought could now be done. He simply washed his hands of the whole affair.

During these days of futile negotiations in Hawaii, the press and public heatedly debated the annexationist issue. The discussion continued to follow to a great extent the party lines which had been laid down when Harrison first submitted the Hawaiian treaty. The Republican newspapers condemned Cleveland for reversing his predecessor's policy and allowing the American flag to be hauled down in Honolulu; the Democratic journals generally lauded his statesmanship and courage in rejecting a program based upon unjustified interference in the affairs of a friendly country. On the one hand the proposal to restore the Queen to power was attacked as "stupid and outrageous" and "an act of national stultification," and on the other it was upheld (though in some cases with grave misgivings) as the only possible remedy for a grave mistake. "Nothing could more strengthen the Administration in the minds of fair-minded and right-thinking men," *The New York Times* stated when the restoration program was first made public, "than the act of justice to Hawaii which is announced in the letter of Secretary Gresham."

The basic issue of annexation was somewhat submerged in the more immediate question of whether the tactics Stevens had followed in supporting the revolutionaries should or should not be upheld. The New York *Commercial Advertiser* nevertheless commented bitterly that the great dream of an American outpost at the crossroads of the Pacific "had been shattered by Grover Cleveland, the Buffalo Lilliputian," while the Chicago *Tribune* declared that should the President's policy allow Hawaii to slip into the hands of any foreign power, "the American people will never forgive the guilty party."

The naval point of view was emphatically expressed by Admiral George E. Belknap. He saw a danger of Great Britain seeking to "get its paw on the group" or at least reviving the idea of some sort of joint protectorate. "We want none of that," the Admiral declared, "—no entangling alliances. We have had enough of such business at Samoa. . . . Westward the star of empire takes its way. Let the Monroe Doctrine stay not its hand until it holds Hawaii securely within its grasp."

In answer to the annexationists, the opponents of any extension of American territory overseas revived all the old anti-imperialist arguments that Seward had had to face in the 1860's. The acquisition of Hawaii would violate the principles on which the Republic was founded and could not be reconciled with the tenets of democracy. Taking this broader view of the question, Carl Schurz argued that, far from strengthening the United

States, taking over the islands would introduce "a future of turbulence, demoralization, and final decay."

The debate continued for a time after Cleveland handed the issue over to Congress, but so confused had the situation become in Hawaii that even the proponents of annexation hesitated to promote it at this particular juncture of affairs. The legislature did not any more know how to deal with this baffling problem than the President. Finally, both House and Senate agreed on a hands-off policy; there was nothing they felt the United States could do. At the same time it was made abundantly clear that such inaction should not be interpreted as meaning abandonment of the historic American interest in Hawaii. Intervention in the islands' affairs by any foreign government, the Congressional resolution explicitly stated, "will be regarded as an act unfriendly to the United States."

Here the matter rested—temporarily. On July 4, 1894, the Provisional Government established the Republic of Hawaii; Queen Liliuokalani perforce accepted her deposition, and the United States recognized the new regime. Nothing was more certain, however, than that annexation would be brought up again as soon as circumstances were more propitious. They were to become so with the return of the Republicans to power in 1897, but nevertheless—as in the case of Samoa—it was not until war with Spain gave a new impetus to the whole imperialist movement that annexation was finally consummated.

To that later chapter in the history of Hawaii we shall return. However, it may perhaps be noted at this point that Cleveland remained irreconcilable.

"Hawaii is ours," growled the former President in a letter to Richard Olney in August, 1898. "As I look back upon the first steps in this miserable business and as I contemplate the means used to complete the outrage, I am ashamed of the whole affair."

CHAPTER VII

The Changing Scene

The development of American interests in Samoa and Hawaii had taken place against the background of a subtle, gradual change in popular attitudes toward the role of the United States in world affairs. During the years in which a few naval officers and a handful of the advance agents of American commerce served as a spearhead for national expansion in the Pacific, new ambitions were beginning to stir among the American people. It was the decade of the 1890's that was most conspicuously marked by the growth of a new imperialist spirit, but even during the late 1870's and the 1880's there were intimations of the shape of things to come.

This had its paradoxical aspects. The slow growth of the idea that the United States might aspire to a larger role on the world stage contrasted sharply with what appeared at the time to be a heightened preoccupation with domestic concerns. Only spasmodically did the public show any active interest in what might be happening beyond the country's continental borders—controversy with Great Britain, a flurry of excitement over German policy in Samoa, the problem of Hawaii. Nevertheless, the final settlement of the West and industrial development, so completely overshadowing any question in the realm of foreign affairs, were at the same time building up the national power and a feeling of national confidence that would lead the American people to envisage a larger destiny than even continental empire. The country was unknowingly passing through a transition which was to mark the end of the classic period of American isolation from world affairs and the beginnings of the international role to which it was to become increasingly committed in the twentieth century.

The contradictions which characterized this transitional stage were especially evident in the 1880's. They have often been described as the most barren years in all the history of American diplomacy, and in many ways they were. Every official declaration of policy reiterated the traditional doctrine that the United States was not concerned with the rivalries of international power, had no interests either to defend or promote beyond its own borders, and was prepared to uphold unreservedly the isolationist policies laid down by the nation's founders.

Available diplomatic resources reflected this attitude. In this period the United States had only some twenty-five ministers resident in foreign capitals—no ambassadors at all; while the State Department's staff consisted of no more than sixty officers and clerks. And to some observers, even this limited personnel seemed too large. In 1889 the New York *Sun* went so far as to suggest the abolition of the diplomatic service on the ground that it had outlived its usefulness. "It is a nurse of snobs," this newspaper stated in what was to become a familiar vein. "It spoils a few Americans every year and does no good to anybody."

Foreign observers were unanimous as to the slight interest both the government and the public seemed to show in external matters. "The one principle to which people have learnt to cling in foreign policy," James Bryce wrote authoritatively in the *American Commonwealth*, first published in 1888, "is that the less they have of it the better." He noted that development of the nation's resources left little time for consideration of anything else, and that the opportunities for commercial and industrial expansion were sufficiently great to absorb national energy. "And into the mind of the people," Bryce added, "there has sunk deep the idea that . . . the true way for the model Republic to influence . . . [the] world is to avoid its errors, and set an example of pacific industrialism."

From a somewhat different angle, Cecil Spring-Rice, the brilliant young secretary of the British legation who would, a quarter of a century later, return as an ambassador, also commented on this total absorption in domestic affairs. He regretted his assignment to Washington in the 1880's—"it seems so far off the line"—and on one occasion wrote home that there was "very little experience of foreign policies here—in fact none."

These foreigners also observed that the American people generally expressed a characteristic antipathy and scorn—Bryce called it "pure and undisguised contempt"—for the Old World. This attitude was of course as old as the foundation of the Republic. At the time of the war of independence, America had rejected not only British rule but all the political and social institutions of Europe—monarchy, class privilege, militarism. The Old World had come to symbolize everything that the New World repudiated—despotism as against democracy, and war as against peace. These deep sentiments were still as strong in the 1880's as in the 1780's. Quite as much as the needs of national security they helped to strengthen the concept of a foreign policy wholly removed from any concern with the complex of European power politics.

When he first came into office in 1885, Cleveland set forth in his inaugural address a view of foreign policy that could not have more clearly reflected contemporary thinking. The genius of the American people, their domestic needs, and the attention demanded for the development of the nation's vast resources, he declared, dictated the scrupulous avoidance of any departure from the policies that the nation had always pursued. He then proceeded to define them: a policy of independence which was favored by geographic circumstances and defended by justice and power; a policy of peace suitable to the national interest, and a policy of neutrality that rejected any share in foreign broils and harbored no ambitions for overseas expansion, but was nonetheless prepared to repel any intrusion of the European powers in the affairs of the New World. What this added up to, Cleveland concluded, was the historic doctrine, bequeathed the nation by Washington, Jefferson, and Monroe—"Peace, commerce and honest friendship with all nations; entangling alliances with none."

This classic statement, however, was in many ways a final and almost nostalgic expression of the historic isolationism growing out of America's geographic position. Cleveland was himself staunchly and consistently to uphold the policy he so warmly praised, not only in avoidance of any entangling alliances but also in opposition to overseas expansion. During his first term of office he never looked abroad, and on his return to the White House in 1893, as we have already seen, he blocked the annexation of Hawaii, disapproved of the tripartite protectorate over Samoa, and also rejected the idea of trying to establish exclusive American control over a possible transisthmian canal. Nevertheless, even in his own day, and in part through his own later actions, the most significant changes were taking place in the country's attitude and in its general approach to world affairs.

The United States was already beginning to broaden its horizons and incorporate remote interests with its own. Granted that the American people remained primarily concerned with domestic problems, the actual course of events was something else again. It was pointing in a quite different direction from that which President Cleveland, drawing upon the past, maintained that the nation should follow.

Even though there was still no involvement in European politics, the 1880's saw the United States taking its first important steps toward the extension of national influence both in Latin America and throughout the general area of the Pacific. To recapitulate what has already been noted: this supposedly wholly quiescent period saw the initiation of Secretary Blaine's program of Pan-Americanism and his strong support, further upheld by his successor, for the principle that any canal linking the Atlantic and the Pacific was a wholly American affair; it witnessed the tightening of American bonds with Hawaii and Samoa as an important stride (Cleveland to the contrary notwithstanding) toward establishing dominant American power in the Pacific, and it found the United States strengthening its ties with Japan and China, opening up Korea, and vying with the European powers for a position of greater influence in eastern Asia.

Also during this period, which has not yet been mentioned, the United States took an unusual and unprecedented step in participating in an international conference held in Berlin in 1884 to deal with the affairs of the International Association of the Congo, established under the aegis of King Leopold II of the Belgians. It is true that the Senate did not approve the consequent General Act of Berlin, signed by the American representatives at the conference, which established the neutrality of what became the Congo Free State. It was unwilling to have the United States make any commitment breaking the isolationist pattern of American foreign policy. But participation in the conference was nonetheless a sign of changing times (not so many years earlier Secretary Seward had refused to have anything to do with even so innocuous a project as the Geneva Convention setting up the International Red Cross), and it dimly foreshadowed a day when even the affairs of distant Africa would engage the attention of a country compelled to assume ever broader responsibilities in the maintenance of world peace.

There were also underlying developments outside the diplomatic sphere that were far more important as demonstrating a quickening of popular interest in the role the United States might have to play beyond its national borders. The steady expansion of foreign trade was creating a demand for more vigorous government support in the development of new markets and the protection of oceanic commercial routes. Linked with this was a growing movement for naval expansion that led to a start toward construction of a modern navy which could operate effectively overseas. Indeed, nothing more signally illustrated—whatever foreign observers might say of the United States' lack of concern with international affairs—a slowly changing climate of opinion than this demand for an effective navy. Americans were beginning to think not only of commercial expansion, important as it was, but of the desirability of their country's being able to speak with a voice of greater authority on the stage of world politics.

"What do the nations of the earth care about your moral power after you leave your own shores?" Senator Charles W. Jones of Florida asked in promoting naval expansion in 1884. "All that they respect when the emergency arises is a decent display of public force."

The naval weakness of the United States before the new building program initiated in the early 1880's got under way was amazing for a nation with its resources and industrial capacity. "Never was there such a hopeless, broken-down, tattered, forlorn apology for a navy," a British journal commented in describing the American fleet, and there was no denying the validity of such a scornful characterization. The entire force was constituted of no more than a handful of obsolescent wooden ships, still relying primarily on sail, at a time when almost every other country already had or was building modern, steel-armored, heavily gunned steam vessels. The American Navy was greatly inferior to those of all the major European states and several of the Latin American nations. The question was raised whether it could even stand up to that of China. After visiting this country Rudyard Kipling was to write in his *American Notes:*

China's fleet today, if properly manned, could waft the entire American navy out of the water and into the blue. The big, fat Republic that is afraid of nothing, because nothing up to the present has happened to make her afraid, is as unprotected as a jellyfish.

The public was becoming aware of this weakness. Want of an effective navy was held responsible in part for the difficulties and delays in settling the fisheries dispute with Great Britain. Its limitations were further driven home by the confrontation with Germany over Samoa. And when in the midst of the controversy with China over immigration the Imperial Government actually did acquire two war vessels larger than any of those in the American fleet, it was cogently suggested that ordinary precaution pointed to the need "to build ships equal in power to the ships of the nation we treat with such contumely."

The basic thesis of the importance of naval power in maintaining a nation's world position was to be most notably elaborated by Alfred Thayer Mahan in his classic study *The Influence of Sea Power upon History*, published in 1890. That same year also saw his ideas on the importance of a powerful navy for the United States incorporated in a special Naval Policy Board report. A full decade earlier, however, Representative Washington C. Whitthorne of Tennessee had marshaled all the historical arguments in support of naval power in a highly significant speech on the floor of the House.

The history of all great nations, from Phoenicia, Carthage, and Rome to Portugal, France, and Great Britain, Whitthorne asserted, showed that those which attained the highest rank of dominion and power, wealth and prosperity, had powerful navies and merchant marines. If the United States were to maintain its well-being and prosperity, and uphold its rightful position in the world, he saw the lesson clearly revealed. It had to build up the American Navy, at a time when it was "worn out, slow in speed, feeble in offensive power, even in the power of running away from danger," to a position that would enable the United States to compete with the rest of the world on the high seas.

The new program first got under way during President Arthur's Administration, when in 1883 Congress authorized the construction of four modern steel cruisers. They were equipped with sail as well as steam, however, and were primarily designed for coastal defense. "It is no part of our policy," the President could still feel justified in saying, "to create and maintain a navy able to cope with that of the other great powers of the world."

When Cleveland came into office two years later, the program received a further impetus largely through the energetic measures taken by his able Secretary of the Navy, William C. Whitney, who worked assiduously both to modernize the Navy Department and to encourage the authorization of new ships. Congress in these years appropriated the funds for five protected cruisers and two battleships (the latter were the *Texas* and the *Maine,* the nucleus of what was to become the famous White Squadron), and by the close of the 1880's still more battleships and cruisers were authorized.

Cleveland supported this naval program. As in the case of Arthur, however, he did not think in terms of a striking power which could challenge the navies of other countries, but of continental defense. It was a sign of the conflicting points of view still prevalent in official circles that the big navy advocates, disciples of the Mahan thesis of sea power, felt it necessary to describe the new ships in the somewhat ambiguous terms of "sea-going coastline battleships."

The next decade saw steadily rising naval appropriations, in line with the recommendations of the Naval Policy Board report in 1890, and the gradual creation of an impressive modern fleet. Congress authorized the construction of twenty-five new vessels, including the first-class battleships *Massachusetts, Indiana,* and *Oregon,* and provided the increased personnel such a fleet would need. By the century's close, the country had a navy which boasted seventeen battleships in being or under construction, six armored cruisers, and a sizable flotilla of monitors, armored cruisers, and gunboats. The United States would soon rank third among the world's naval powers, its fleet inferior only to those of Great Britain and France.

National pride had been perhaps the greatest force in building the new navy. "We stand among the great powers of the world and we should make ourselves respected," declared one congressman in supporting the increased naval appropriations; and another asserted with equal fervor that for the United States to remain helpless before the navies of Europe "was not a fit position for this great Republic to occupy." Even President Cleveland, for all his isolationist and anti-imperialist views, had come to decry the disadvantage the country would suffer if in the conduct of its relations with other nations, the United States could not enforce "the terms dictated by its sense of right and justice."

The sense of national pride, constantly swelling as the new navy took on shape and form, was soon to spill over into an aggressive jingoism which, well before the days of the war with Spain, found many Americans apparently spoiling for a fight that would test the country's new fleet. This latent chauvinism had been manifest in the fisheries dispute with Great Britain and the quarrel with Germany over Samoa. It flared up even more dangerously when Harrison succeeded Cleveland in 1889, and with Secretary Blaine back at his old post in the State Department, the United States embarked on what was described as a more "spirited" foreign policy.

Rudyard Kipling had something to say at this very time about jingoism, as well as about the still woeful state of the American Navy. Its anti-British manifestations naturally interested this English writer the most, and he apparently had a revealing experience of what Americans still thought about the Mother Country at a banquet in San Francisco:

It was my first introduction to the American Eagle screaming for all its worth. . . . I sat bewildered on a coruscating Niagara of—blatherskite. It was stupendous. . . . Then, according to rule, they . . . hurled defiance at "our natural enemy . . . with her chain of fortresses across the world." Thereafter they glorified their nation afresh . . . in case any detail should have been overlooked.

The most blatant example of the jingoist spirit during these years occurred during a quarrel with Chile which grow out of a riot in Valparaiso, on October 16, 1891, involving a party of American sailors on shore leave from their ship, the U.S.S. *Baltimore*. The Chilean people were feeling bitterly anti-Ameri-

can at this time because of the policy the United States had
followed during a recent revolution, and what had started out
as a casual saloon brawl soon took on heroic proportions. An
angry mob attacked the Americans and beat them up so severely
that two men died and several others were badly injured. Then
to make matters worse, the Chilean police, who had stood by
complacently during the riot, carried the hapless American
survivors off to jail.

Captain W. S. Schley of the *Baltimore* entered an immediate
and vigorous protest with the Chilean authorities, and when
shortly afterwards Captain "Fighting Bob" Evans arrived at
Valparaiso with the gunboat *Yorktown,* he also called for prompt
reparation for the injuries inflicted on the American sailors. The
two naval officers differed only in describing the condition of
the men who had gone ashore. Captain Schley insisted they were
sober, quiet, and peaceful; Captain Evans admitted they were
"probably drunk, properly drunk," and that many of them had
indeed gone ashore "for the purpose of getting drunk." But
whether drunk or sober, it was insisted that the members of the
Baltimore's crew were entitled to police protection and had
instead been "foully murdered" by Chilean roughs.

The State Department fully sustained the position taken by
Captains Schley and Evans and in turn demanded "prompt and
full reparation." When no immediate reply was forthcoming
from the Chilean Government, tempers began to rise in Washington. Surprisingly enough Secretary Blaine, who in an earlier
day had earned the sobriquet of "Jingo Jim," was to find himself
in the unusual position of seeking to restrain a far more bellicose
President.

A self-important little man, whose aloof austerity was in
marked contrast with Blaine's easygoing, genial good nature,
Harrison had been a Civil War soldier, prided himself on his
patriotism, and perhaps more than any other man in public life
mirrored the jingoistic spirit of the day. He was not one to
brook any injury done his country. When Blaine tried to counsel
a patient attitude in dealing with Chile, the President retorted

sharply, "Mr. Secretary, that insult was to the uniform of United States sailors." On hearing nothing from Chile for nearly two months, Harrison reported to Congress in December that if there were any further delay in receiving a full apology and reparation for what had happened in Valparaiso, he would bring the matter to it again "for such action as may be necessary."

This ominous warning—for, why would the President submit the dispute to Congress unless he had forceful military measures in mind?—stirred the Chilean Foreign Minister to action, but hardly the action that would soothe ruffled feelings in Washington. He stated that the information on which the President had based his report on the riot was "erroneous or deliberately incorrect," assailed the American Minister to Chile for what he declared to be an unfriendly attitude toward the country to which he was accredited, and belligerently concluded that the rights and dignity of his own country would be upheld "notwithstanding the intrigues which proceed from so low a source and the threats which come from so high a source."

This was adding further insult to injury. With publication of the note, jingoes throughout the United States seized such an opportunity as had never before been presented them. There were some few voices of moderation. The Charleston *News and Courier* said that to make such a fuss over Chile's attitude was "like John L. Sullivan shaking his fist at a little street gamin." The New York *Tribune* soberly commented that "a nation really great does not permit itself to lose its temper—but waits." Far more generally, however, the press screamed for blood. If there was not an immediate apology, the New York *Sun* insisted that "we must teach men who will henceforth be called snarling whelps of the Pacific that we cannot be snapped at with impunity"; and the Chicago *Tribune* bellicosely called on the Administration to get American warships on the coast and enforce its demands, if necessary seizing and holding the Chilean nitrate beds. "There must be no fear of fractious or partisan opposition to a declaration of war," it added. "The whole nation would demand it."

The capital seethed with rumors. The entire cabinet was said to be in favor of war; the Navy Department, headed by the able and imperialist-minded Benjamin F. Tracy, was impatiently anxious to test its lovely new ships; preparations were reported to be under way to call out the troops. A young man who will repeatedly return in later stages of this narrative, Theodore Roosevelt, at this time a member of the Civil Service Commission but very active politically, was almost hysterically calling for war as a means of reviving the national spirit. He was described (in a letter from John Hay to Henry Adams) as going about Washington "hissing through his clenched teeth that we are dishonest. For two nickels he would declare war himself . . . and wage it sole." Excitement mounted throughout the country. Reporting on the general situation, the Britisher Cecil Spring-Rice wrote home that Secretary Blaine's influence was for peace, and he was doing everything he could do to preserve it, but that the President appeared to be bent on hostilities.

On January 21, 1892, a stiffly worded note that Harrison himself had drawn up was dispatched to the Chilean Government. It unequivocally declared that the United States would have no alternative to breaking off diplomatic relations unless an immediate apology was received, both for the failure of the police in Valparaiso to provide adequate protection for the *Baltimore's* shore party and for the offensive statements of the Chilean Foreign Minister. After waiting but a brief four days for a reply, the President then sent another message to Congress submitting the issue to it for such action as it deemed appropriate.

Fortunately, the Chilean Government had already come to the conclusion that any further delays or evasions on its part would almost surely push the United States into war. It was prepared to beat a hurried retreat, and its capitulation reached Washington just in time. In answer to Harrison's virtual ultimatum, Chile apologized for the slurs that had been cast upon the President and the American Minister, and promised to pay an indemnity for the loss of lives in the rioting at Valparaiso.

Even the most rabid jingoes, whether within or without the

Administration, had to admit themselves satisfied by Chile's back-down. There could be no further pretext for hostilities. Blaine was able to make a friendly response to the Chilean Government ("it may seem to you too cordial," he almost apologetically wrote the hot-headed President, "but I believe it to be in the highest sense expedient"), and a dangerous threat of war completely subsided.

"The triumph for peace is great," wrote the Philadelphia *Press,* and then added a note which marked what the incident had meant for a patriotic, restive, excitable people: "There is not an American who does not thrill with a sense of national power exerted for international right."

The jingoism inflamed by the Chilean war scare would con-tinue to exert a powerful influence on popular sentiment. It was not only Roosevelt who felt that war might revive a national spirit which was felt to be becoming weak and flabby. But it must be remembered that the generation of the 1890's did not think of possible hostilities in terms of a dangerous worldwide conflict. "War now not only occurs more rarely," Captain Mahan was to write, in pointing up what could hardly have been a more different situation than that to develop over a not too distant horizon, "but has rather the character of an occasional excess, from which recovery is easy." The jingoes of this earlier age thought in terms of picturesque naval battles and exciting cavalry charges; they dreamed of national glory and the easy rewards of heroism.

Nonetheless, the more conservative-minded were greatly con-cerned over what was happening. A contributor to the *North American Review* commented that the American people ap-peared to be "inflated with a national vanity" that made them supersensitive in their relations with other countries, and an article in the *Arena* stated that unless all signs failed, the United States seemed to be initiating a foreign policy "which will soon reflect our worst characteristics."

The *Nation* carried on a relentless campaign against what it called the "professional frothings of the incurable jingoes." In a trenchant editorial in 1894, Edwin L. Godkin took the country severely to task for giving way to such dangerous nonsense:

The number of men and officials in this country who are now mad to fight somebody is appalling. Navy officers dream of war and talk and lecture about it incessantly. The Senate debates are filled with predictions of impending war and with talk of preparing for it at once. . . . Most truculent and bloodthirsty of all, jingo editors keep up a din day after day about the way we could cripple one country's fleet and destroy another's commerce, and fill the heads of boys and silly men with the idea that war is the normal state of civilized country.

From prudently minding its own business, the country seemed all too ready to interfere in the affairs of other nations. "The United States has ceased to be the China of the Western Continent," exuberantly declared Senator Cushman K. Davis, later a leader among the imperialists. "We are alive, thank God, and must not be insulted by any power in the world, great or small."

The policy of the Harrison Administration reflected this often irresponsible chauvinism and also a latent imperialism in other instances than in the stand it had taken in upholding national honor in the dispute with Chile. We have already seen that it vigorously defended American rights in Samoa against any possible infringement by Germany, and that in its closing days it rushed through a treaty for the annexation of Hawaii. It also reaffirmed national support for exclusive American control over a Nicaraguan canal, and renewed earlier efforts to secure naval bases in the Caribbean.

Discussions were begun with Haiti for leasing a coaling station, with three warships sent to the coast in what turned out to be a futile effort to persuade the Haitian Government to grant the American request. Offers were made to Santo Domingo for a lease of Samaná Bay. It was clear that President Harrison had decided expansionist ambitions. His policy was attacked by his Democrat opponents as one of "irritation and bluster," but the

Republicans defended it as seeking the "achievement of the manifest destiny of the Republic in its broadest sense."

Had Harrison continued in office, it was widely believed that a still more aggressive foreign policy would have been one of the most marked features of his second administration, and that the United States might then and there have acquired a string of naval bases in the South Atlantic and the Pacific. Moreover, the chancelleries of Europe were quite aware of what was described as "the chauvinistic tendencies" of the American Government. They were beginning to worry over where they might carry a nation so steadily building up its naval power. There was a feeling in some quarters, as expressed by the German Minister in Washington during the Samoan imbroglio, that America was becoming "overconfident . . . and yielding to the temptation to measure its exuberant strength against a European enemy." Even though any such challenge might be chimerical, President Harrison's approach to foreign affairs appeared to herald a significant change in America's outlook on the world.

Harrison was not re-elected in 1892, however; the conservative Cleveland was returned to office after his four-year retirement to the side lines. And he remained as ardently opposed as ever to a jingoistic or imperialistic foreign policy. He still clung to the past on taking office again in 1893; he stoutly reaffirmed those basic principles he had set forth in his inaugural address in 1885. Yet in the spirit of the times he was all unwittingly to help usher in a quite different future.

CHAPTER VIII

Cleveland and Venezuela

The nation was torn and distracted when Grover Cleveland began his second term. Apart from those years when it has been confronted by war, the mid-1890's was one of the most perilous periods in all its history. The tremendous economic advance that had marked the years since the Civil War appeared to have ground to a halt. Depression lay heavily over the entire land. The farmers had risen in sullen revolt against governmental policies which they held responsible for a catastrophic decline in agricultural prices; downtrodden workers in industry and on the railroads challenged their employers in embittered industrial strife.

This situation on the domestic front was directly and importantly to influence foreign affairs. It further encouraged the spirit of jingoism and the idea of foreign adventure. A number of political leaders were to support overseas expansion primarily as a means to divert popular attention from domestic ills and to escape the dangerous impact of internal unrest. They believed (reminding us of Seward's "Thoughts" in 1861) that only through an aggressive foreign policy could a shattered national unity be effectively restored. Some newspaper editors and congressmen were frankly to say that war would be a godsend in allaying class and sectional strife. As one of the latter rather inelegantly expressed such an extreme view, it would "knock the pus out of the anarchistic, socialistic, and populistic boil."

Even though President Cleveland was never to approve an expansionist policy, as has so repeatedly been demonstrated, no one was more firmly committed than he was to defending the national interest and upholding the national honor as he interpreted these sometimes vague abstractions. He had temporarily set back the cause of imperialism in rejecting the annexation of Hawaii and in speaking out so strongly against any other move toward acquiring overseas colonies. At the same time he took such a determinedly nationalistic stand in handling the most important foreign problem of his administration that perhaps more than any of his predecessors he strengthened the underlying forces that were to launch the United States on its new career as an imperialistic world power.

This problem was the quarrel that arose with Great Britain in 1895—the last of that series of controversies which had bedevilled Anglo-American relations ever since the Civil War—over the boundaries between British Guiana and Venezuela. The dispute regarding the frontier of this little colony (the British had taken it over from the Dutch during the Napoleonic Wars) and its Latin American neighbor could be traced back to 1841. It was more than fifty years later, however, that further developments led to the direct involvement and intervention of the United States.

The line marking the boundaries between Venezuela and British Guiana had originally been drawn by Sir Robert Schomburgk, a British geographer. Venezuela had never accepted this line, however, and when the British later encouraged new settlements in the disputed area, encroaching even farther into territory that Venezuela considered its own, the Venezuelan Government was outraged. The land in question was some fifty thousand square miles of largely uninhabited jungle, but it controlled the mouth of the Orinoco River, and with the discovery of gold fields in the general area around 1875 it also took on an additional and unforeseen economic value. Venezuela insisted that the dispute be submitted to arbitration. Great Britain was willing to consider adjudication of the title to the new settlements west of the Schomburgk line, but it insisted on the validity of the original boundary, flatly rejecting the Venezuelan demand that it be included in any arbitration proceedings. In these circumstances Venezuela broke off diplomatic relations in 1887, and the controversy continued to fester.

The United States on several occasions showed a willingness to extend its good offices in trying to heal the breach, and in 1894 President Cleveland renewed these offers, expressing the belief that it was of the utmost importance "to remove from this hemisphere all causes of difference with powers beyond the sea." Still maintaining its intransigeant attitude toward inclusive arbitration, Great Britain rejected these friendly overtures, and its Foreign Secretary, Lord Kimberley, even hinted that his country was now determined to hold on to the new British settlements west of the Schomburgk line. British imperialism appeared to be on the march at the expense of a weak and almost defenseless Latin American republic.

There was also the further factor that the expansion of England's influence anywhere in Latin America might endanger American commercial interests. Cleveland was no less aware than his successor William McKinley would be of the importance to the United States of a growing foreign trade, and even though earlier efforts for its extension in Latin America had not succeeded, the countries south of the Rio Grande were still regarded as important potential customers for American manufactured products. Great Britain in control of the Orinoco River would be in a favored commercial position. And while much more was to be said about it in later years, the need for a more aggressive foreign policy to safeguard American trade was already being stressed in many quarters.

One spokesman for such a policy was Don Dickinson, a

prominent Michigan Democrat who was known to be very close to Cleveland. "We need and must have," Dickinson declared significantly in attacking Great Britain's policies in Latin America, "open markets throughout the world to maintain and increase our prosperity." The Venezuela controversy was not an isolated incident in the evolution of American foreign policy. In some respects it was a link between the Pan-Americanism of Secretary Blaine and the expansionism of President McKinley.

As it became known that Great Britain was paying no attention to the pressure for arbitration of its dispute with Venezuela, the American public began to show a lively interest in a situation which it had heretofore largely ignored. Its natural sympathies for Venezuela were then reinforced when in October, 1894, William L. Scruggs, the former American Minister in Caracas now serving as an agent of the Venezuelan Government, published a sensational pamphlet with the inflammatory title, "British Aggressions in Venezuela, or the Monroe Doctrine on Trial." Scruggs distributed this pamphlet widely (it ran through four large editions before the end of the year), and newspapers throughout the country began calling for decisive measures to meet what they had become convinced was a dangerous challenge to the basic principles of American foreign policy in Latin America. Congress in turn responded to this popular agitation and in February, 1895, unanimously adopted a joint resolution calling upon Great Britain and Venezuela to accept arbitration of the disputed boundary.

In the face of such pressure, which was intensified by popular criticism of the attitude Great Britain was at this same time displaying in another controversy with Nicaragua, Cleveland was strengthened in a resolve he had already reached to take some action to bring the Venezuelan business to an end. He was under attack, as a result of his withdrawal of the Hawaiian annexation treaty, for following a weak foreign policy, and politics as well as his own sense of frustration with Great Britain's disregard of his arbitration proposals undoubtedly influenced his attitude. Democratic party leaders were advising that a forthright, aggressive stand on such a popular issue as defense of the Monroe Doctrine would build up the Administration, divert the country's attention from disruptive problems nearer home, and enhance the party's political prospects in the next Presidential election. But while politics may have initially affected Cleveland's position on Venezuela, his policy was soon to gather an irresistible momentum of its own.

In any event, Cleveland decided to send a sharp protest to Great Britain. While it was still being prepared, Secretary of State Gresham died and was replaced by Attorney General Olney. In contrast with his cautious and pacific-minded predecessor, Olney was imperious and demanding, no man to brook opposition to any course on which he had decided, and not unduly blessed with diplomatic tact. As Attorney General he had forcefully suppressed the Pullman strike of 1894, and he seemed ready to deal with Great Britain somewhat in the manner he had treated the striking railwaymen. As he later admitted, the note that he now sent to the British Foreign Office—on July 20, 1895—was "undoubtedly of the bumptious order." It was drawn up along such lines, however, by calculated design. "In English eyes," Olney revealingly wrote, "the United States was then so completely a negligible quantity that it was believed only words the equivalent of blows would be really effective."

The note set forth a bold and ringing assertion of the principles underlying the Monroe Doctrine and of the position which the United States had attained in the Western Hemisphere and was ready to defend. In the light of such circumstances, Olney thereupon declared, the controversy between Great Britain and Venezuela was one which directly concerned the United States. It could not countenance interference by any European government in the affairs of the Western Hemisphere. Should Great Britain persevere on a course of seeking to enlarge the bounds of British Guiana, this policy could not but be interpreted as amounting in substance to an invasion and conquest of Venezuelan territory. For the United States to fail to protest such action or to fail to warn Great Britain that it would be considered injurious to the interests of the people of the United States would be to ignore an established national policy with which the honor and welfare of the country were deeply identified.

And in the course of this cogent statement Secretary Olney, with magnificent abandon, defied all Europe:

That distance and three thousand miles of intervening ocean make any permanent political union between an European and an American state unnatural and inexpedient will hardly be denied. . . . Today the United States is practically sovereign on this continent, and its fiat is law upon the subjects to which it confines its interposition. . . . Its infinite resources combined with its isolated position render it master of the situation and practically invulnerable as against any or all other powers.

Both President Cleveland, who fully approved the note, and his Secretary of State had quite consciously issued a direct and unequivocal challenge to Great Britain. They felt certain, however, that once the British Foreign Office realized how strongly the United States felt about the Venezuelan issue, it would move quickly to accept arbitration. They waited confidently for the reply which would enable the President to demonstrate how forcefully—and successfully—the Administration had defended the national interest.

They waited almost five months. The British Government had not really been awakened to the gravity of the issue as viewed in the United States (in part due to reassurances by the overly pro-British American Ambassador, former Secretary of State Thomas F. Bayard), and neither Lord Salisbury, the Prime Minister, nor Joseph Chamberlain, the Colonial Secretary, were seriously disturbed by the possible implications of Olney's note. Their casual attitude, it would appear, did much to justify the Secretary of State's later comment that in British eyes the United States was still "a negligible quantity." And when Lord Salisbury finally got around on November 26 to sending the reply which Olney had specifically requested before the President had to forward his annual message to Congress, he made not a single concession to the American position.

The tone of the British note, clearly reflecting resentment of Secretary Olney's own arrogant claims, was highhanded, self-righteous, and dogmatic. Lord Salisbury questioned the very bases of the Monroe Doctrine, declaring it had no validity whatsoever in international law. Even if it were taken more seriously than it deserved to be, he then stated, it still did not give the United States any rights in the current controversy—"the disputed frontier of Venezuela has nothing to do with any of the questions dealt with by President Monroe." The Prime Minister then blandly reiterated that so far as the Schomburgk line was concerned, Great Britain could not accept the American suggestion that the dispute be submitted to arbitration.

When this belated and supercilious reply was received in Washington, President Cleveland (hastily summoned back from a duck-shooting expedition) was reported to be "mad clear through." He had characterized Olney's note as "the best thing of the kind I have ever read" and was ready to back up his Secretary of State to the hilt. There was apparently in his mind no comparison between the nationalistic stand he was prepared to take on this issue and those manifestations of an imperialistic or jingoist spirit which he had so often condemned in the past.

What he believed was at stake were the basic, underlying principles of the Monroe Doctrine whose defense, as he would say, was "essential to the integrity of our free institutions and the tranquil maintenance of our distinctive form of government." And there were also the "practical benefits" of the Doctrine in safeguarding American commercial interests against what might prove to be the dangerous encroachments of European powers in a part of the world where the United States had such great opportunities to extend its trade. Moreover, to defend the Monroe Doctrine was in his eyes to sustain the most fundamental precepts of American foreign policy rather than in any way to depart from them. Cleveland felt it to be his clear duty, over and above everything else, to uphold the position that Secretary Olney had made so clear in first calling Great Britain to account.

The public, which had not been informed of Secretary

Olney's note, was in the meantime growing restive over the apparent passivity of the Administration. Reflecting such feelings the Washington *Post* declared that the United States should be ready to defend the national interest whatever Great Britain might do. An article appearing in the June issue of the *North American Review* by the new, young senator from Massachusetts, Henry Cabot Lodge, even more explicitly expressed a jingoist point of view. It had much—highly critical—to say on other phases of current foreign policy, but on the Venezuelan issue was especially forthright. "The supremacy of the Monroe Doctrine," Lodge wrote, "should be established and at once—peaceably if we can, forcibly if we must."

Cleveland needed no prodding. He knew what he felt he should do, and after receiving Lord Salisbury's reply he sent a special message to Congress in which he drew no punches. Following a review of the entire Venezuelan controversy, he vigorously upheld the thesis that in refusing to accept arbitration over title to the entire disputed area, Great Britain was directly challenging the Monroe Doctrine. He was not concerned with the niceties of international law but with American rights, American honor, and American prestige. After outlining his case, Cleveland consequently asked Congress to appropriate the necessary funds for an investigation of the boundary between British Guiana and Venezuela, and then stated that when the investigation had been completed, the United States should be prepared by every means in its power to resist any attempt on the part of Great Britain to assert authority over territory that "we have determined of right belongs to Venezuela." In conclusion, the President somberly told Congress, "I am fully alive to the responsibility incurred, and keenly realize all the consequences that may follow."

The consequences of such a belligerent stand—the assertion of an American right to determine the disputed boundary by unilateral action—were of course possible war with Great Britain. The conservative, responsible, antijingo Cleveland was ready, if it should prove necessary, to uphold the position he had taken in the name of the United States by force of arms.

A startled country accepted in full stride the implications of this emphatic message. In reporting on the popular reaction the *Literary Digest* stated that "the overwhelming majority of the newspapers applaud the message as American, vigorous, and eminently just." Among typical comments was that of the Atlanta *Journal.* "In supporting the President in this position," it wrote, "the people of this country will stand as one man. Party lines will vanish like smoke and sectional divisions will be forgotten. The honor of the country is at stake. We have a President who means to defend it." The Congress promptly, excitedly, and unanimously passed a bill providing the necessary appropriation for setting up the commission to determine the Venezuelan boundary line.

True to its conservative traditions the *Nation* was one journal which from the outset opposed such a belligerent stand and such dangerous defiance of Great Britain. Its comment, however, also revealed in how much of a minority the critics of Cleveland's policy found themselves in this first excited reaction to his message. The "rational sober-minded people," wrote the *Nation's* editor, were driven to silence in fear that any opposition to the President would lead to their being charged with the crime of "un-Americanism."

In the more extreme jingoist circles the prospect of possible war seemed to be wholly alluring. Theodore Roosevelt was as ready to welcome hostilities with Great Britain as he had been hopeful of their breaking out against Chile. "Let the fight come if it must," he wrote a friend with characteristic bellicosity. "I don't care whether our seacoast cities are bombarded or not; we would take Canada." Lodge was reported as "bubbling over with delight" and privately exulted: "We are all jingoes now."

However, there was a sharp reaction to such uncontrolled hysteria once the enormity of possible war with Great Britain was more fully realized. Few Americans really wanted to face the frightening consequences of conflict between the two Anglo-Saxon nations over a boundary dispute in the distant jungles of South America. On more sober second thought, the public grew increasingly alarmed over the unspeakable tragedy that might result should matters be allowed to drift any further. The conservative and financial interests of the country, as well as liberals and intellectuals, exerted all their influence in seeking to calm the popular excitement.

So influential a Democratic newspaper as the New York *World* took the lead in this movement. Only four days after Cleveland's message, it said editorially that there was no menace to the United States in a dispute over Venezuela's boundary— "it is not our frontier," and declared that "to raise the spectre of war over a false sentiment, and a false conception, is something more than a grave blunder. If persisted in, it will be a colossal crime." Seeking out the responses of leading public figures both in the United States and in England, it was then able to publish their overwhelming condemnation of war, and the conciliatory statements of such prominent British figures as the Prince of Wales, the Duke of York, and William Gladstone did much to turn the tide. The British Ambassador in Washington was soon able to report to his government that there was "a strong undercurrent in opposition to the warlike attitude of the United States."

At the same time public sentiment in England, shocked to discover that a seemingly minor controversy could have such grave repercussions in the United States, was rallying even more strongly in support of a peaceful resolution of the dispute. Aroused by the possibility of a war which even the Colonial Secretary (however casual his attitude during the first exchange of notes) now called "an absurdity as well as a crime," some 350 members of the House of Commons signed a memorial calling for the arbitration of any dispute with the United States. Other groups, including one made up of British writers, sent appeals to America urging an amicable settlement. On the very day that the British Ambassador in Washington was describing the more peace-minded atmosphere in the United States, the American Ambassador in London cabled that he had heard "nothing but sorrow, alarm and indeed horror, expressed at the suggestion of a conflict of force."

Against this background of mounting concern on both sides

of the Atlantic, the two governments moved rapidly toward more conciliatory policies. The United States was not prepared to sacrifice the principles on which it had taken its stand, but it had no idea of pushing matters too far. Great Britain was particularly constrained to re-establish friendly relations because political developments in Europe at just this juncture of affairs heavily emphasized the importance of Anglo-American understanding. On January 3, 1896—Congress had just passed its bill establishing the commission to investigate the Venezuela boundary—the German Kaiser sent a famous telegram to the Boers in South Africa congratulating them on their repulse of an English-led raid into the Boer republic of the Transvaal. Although Lord Salisbury was already anxious to find a solution of the Venezuela crisis, nothing could have driven home more forcibly the value of American good will than this suggestion of Germany's sympathy for England's foes in the threatening Boer War.

The British Government, in any event, now agreed to accept in principle the all-inclusive arbitration that it had heretofore so stubbornly rejected ever since the Venezuela dispute had first arisen. If little could be said for the hazardous diplomatic methods which it had employed—the "brinkmanship" of a later day— the United States had won a signal victory in support of its interpretation of American rights under the Monroe Doctrine. "Never again," exulted the Chicago *Journal*, "will a European nation put forth claims to American territory without first consulting the Government of the United States."

The diplomatic correspondence prescribing the terms of arbitration strung out tediously, both the American and British publics now having lost all interest in the matter, but finally in February, 1897, an arbitration treaty was duly signed between Great Britain and Venezuela. It caused hardly a ripple of interest. Two years later the arbitral commission made its award in an even more deafening silence. Its settlement of the disputed boundary generally followed the fifty-year-old Schomburgk line but granted Venezuela some slight additional territory and control of the mouth of the Orinoco River.

President Cleveland's bold assertion of American rights in the Western Hemisphere not only revived popular interest in the Monroe Doctrine but it created among the American people— and also among the peoples of Europe—a new sense of the potential power of the United States. Even though its implications were not fully foreseen at the time, the stand taken in the Venezuela dispute thus marked a dividing line in the evolution of American foreign policy. It strengthened the forces of nationalism, encouraged further naval construction, and revealed that America was prepared to act as a great power.

It still remained highly ironical that it was Cleveland who so greatly encouraged this new, chauvinistic outlook on foreign affairs which was soon to have the imperialistic consequences that he so greatly deplored. He himself could never quite understand how he could in any way be charged with fostering the latent jingoism that had already made itself manifest in the United States' earlier but less significant disputes with England, with Chile, and with Germany. He had not wished to stir up any trouble, he was later to write somewhat naïvely to Ambassador Bayard in London, and had been greatly disappointed in the attitude of the British Government when he had come to the defense of the Monroe Doctrine. He could not see why it had failed to appreciate his position "in the midst of all this administration has had to do in attempts to stem the tide of 'jingoism.'"

It has sometimes been maintained that throughout the whole controversy Cleveland acted as he did solely because of political pressures and public opinion. As already suggested such influences may well have influenced him initially, and at no time could he have been wholly immune to them, consciously or unconsciously, but he was acting entirely in character. Few presidents have ever been more independent—or stubborn—in upholding and supporting their own views on foreign policy. The belligerent stand he took after Great Britain's refusal to accept arbitration with Venezuela reflected his own conviction that British policy did indeed challenge the Monroe Doctrine. He was prepared in good conscience to accept whatever consequences might flow from the virtual ultimatum incorporated in his message to Congress.

It might be remembered that in his statement on American isolationism in 1885, he had strongly emphasized that while rejecting any share in foreign broils, he had considered a major tenet of American policy the repulsion of any intrusion of the European powers in the affairs of the New World. Moreover, he had always stressed the vital importance of maintaining intact both the honor and prestige of the United States. This aspect of his attitude foreshadowed the position that Woodrow Wilson was to take some twenty years later, when he in turn expressed the conviction that the maintenance of national honor was essential if America was to retain the respect of the world.

In the message which Cleveland sent to Congress in December, 1895, he had said:

There is no calamity which a nation can invite which equals that which follows upon supine submission to wrong and injustice, and the consequent loss of national self-respect and honor, beneath which are shielded and defended a people's safety and greatness.

A further consequence of the Venezuela dispute, as important for the long run as its more immediate results in stimulating an enhanced nationalism, was the impetus it somewhat paradoxically gave to the movement toward a lasting Anglo-American *rapprochement.* The confrontation over the Monroe Doctrine had brought the two countries so much closer to the brink of war than the dispute over the *Alabama* claims or the controversies over fishing and sealing rights, that it drove home with compelling force the imperative need to prevent anything like it ever happening again. If the American and English people were both now agreed that war between their two countries was "unthinkable," some substitute had to be found to provide the means for a peaceful solution of whatever controversies might arise in the future.

To this end Secretary Olney and the British Ambassador in Washington, Lord Pauncefote, undertook to negotiate a general arbitration agreement, and on January 11, 1897, such a pact was signed. It had widespread popular support, one newspaper hailing it as "one of the grandest triumphs of humanity." Nonetheless, it encountered stubborn opposition in the Senate. To some extent this may have reflected the age-old suspicions of Great Britain, but it was perhaps due more to the reluctance of the Senate to surrender its prerogatives in the conduct of foreign policy by approving in advance any program of general arbitration. Whatever the decisive factor may have been, the Olney-Pauncefote Convention was defeated.

This was a disappointment keenly felt in wide circles in both the United States and Great Britain, but rejection of the convention did not halt the continued growth of more friendly feelings between the two countries. There would not again be the irresponsible warmongering which had flared up so dangerously at the close of 1895.

"There is a patriotism of race as well as country," Olney himself was to declare only three years after he had fired off against Great Britain what Cleveland had called his "twenty-inch gun," "and the Anglo-American is as little likely to be indifferent to the one as the other." While Olney freely recognized that the two peoples might again become involved in "family quarrels," he felt that it was not permissible to doubt that they would in the future be found "standing together against any alien foe by whom either was menaced by destruction or irreparable calamity."

Equally prophetic were two other interpretations of the consequences of the Venezuela controversy. Alfred Thayer Mahan wrote that the stand taken by the United States indicated "the awakening of our countrymen to the fact that we must come out of our isolation . . . and take our share in the turmoil of the world." In rather more flamboyant terms, Henry Watterson, the colorful editor of the Louisville *Courier-Journal,* declared that the United States was henceforth destined "to exercise a controlling influence upon the actions of mankind and affect the future of the world as the world was never affected, even by the Roman Empire itself."

When Grover Cleveland relinquished his high office to William McKinley after the Republican triumph in the election of 1896, the contradictory and unforeseen consequences of his foreign policy became more than ever apparent. He had for a time blocked overseas expansion but encouraged the forces that were to make such expansion almost inevitable. He had upheld the country's traditional isolation and yet helped prepare the way for its imminent breakdown. He had refused to venture overseas but for the first time made the European powers aware that America was a great power.

The underlying forces in American life making for a shattering of continental boundaries had indeed received a powerful impetus. What was soon to be discovered was that they were far stronger than any controls that might be exercised by conservative policy-makers in Washington. The nation's emergence on the world stage could no longer be delayed.

CHAPTER IX

Background of Adventure

Over and beyond everything else in accounting for the new position in world affairs that the United States had attained at the
time of the Venezuela incident and that would be further bol-
stered by the century's close, was its economic and industrial
growth. The depression of the early 1890's soon receded into the
past. The nation was to find itself, as a consequence of the further
acceleration of the only briefly interrupted progress under way
ever since the Civil War, at a new pinnacle of strength and self-
assurance. It led all the world in the production of such basic
resources as wheat, coal, and iron; the value of its manufactured
products equaled that of its two closest rivals, and foreign trade
was steadily expanding.

"Behold a republic increasing in population, in wealth, in
strength and in influence, solving the problems of civilization,"
cried William Jennings Bryan; and with no less confidence
Andrew Carnegie declared, "The old nations of the earth creep
on at a snail's pace; the Republic thunders past with the rush of
the express. . . . America already leads the civilized world."

Both the Great Commoner and the Great Steelmaster were
later to take a strong stand against imperialism and the acquisi-

tion of overseas colonies. Their sense of America's gathering power and glowing destiny was nonetheless a significant reflection of what the people as a whole were beginning to feel about their country's dynamic potentialities. Through its spectacular economic development it had broken the bonds of the past, outgrown its one-time provincialism, and held the future in its hands.

The final settlement of the West had accompanied the nation's industrial triumphs during the latter half of the nineteenth century. The broad prairie lands that had been bypassed in the first thrust to the Pacific in pre-Civil War days were finally cultivated to corn and wheat, and with their population rapidly growing, the territories of the Great Plains were carved into new states. By the 1890's the frontier, as it had traditionally existed throughout all prior American history, finally disappeared. Even though much free land still remained to be taken up as homesteads, an end had come to the great epic of continental expansion. In their restless energy the American people had spread out across the land from the Atlantic to the Pacific, and as they stood poised on the shores of the Western Ocean the question arose as to whether this indeed marked an end to territorial growth.

There were those who did not think so. The subjugation of a continent had been sufficient to keep the American people busy at home for a century, declared a writer in the *Overland Monthly*, published in San Francisco, but now that the continent was subdued, "we are looking for fresh worlds to conquer." Stressing as would so many contemporary commentators "the colonizing instinct" of the Anglo-Saxon people, he predicted that whether conservative stay-at-homes liked it or not, this instinct could not be denied.

It was no longer enough, such expansionists felt, for Americans to be content with cultivating their own land and developing their own resources. They questioned the belief that even with everything the country itself had to offer, the United States could make itself completely self-sufficient—independent and aloof from the outside world. The harsh circumstances that had cast a shadow over the Midwest when in the early 1890's it was sorely irked by drought, dust storms, and insect plagues had shaken popular faith in that historic "myth of the garden" which envisaged the Mississippi Valley as the unassailable granary of the world. It was argued that the time had come when the United States could not rely entirely on its internal strength, great as that might be, but should expand the area of its influence and power. Americans must begin to look beyond existing national horizons and seek to project their great achievements at home on the broader stage of a beckoning world.

When the excitement of the Spanish-American War gave a fresh impetus to such ambitious ideas, the Washington *Post* was to go even further than the *Overland Monthly* in stressing the country's new expansionist spirit. "A new consciousness seems to have come upon us," it exclaimed enthusiastically, "—the consciousness of strength—and with it a new appetite, the yearning to show our strength." There could be no avoiding the destiny opening up before the nation, the *Post* continued: "it means an imperial policy, the Republic renascent, taking her place with the armed nations."

The commercial needs of the country appeared to provide a more practical argument for a program of overseas expansion. The growth of industry was producing a surplus of manufactured goods which the domestic market seemed incapable of absorbing. If the United States were to maintain its prosperity, this thesis ran, it had to develop further its foreign trade by finding new outlets for the products of both its farms and its factories. Faced with the mounting competition of the commercial powers of Europe, it could not stand aside while they extended their control over world markets and, through their naval power, exerted an influence that might exclude the United States from its share of international trade.

Innumerable quotations could be cited from the literature of the 1890's and the statements of public men on what appeared to be this overpowering need to obtain new foreign markets. It was a constant and recurring theme, and its reiteration has led to its being given a sometimes exaggerated significance in the eyes of historians seeking economic causation as the all-inclusive reason for overseas expansion. Nevertheless, interest in foreign trade became increasingly widespread. There was no alternative to finding new commercial markets beyond the national borders, as one contemporary economist stated the prevailing view, "in order to prevent business depression, idleness and suffering at home," and it had consequently become necessary by the very instinct of self-preservation for the United States "to enter, however reluctantly, upon the field of international politics."

The geographic area where it was believed the United States could most successfully develop new outlets for its products was eastern Asia. In keeping with the well-founded tradition that had always led the United States to look out across the Pacific, the old dreams of the immense potentialities of the China market were once more revived. Moreover, it seemed imperative that something be promptly done to strengthen the American position in that part of the world. The spheres of influence, the colonies and dependencies, that the European powers were establishing there, appeared gravely to threaten American interests unless the United States effectively challenged its commercial rivals' exclusive ambitions.

The businessmen and traders in the United States were not generally to be converted to the need for direct action along these lines until after the Spanish-American War. In the mid-1890's newspapers and magazines expressing their point of view were fearful of the disturbing effects of any sort of overseas adventure on an economy not yet fully recovered from depression. Opposing both the annexation of Hawaii and any attempt to control a transisthmian canal, the New York *Journal of Commerce* stated as late as 1897 that there was "no excuse whatever in our commercial or political interests" in taking the risks such moves would involve. The ultimate need for extending American influence in the Pacific and in eastern Asia was, however, being stressed in many other quarters.

This program was the basis for what Alfred Thayer Mahan,

whose significant and direct influence on the creation of the new Navy has already been noted, was to call "mercantile imperialism." Drawing together both the naval and commercial arguments for overseas expansion, he declared that the United States had to develop its foreign commerce as a material factor in attaining a position of world power, and was therefore called upon to provide the means for its defense in time of war as well as in time of peace. If our future trade were to be adequately safeguarded, there was an obvious necessity for a strong navy and for the overseas bases that would enable such a navy to operate effectively should the nation's extended interests ever be threatened. Mahan was confident that both the resources of the country and the spirit of the people destined America to future greatness, and he was constantly calling upon his countrymen to look outward and think in terms of a new and comprehensive global policy.

"The annexation, even, of Hawaii," Mahan wrote as early as 1893, "would be no mere sporadic effort, irrational because disconnected from an adequate motive, but a first-fruit and a token that the nation in its evolution has aroused itself to the necessity of carrying its life . . . beyond the borders which have heretofore sufficed for its activities."

The threefold strands of an extended commerce essential for the nation's continued prosperity, a powerful navy that would enable the United States to provide adequate protection for this trade, and the bases that would make overseas operations feasible, were thus combined to present a cogent case for national expansion. How else could the United States feel really secure in a world of mounting imperialistic rivalries?

"I do not mean that we should enter on a widely extended system of colonization," Henry Cabot Lodge once defended his own position. "That is not our line . . . [but] we should take all outlying territory necessary for our own defense, to the protection of the Isthmian Canal, to the upbuilding of our trade and commerce, and to the maintenance of our military safety everywhere." This was perhaps a rather tall order—what could con-

trast more sharply with the position maintained by Cleveland?—
but as the 1890's advanced, such views were gaining a good deal
of popular support.

Another source for what was to become the new imperialism,
apart from its commercial and strategic roots, was the historic
sense of America's mission in the world. Americans had always
believed not only that they were destined to be an example for
all other peoples in their commitment to liberty, but that they
were further called upon to spread abroad the concepts of freedom and democracy for which the New World stood in contrast
with the Old World's tyranny and despotism. At the close of the
nineteenth century this almost instinctive conviction of America's
predestined role in the world, with all its emotional and religious
undertones, was strengthened by the theory of social Darwinism
which sought to apply to races and peoples the thesis of survival
of the fittest accepted as the basis of evolution in the biological
world.

The processes which accounted for the superior development of man were said to be equally responsible for the unique
virtues with which the Anglo-Saxon people (and especially the
Americans) were endowed in comparison with all other races. It
was not enough, however, to accept passively this obvious superiority. The social Darwinists declared that the Anglo-Saxons were
under an obligation to extend to other people the blessings of
their religion, their political principles, and their institutions. In
its simplest terms, so happily expressed as the White Man's
Burden, this meant no more than that Great Britain and the
United States were fated, by the laws of evolution as well as
the sanctions of religion, to extend their authority throughout the
greater part of the world. Any possible contradiction between the
principles and ideas in which Anglo-Saxons believed and those
upheld by other peoples was easily resolved in the former's favor.
The Anglo-Saxons naturally knew best. And by the same reasoning, there could be no question of the ultimate justice in their

seeking to impose their beneficent rule over less advanced peoples.

Among the several popular and influential exponents of such ideas well before imperialism came into full flood was the well-known Congregational minister and evangelist Josiah Strong. In 1885 he published *Our Country,* a highly popular little book that rapidly went through a succession of cheap editions and was also widely quoted in newspapers and magazines throughout the country. Strong drew heavily on the ideas of John Fiske, the popularizer in the United States of evolutionary theory and an unflagging advocate of "the manifest destiny" of the American people, but he gave a uniquely religious cast to his application of social Darwinism to the national future.

Strong argued that it was through their convictions on spiritual Christianity and civil liberty that the Anglo-Saxons had risen, through the processes of natural selection, to their proud eminence throughout the world. Moreover, the United States was destined in his view to become the principal seat of Anglo-Saxon influence and power. From this home base he saw his country-men moving down upon Mexico, upon Central and South America, to the islands of the sea, and across to Africa. "Can any one doubt," he asked rhetorically, "that the result of this competition of the races will be the survival of the fittest?" In terms which now neatly brought together God's will and biology, he was expressing the age-old dream of the New World's regeneration of all mankind. "As America goes," the preface to his book stated with concise brevity, "so goes the world."

When Strong wrote *Our Country* in 1885 he was still think-ing in terms of the ennobling influence of a higher civilization in raising the spiritual and social standards of the peoples of Latin America, Asia, and Africa. The Anglo-Saxons were to exercise a peaceful influence, and by their preaching and example inspire the evangelization of mankind. But the views he presented so persuasively of the innate superiority of American religion, Amer-ican political principles, and American social institutions, and the consequent moral duty of the American people to carry them overseas, provided the greatest possible support for "the imperialism of righteousness." Strong was to become himself an ardent advocate of the acquisition of overseas territory, because he saw it as providing the most effective means for enlightening the inferior races. In a later book entitled *Expansion under New World Conditions,* he called upon his countrymen to dismiss "the craven fear of being great" and to accept the role which God had called them to play in carrying out the obligations devolving upon them in behalf of Christian civilization.

The emphasis on racial superiority that ran through all Strong's writing was typical of the thinking of his day, and it was to characterize the whole imperialist movement. It also had other manifestations at the close of the century: the exclusion laws as applied to the Chinese, the growing agitation for a quota system for immigrants from southeastern Europe, and the new discriminatory laws directed against the Negroes at home. Although the assumption of racial superiority was often the rationalization of a bigoted color prejudice, or in some cases a cloak for the promotion of wholly selfish economic interests, the feeling was general that the white race was the superior race. Throughout all the controversy over imperialism, it made it easily possible for many people to believe that the United States had an inescapable obligation to extend its control over the "lesser breeds beyond the law."

While the moral core of the expansionist argument was the benefit to these inferior peoples of the imposition of the ideals of democracy and freedom, and all the other benefits of American civilization, the imperialists would appear to have been singularly insensible to the probable consequences of their noble purpose. For rarely in the literature of this period is there any suggestion that the infiltration of democratic ideas might result in the ultimate assertion by the subject races of their own right to self-government and independence. The comfortable assumption of racial superiority, which would enable the Anglo-Saxons to maintain their benevolent rule indefinitely, seemingly blinded the imperialists to even the possibility of a revolution of rising expectations among the peoples they were so obligingly ready to train in democracy.

The varied influences—political and economic, emotional and psychological—that created the imperialist climate of the late 1890's had their most persuasive spokesmen in a closely knit little group of writers, publicists, and politicians centering in Washington. In and out of season, in varied magazine articles and lengthy speeches on the floor of Congress, in countless newspaper editorials, they vigorously urged the importance to the United States of an expansionist program.

Foremost among them was Captain Mahan who constantly elaborated on his ideas of mercantile imperialism in a flood of articles for the popular magazines. He not only called for the annexation of Hawaii as "a first fruit" of the new expansionist spirit, but urged the necessity of building an American-controlled isthmian canal and obtaining the naval bases necessary for its protection. He envisaged the United States as both dominating the Caribbean and extending its power out across the Pacific.

Theodore Roosevelt and Henry Cabot Lodge, those two irrepressible jingoes who had hailed Cleveland's stand on Venezuela so enthusiastically, were among his earliest converts and closest political associates. They accepted his whole expansionist thesis ("You are head and shoulders above all of us," Roosevelt once wrote), and did everything within their power to win acceptance for it in government circles. How close was the relationship between the three men is interestingly revealed in a letter Roosevelt wrote Mahan on May 3, 1897. After discussing the possible annexation of Hawaii ("hoist our flag over the island, leaving all details for after action"), Roosevelt continued:

I need not say this letter must be strictly private. I speak to you with the greatest freedom, for I sympathize with your views, and I have precisely the same idea of patriotism and of belief in and love for our country. But to no one else excepting Lodge do I talk like this.

Roosevelt was exceedingly brash and cocky; his martial fervor knew no bounds. Believing in an imperial destiny for the United States and ready to welcome war as a means of reviving the national spirit, he had the greatest scorn for the anti-imperialist, antijingo forces in the country. "These solemn prattlers," he once wrote of them, "strive after an ideal in which they shall happily unite the imagination of a green grocer with the heart of a Bengalese baboo."

When he became Assistant Secretary of the Navy in 1897, Roosevelt was in a position to exercise some direct influence on the McKinley Administration, and he attempted to do so on every possible occasion. On the eve of war with Spain he privately wrote of one time when he "advised the President in the presence of his cabinet . . . as strongly as I know how, to settle this matter instantly by armed intervention." Possibly the always impetuous Roosevelt overplayed his hand, for five days later he reported to another friend that the President "will no longer see me."

Henry Cabot Lodge was perhaps less of a jingo but certainly just as much of an imperialist as Roosevelt. Chilly and aloof, marked by what a contemporary described as "an air of well-bred hauteur," Lodge had quickly won a reputation in Washington as an able parliamentarian, effective speaker, and hard-working senator. He was almost obsessed by the idea of driving the European nations out of the Western Hemisphere, repeatedly affirmed the Mahan thesis on the importance of sea power, and also insisted, as already noted, on America's need to obtain "the necessary outworks" to safeguard its continental position. In a notable speech before the Senate on March 2, 1895 ("I was in desperate earnest," he wrote his mother), he outlined an imperialistic program that called not only for the annexation of Hawaii and Samoa but also that of Canada.

A good many years later Lodge was to be assailed for his narrow isolationist views in opposing American membership in the League of Nations, but in the 1890's he worked incessantly in favor of a broader role for the United States in world affairs. He would not himself have seen any inconsistency in these seemingly contradictory stands. He interpreted overseas expansion as a logical projection of traditional American policy. The "outworks" he sought were necessary for the defense of the "citadel" of American power. He was just as opposed in 1899 as he would be in 1919 to the United States becoming "entangled" in any sort of an alliance with a foreign power. He considered his program as one breaking away from the continental isolation of the past but as nevertheless strengthening American independence. It was the only course American statesmen could follow, Lodge declared, "if they would prove themselves worthy inheritors of the principles of Washington and Adams."

Within the social circle in Washington in which Roosevelt and Lodge moved were a number of other prominent figures and close friends who favored a new and more aggressive foreign policy. Henry Adams and his brother, Brooks Adams, helped to provide what might be described as the intellectual basis for the idea of America's assumption of a larger role in world affairs. They both felt that the nation could not possibly avoid the consequences of its growing power, and placing a primary emphasis on economic factors, foresaw an increasing rivalry with Europe. "Brooks Adams had taught him," Henry Adams was to write, "that the relation between civilizations was that of trade." He believed that in the competition of nations, the United States could save itself only by moving out across the Pacific and winning for itself the commerce of the Orient.

Henry Adams did not play such a direct role in politics as did Roosevelt and Lodge, but he was an influential figure through his many friendships in Washington. "Stableman to statesman," he once described himself. Together with Brooks Adams, he had a remarkably prophetic vision of the nation's future as a great center of power.

From the point of view of his later role in formulating American foreign policy, John Hay was another very important member of this closely knit, imperialist-minded clique. The future Secretary of State, an intimate friend of Henry Adams and also a good friend of both Roosevelt and Lodge, was at the onset no imperialist, let alone a jingo. A man of easy adaptability rather than firm convictions, he was won over to the expansionist cause, however, and came to believe strongly in "our Pacific work." His own interpretation of his swing to imperialism—and that of the McKinley Administration—did not suggest so much personal conversion to the cause his friends espoused so warmly but rather an almost helpless submission to the prevailing climate of opinion.

"No man, no party," Hay wrote, "can fight with any chance of success against a cosmic tendency; no cleverness, no popularity, avails against the spirit of the age."

Among others in this group whose letters reveal how often they met and how congenially they discussed public affairs were a number of expansionist-minded diplomats and senators. The former included Henry White, who was to win great distinction as the country's foremost envoy in European courts, and William W. Rockhill, the future architect of the Open Door policy in China. The senators were J. Donald Cameron of Pennsylvania ("the relation was almost daily," Henry Adams wrote of this association), John T. Morgan of Alabama, Cushman Davis of Minnesota, Redfield Proctor of Vermont ("A jingo!" Roosevelt exclaimed on one occasion, "and it is a relief to see a man who can't be touched by the timid people of wealth"), and, somewhat later, the brilliant young Senator Albert Beveridge of Indiana, the most dedicated and eloquent imperialist of them all.

And finally, in the wings, but often coming into social contact with these men, were such almost rabid expansionist editors as Whitelaw Reid of the New York *Tribune*, Albert Shaw of *Review of Reviews*, and Walter Hines Page of the *Atlantic* and subsequently *World's Work*.

Looking back on the imperialist movement from the vantage point of 1902, Alfred Thayer Mahan was to minimize the influence of this little circle for which he himself served in some measure as mentor. "No man or group of men," he wrote, "can pretend to have guided and governed our people in the adoption of a new policy, the acceptance of which has been rather instinctive—I would prefer to say inspired—than reasoned." These particular men, true enough, were not engaged in a conspiracy; indeed, they had no organized program in mind. Nevertheless, their vigorous support for overseas expansion spearheaded the movement that grew out of the spirit of the times, and they helped to shape the course that it ultimately took.

Whatever the relative importance of the more imponderable forces at work and the immediate activities of imperialist-minded leaders, there is no question whatsoever of the dramatic transformation in the popular attitude toward foreign policy in the late 1890's. The beginnings of this transformation may be pushed much farther back, as we have seen, to the awkward transitional period of the previous two decades. Old ambitions were now, however, coming to a new peak.

There were to be many warnings. The Englishman James Bryce advised against the danger of a nation wanting to expand overseas, as he saw it, for no other reason than "to see marked on the map of the world, dominions beyond her natural borders." But the taste of empire was in the mouth of the people; their emotions were too deeply engaged to judge the country's course by logic alone. The paths of glory seemed to lie out and beyond the national domain in proudly joining the world competition for trade, naval power, and overseas colonies.

CHAPTER X

War with Spain

In one of his many shrewd comments on American foreign policy, former Secretary of State Olney once wrote that, while historians would probably date the abandonment of isolation from the war with Spain, "the change was inevitable, had been long preparing, and could not have been long delayed." This has certainly been demonstrated by the events related in the course of this narrative. The United States had almost in spite of itself become a great power well before the close of the century.

It was nevertheless the war undertaken in 1898 to bring freedom to the people of Cuba that finally launched the nation on the course that broke through and ultimately shattered the patterns of the past. It not only greatly intensified the imperialist spirit already so evident in many quarters, but it provided the actual opportunity for the acquisition of new overseas territories. And in its broader consequence, the war caused the other nations of the world to realize as never before that America had become a nation whose inherent strength and newly awakened ambitions would enable it to exert a decisive influence on the international balance of power.

Intervention in Cuba was a consequence of the revolutionary situation prevailing in that Spanish colony in 1898, but the United States had long had an interest in the rich, tropical island lying so close to its shores. Annexationists had always had their eyes on so valuable a prize, and there had been occasional attempts in the past to purchase it from Spain. Geography if nothing else linked Cuba and the United States so closely that whatever affected Spain's last possession in the New World was always of immediate concern to the American people.

An opportunity to come to the support of the Cuban people in their perennial struggle to win freedom from Spain—under quite as justifiable circumstances as those that developed in 1898— had occurred a quarter century earlier during the bloody and savage insurrection known as the Ten Years' War. But in spite of some popular agitation for intervention at that time, Secretary of State Fish was strongly opposed to any such direct action. Instead, he offered to mediate the conflict, proposing that Spain grant Cuba its independence in return for an indemnity of $150 million to be guaranteed by the United States. When Spain summarily rejected this offer, the advocates of intervention, aroused by what they considered the arbitrary attitude of the Madrid Government, renewed their efforts to spur the Administration into taking more positive measures. In February, 1870, they introduced a joint resolution in Congress calling for recognition of the Cuban belligerents. President Grant had himself earlier favored such recognition, but again Secretary Fish stood in the way of a step that might well have invited war. He persuaded the President to throw his influence against the proposed resolution, and it failed to pass.

Three years later the interventionists found a more compelling pretext for action in the *Virginius* affair. Filibustering expeditions from the United States in aid of the rebels were already commonplace, and Spain was ready to do anything to prevent their reaching Cuba. In October, 1873, a Spanish gunboat seized the *Virginius,* a filibustering ship flying the American flag, and took her in to Santiago. There, after a summary court martial, the authorities executed fifty-three of her passengers and crew (including several American citizens) as pirates.

It was later learned that the papers under which the *Virginius* was sailing had been obtained by fraud and she was not an American vessel, but this was not known at the time and the public was incensed by what it considered an outrageous insult to the flag. Protest meetings in many parts of the country called for punitive action against Spain, and foreshadowing the attitude taken after the sinking of the *Maine* a quarter century later, many newspapers throughout the country called for war.

Secretary Fish still refused to be swept off his feet, but realizing the seriousness of the situation, he demanded redress from Spain and threatened to break off diplomatic relations if it was not promptly forthcoming. Spain thereupon released the seized vessel and agreed to an indemnity of $80,000 to be paid to the relatives of the Americans executed at Santiago. The United States accepted this solution to the unhappy incident, and with Secretary Fish exercising all his influence in favor of a peaceful accommodation, popular excitement subsided. There was neither intervention in Cuba nor war with Spain.

The contrast between the course of events in 1873 and the situation that was to develop in 1898 significantly reflects the different spirit prevailing in the country in these two years. Too absorbed in domestic matters in the 1870's to yearn for foreign adventure, the American people could be aroused from their own concerns neither by the shocking conditions prevailing in Cuba nor by the Spanish Government's seizure on the high seas of what was believed to be an American vessel. The country applauded Fish for peacefully resolving a crisis that in the hands of a more belligerent or irresponsible Secretary of State might conceivably have led to war over Cuba a quarter century before it actually occurred.

Spain finally suppressed the earlier insurrection, but it could not extinguish the smoldering fires of Cuban discontent. In 1895 they flared up again in what was to prove to be a consuming conflagration. Economic distress, growing in part out of new American tariffs imposed on sugar, fed the flames of the new revolt, and the Cuban rebels were this time determined to break the power of the Spanish Government at whatever cost. They were prepared to destroy the sugar plantations and the cattle ranches, their manifestoes ringingly declared, and if necessary unfurl the flag of the republic of Cuba over a country reduced to ruins and ashes.

Drawing their funds and many recruits from exile commit-tees in the United States, as they had in the earlier insurrection, the rebels sought by all possible means to win American sympa-thy. A junta—or central revolutionary committee—organized a highly effective propaganda campaign, and from its New York headquarters provided newspapers throughout the country with sensational articles depicting the cruelty of the Spanish admin-istration and the sufferings of the Cuban people. Moreover, in the accepted tradition of their policy whenever revolt flared in the harassed island, the revolutionary exiles in the United States again flagrantly disregarded the laws of neutrality in launching their filibustering expeditions from American territory.

The Spanish Government's response to the destructive tactics of the Cuban rebels was a ruthless campaign of suppression and terror. The commanding general on the island, General Valeriano Weyler, who was soon to win throughout the United States the sobriquet of "Butcher Weyler," herded the villagers—men, women, and children—into concentration camps in order to break up the guerrilla bands and instructed the Spanish forces to shoot on sight anything that moved in the depopulated areas. The conditions in these camps, without adequate housing, food, or sanitation, soon became appalling. Described in 1898 by Sen-ator Redfield Proctor of Vermont in a telling indictment on the floor of Congress, they had a tremendous impact in strengthening the natural American sympathy for the rebel cause:

Torn from their homes, with foul earth, foul air, foul water, and foul food or none, what wonder that one-half have died and that one-quarter of the living are so diseased that they cannot be saved? . . .

Little children are still walking about with arms and chest terribly emaciated, eyes swollen, and abdomens bloated to three times the natural size.

Even before such disclosures of the consequences of the con-centration-camp policy, the inevitable popular demand had arisen for American intervention in the name of peace and humanity. The United States had officially declared its neutrality when the insurrection first broke out, but in the spring of 1896 both houses of Congress passed concurrent resolutions, by overwhelming ma-jorities, which called for recognition of Cuban belligerency and the proffering of American good offices in seeking to bring the conflict to an end on the basis of Cuban independence. Secre-tary Olney was nevertheless as anxious as Secretary Fish had been, with (in this instance) strong support from President Cleveland, to block any precipitate action. Even though the Administration had taken a strongly nationalist stand in defense of the Monroe Doctrine during the Venezuela dispute, it had no desire whatsoever to become embroiled in a quarrel over Cuba that could lead to war with Spain.

In these circumstances Olney sought out a middle ground. He proposed to the Spanish Government that a way might be found, through American mediation, to bring the rebellion to an end on the basis of due regard for Spain's rights but also satis-faction to the reasonable demands and aspirations of the Cuban people. This proposal was studiously ignored. Even in the face of such a rebuff and further popular clamor at home, Olney still refused to take any step toward recognition of the insurgents. He nevertheless did inform the Spanish Government that the United States "cannot contemplate with complacency another ten years of Cuban insurrection" and warned that if a new administration came into office after the Presidential election of 1896, it might not be able to curb the popular hostility to Spain.

The issue was largely subordinated to domestic questions, especially the great controversy over free silver, during the en-suing election, but when the Republicans were returned to power under President McKinley, antagonism to Spain gained a fresh impetus. It was fanned from many quarters. The jingoes and imperialists urged intervention as a means to drive Spain out of the New World once and for all. Even if the United States did not actually add Cuba to the national domain, it should at least seize the opportunity to establish unquestioned American supremacy in the Caribbean. They welcomed possible war. Theodore Roosevelt was to write that he would view it from two angles: its advisability on the ground of both humanity and self-interest in taking one more step to free the Western Hemisphere from all foreign domination, and the benefit that would accrue to the American people by giving them something else to think about other than material gain. His belligerency was echoed by many congressmen. One representative greeting possible war in glowing terms was Henry F. Thomas of Michigan. "The blue and the gray," he declaimed, "shall be blended into one vast army, flying the banner of freedom, keeping step to the heartbeat of humanity, and moving upon the last contingency of despotism."

The popular newspapers were less concerned with victories for liberty than with their own sales through making the most of a good news story. By excitedly playing up the most lurid accounts of Spanish atrocities in Cuba and shrilly beating the drums of war, as is so well known, they greatly magnified the already widespread spirit of jingoism. In New York, where Hearst and Pulitzer were engaged in their famous circulation war, the *World* and the *Journal* sought to outdo each other in piling sensation on sensation through their correspondents' reports from Cuba. Their coverage of the rebellion could hardly have been more inflammatory. Nor was it only the New York yellow press which fed the country's martial fever. Newspapers throughout the land, often given their material by the Cuban junta, printed the most exaggerated accounts of what was taking place, and in their editorials they almost universally emphasized the need for American intervention if peace were ever to be restored to unhappy Cuba.

The feeling that the United States could not indefinitely

stand aside while the island was torn apart by bloody strife and its people beaten to their knees by Spanish ruthlessness had, however, deeper roots than jingoist outbursts and newspaper sensationalism. The interests of the American people were deeply engaged because of their age-old convictions as to the right of every people to liberty and freedom. The shocking spectacle of a colonial government starving and killing men, women, and children who were bravely struggling for their natural rights, on an island only one hundred miles off the American coast, awoke every idealistic impulse for the underdog and for fair play. In the new temper of the times—patriotic, restless, jingoist—it was little wonder that the public became increasingly outraged by Spain's refusal to grant the Cubans their freedom and more and more determined to come to their support. The popular demand for decisive action gathered day by day an almost irresistible momentum.

Economic considerations had little to do with the popular sentiment of 1898. American investments in Cuba amounted to some $50 million, and the annual trade between Cuba and the United States totalled $100 million. But, while the insurrection had led to widespread property destruction and the almost complete disruption of trade, even those Americans suffering directly from these developments did not favor intervention. They sought American diplomatic protection for their property rights, but on highly practical grounds feared that their losses would be still greater should the United States become involved in actual hostilities.

As for the business community as a whole, it generally opposed war. With the country finally recovering from the hard times of the early 1890's, the last thing the financial, industrial, and commercial interests wanted was to see any step taken that might imperil further economic gains. In their belligerent resolutions calling for action, the war-minded invariably castigated what they termed the selfishness and cowardice of men of wealth in opposing Cuban intervention. There is the well-known story of an incensed Roosevelt shaking his fist at Senator Mark Hanna of Ohio, the outstanding political spokesman for the business community, and shouting, "we will have this war for the freedom of Cuba in spite of the timidity of the commercial interests."

The drive for intervention was based not on possible economic benefits, but on the high ground (however exploited by the yellow press) of freedom, morality, and humanitarianism.

Cleveland had hoped to convince Spain of the necessity of making adequate concessions to the Cuban rebels in order to combat a rising war fever, which he bluntly characterized as an "epidemic of insanity." McKinley was no less anxious to avoid war if it could possibly be done, promising that there would be no "jingo nonsense" in his Administration. The new President was not, however, the man of unbending convictions and strong will that his predecessor had been. Easygoing and affable, looking very much like a president with his fine, massive head and handsome features, McKinley was throughout his career inordinately concerned with what the public seemed to want and the political fortunes of his own party. It was not that he was lacking in either patriotism or a strong sense of duty, but he simply did not have the qualities that made for really effective leadership on the national stage. While his weakness has sometimes been exaggerated, he was nevertheless a man to swim with the tide rather than battle against it. In the Cuban situation he was unhappily to let himself become the victim of events instead of making any really determined effort to control them. Perhaps no man could have done so, but McKinley in any event completely failed.

Nevertheless, for a time at least he assiduously tried to do everything possible to induce Spain to pacify Cuba before an uncontrollable crisis arose in Spanish-American relations. From the first he made it very clear that the United States did not want either to annex Cuba or to establish an American protectorate, and that in offering its good services its only interest was in bringing peace to the war-riven island. In negotiating along such lines through the American Minister in Madrid, Stewart L.

Woodford, the President's tone was invariably friendly and courteous.

In the autumn of 1897 his patient policy appeared to be making some impression on the Spanish Government. A new ministry came into office in October, and while internal considerations rather than American pressure may have in fact been responsible for its moderate attitude, it significantly liberalized the harsh program Spain had been following. It recalled General Weyler, modified the concentration-camp program, and appeared to be ready to grant the Cuban people a large measure of autonomy.

"No War with Spain—All Indications Point to Peace," the Washington *Post* headlined on November 6 in reporting this shift in Spanish policy. The agitation in favor of intervention seemed to be subsiding; the newspapers calmed down and began to emphasize news other than Cuba. When President McKinley sent his annual message to Congress in December, he was reasonably optimistic. But he also voiced a note of caution. On the one hand he took occasion to warn Congress against any overt act that might still precipitate Spanish-American hostilities, and on the other he forcefully reminded Spain that should she fail to carry out her pledges and should the insurrection continue in Cuba, the United States might find its patience exhausted.

The breathing spell during the winter of 1897–1898 proved, however, to be the lull before the storm. Conditions had not really improved in Cuba, and the point had been passed where the insurgents might have been satisfied with autonomy. Moreover, a series of unforeseen incidents, of which both the jingoes and the yellow press took every advantage, rapidly deepened the rift between the United States and Spain into what was to prove to be an unbridgeable gulf. Although these incidents did not necessarily bear on the basic issue in dispute—the status of Cuba —they convinced the general public of the perfidy of Spain and of the futility of trying to seek any just solution of the Cuban problem by diplomatic negotiations. The war fever was not only revived but soon gave way to a mounting wave of national hysteria.

A first incident was the publication, on February 9, 1898, of a personal letter which the Spanish Minister in Washington, Dupuy de Lôme, had written to a friend in Havana where it had been intercepted by agents of the Cuban junta. In this letter de Lôme described President McKinley, head of state of the country to which he was accredited, as "weak and a bidder for the admiration of the crowd, besides being a would-be politician who tries to leave the door open behind himself while keeping on good terms with the jingoes of his party." De Lôme promptly resigned when his indiscretion became known, and after a somewhat belated apology by the Spanish Government, the incident was closed in official circles. The American public, however, interpreted the Minister's remarks as a studied insult to the President of the United States which inadvertently revealed the real attitude of Spain and the unlikelihood of its ever dealing fairly with either the United States or the Cuban rebels.

The second incident was far more important and has ever since had its special niche in American history—the sinking of the *Maine*. This battleship, one of the proud new vessels of the young American Navy, had been sent to Havana as an "act of friendly courtesy." When it mysteriously blew up on February 15 with the loss of 260 officers and men, an already worked-up public went wild. There were occasional cautionary voices urging that judgment should be withheld until an official investigation could determine the cause of the *Maine*'s destruction, but they were scarcely heard in the noisy clamor demanding immediate retaliation against Spain as without question being responsible for the disaster.

The New York *Journal* set the pace for the general treatment of the story, its headlines shrieking that the *Maine* had been blown up "by an enemy's secret infernal machine," and equally inflammable newspaper "extras" were hawked on the streets of every city throughout the land. Congress unanimously voted a $50 million emergency fund for national defense; army recruitment stations found themselves flooded with eager volunteers. Roosevelt excitedly wrote that "the blood of the murdered men of the *Maine* . . . calls for the full measure of atonement which can only come by driving the Spaniard from the New World"; Lodge declared with equal vehemence that "this gigantic murder, this last spasm of a corrupt and dying society . . . cries aloud for justice."

Then, in the midst of this excitement, Senator Proctor made his telling indictment of the suffering of the Cuban people in the concentration camps. Popular anger surged through the country even more furiously, and the war fever infected even the religious press. "And if it be the will of Almighty God," declared the *Evangelist*, a Presbyterian journal, "that by war the last trace of this inhumanity of man to man shall be swept away from this Western Hemisphere, let it come!"

Finally on March 28 the committee investigating the *Maine* disaster published its excitedly awaited report. It stated that the warship had been blown up by a submarine mine, but it did not attempt to fix responsibility for the disaster. The committee's caution made no difference whatsoever. Hysteria had taken hold and there was no quelling it.

> *Remember the* Maine!
> *To hell with Spain!*

Politics now had its innings to a far greater extent than during the Presidential campaign of 1896. With Democrats and Populists taking up the cry for intervention ("Humanity demands that we shall act," cried William Jennings Bryan), Republican newspapers and party leaders increased the pressure on a harassed President to assert a more vigorous leadership. If nothing were done, the Chicago *Times* warned, a war for Cuban liberty would become the Democrats' rallying cry in the next election. "And who can doubt," it asked rhetorically, "that by that sign, held aloft and proclaimed by such magnetic leaders as William J. Bryan, they will sweep the country like a cyclone."

The conservative business leaders in the Republican party, men like Mark Hanna, continued to oppose hostilities and to do everything they could to calm national excitement, but with rallies, mass meetings, and popular demonstrations whipping up the war fever, they appeared to be helpless. The Republican rank and file, believing that certain political defeat stared them in the face if the Cuban war was allowed to drag on until the midterm elections in the autumn, could not be restrained.

Congress was also becoming increasingly belligerent—if possible even more so than the public. The New Orleans *Times Picayune* (where the Cuban junta had supposedly planted one of its agents) reminded it that if the President did not have the backbone to do anything, it had in its own hands the constitutional authority to declare war. However, in both the Senate and the House there were firebrands who hardly needed to be reminded of this power. They excitedly called for the action the President still seemed unwilling to propose.

Cruelly torn by his desire to please his constituents and his sincere hopes for a peaceful solution of the mounting crisis, McKinley was following a tortuous course. He exercised great restraint when the insulting de Lôme letter was published, and he also urged the public to suspend judgment after the sinking of the *Maine*. As March drew to a close, however, his position was becoming more and more difficult. A sterner note began to creep into his diplomatic negotiations, and in his instructions on the twenty-seventh to Minister Woodford in Madrid, he outlined what was virtually an ultimatum for the Spanish Government.

The President proposed that Spain grant the Cuban rebels a temporary armistice, to last until October; initiate fresh negotiations with them, and if a peaceful settlement could not be reached, allow him to act as final arbiter in the dispute. He did not make it entirely clear at the time what the United States would consider a satisfactory settlement, speaking of "full self-government with indemnity," but on Woodford's request for a further explanation, he acknowledged that this in fact meant Cuban independence.

The Spanish Government was now ready to make further substantial concessions, but it could no more go the whole way in accepting American policy—that is, allow the United States to dictate its attitude toward Cuba—than this country could have permitted foreign intervention in its own Civil War. The Spanish people had their sense of national honor, however hard-pressed the Government might feel. While the authorities in Madrid were increasingly anxious to discover a path to peace, they were convinced that to surrender to foreign pressure would mean the outbreak of insurrection at home and the collapse of the monarchy.

In replying to McKinley's overtures, the Government would appear to have given in as much as it felt it could at the time. It officially announced that it had withdrawn the orders maintaining the concentration camps and was prepared to consider plans for Cuba's pacification. It did not, however, give any indication of being willing either to grant an armistice or to accept the President's mediation. Woodford was nevertheless convinced that it was seeking to find an honorable way out of the impasse. His earlier dispatches had been anything but encouraging; he was constantly exasperated by the indecision and wavering of the Spanish officials. But he now pleaded for still greater patience on the part of the President.

"If you can still give me time and reasonable freedom of action," he optimistically cabled on April 3, "I will get the peace you desire so much and for which you have labored so hard."

Further developments in the next few days seemed to give some justification for these hopes. Spain had been desperately seeking support for its position among the European powers, but while they were highly sympathetic, no one of them was ready to intervene actively in its behalf. Madrid realized that the government would have to make further concessions if Spain were to avoid a war in which it would necessarily stand alone against the superior power of the United States. Following on the urging of the Pope, whose intercession provided a more honorable basis for such a retreat than American pressure, the Queen announced on April 9 that Spain was granting an armistice in Cuba, to last as long as the military commander on the island felt it to be prudent, in order that efforts might be renewed "to facilitate the peace earnestly desired by all."

More confident than ever before that the issues at stake could now be peacefully resolved, Woodford reported on the basis of this announcement that the Spanish Government "is going, and is loyally ready to go, as fast and as far as it can." He believed that if Spain were given time to work out its own internal problems, one of three courses would be followed: provision for Cuba's autonomy on terms acceptable to the rebels, complete independence, or the cession of Cuba to the United States. "With your power of action sufficiently free," Woodford concluded, "you will win the fight on your own lines."

At home, however, the pressure for immediate intervention, regardless of any possible Spanish concessions, was building up to such a pitch that McKinley had already let himself become convinced that he has lost all freedom of action. In later years he was to say that if he had been let alone, he could have secured Spain's withdrawal from Cuba without war. But he was not left alone. In these early days of April he was under a constant and growing strain that was steadily weakening his power to resist the popular clamor for war. As early as April 4 his Secretary of War noted in his diary that the President was so worn down by the mounting tension and his consequent lack of sleep that "his mind does not work as clearly and self-reliantly as it otherwise would."

The members of his cabinet still favored peace. The conservative leadership in the Senate, men from his own party, were reported to be "ferociously against war." The Speaker of the House, Thomas B. Reed, was adamantly opposed to intervention. Yet in spite of such powerful allies, McKinley felt helpless. The people themselves, and perhaps even more the belligerent majority in Congress, were forcing his hand. He was convinced that unless he followed the course that the public seemed to be demanding, he not only gravely endangered the solidarity of the Republican party, to which he was so consistently loyal, but the unity of the nation itself.

In spite of Woodford's optimism, McKinley may also have felt (we have no record—no diary, no letters—revealing his personal point of view) that the Spanish Government was not in fact prepared to yield as much as was suggested. It had delayed so long and procrastinated so much in coming to grips with the situation in Cuba as perhaps to justify a lack of confidence in its apparent change of policy. The question still remained as to what peace terms it might actually offer the Cuban rebels, and at no time had it officially agreed to American arbitration of the dispute should negotiations with the insurgents break down. There was always the possibility, in the belief such a stand was necessary to preserve the Spanish monarchy and uphold Spanish honor, that the Government would at the last moment block any grant of independence. Yet, from the American point of view—as well as that of the rebels—independence was now considered the only permanent solution for the Cuban problem.

In any event, the President had already reached a decision. Believing he had done "all that in honor could be done to avert war," he was ready to submit the issue to Congress and let it determine the next step. On April 11 he thereupon forwarded a message which marked the end of his negotiations with Spain and constituted in effect the acceptance of war.

After reviewing the whole history of the insurrection, McKinley stated that it had become apparent that neither side could prevail in the fighting in Cuba, and that consequently the only way in which peace could be restored to the prostrate island was through the intervention of the United States. He had only the power to propose, he told Congress; it had the power to act. However, "in the name of humanity, in the name of civilization, in behalf of endangered American interests," he asked for the necessary authority to use the army and the navy to end the war and secure a stable government for the Cuban people.

This message was sent to Congress two days after Woodford's cable telling of Spain's latest concessions on an armistice. But it had been drawn up several days earlier and its delivery postponed to allow time for the American citizens in Cuba to leave the island. No change was suggested after the reception of the message from Madrid. His mind made up, the President only added a brief summary of Woodford's latest dispatch, without either interpretation or comment. "The issue," he succinctly stated, "is now with Congress."

In spite of its clear intent, the rather ambiguous phraseology of the Presidential message left some question as to just what the next immediate step should be. Congress wrangled for eight days over the exact terms of the resolution it might adopt. During this uneasy interval, the European powers considered a final effort to maintain peace. They had earlier agreed upon an appeal to the "humanity and moderation of the President" which McKinley had politely but noncommitally acknowledged, and their envoys in Washington now prepared a joint note which would have more urgently protested American intervention in Cuba in the light of Spain's concessions. It was never delivered. The outspoken opposition of the British Foreign Office ("it seems very doubtful whether we ought to commit ourselves to a judgment adverse to the United States") and also somewhat surprisingly that of the German Kaiser ("we would put ourselves in wrong with the Americans") led to abandonment of the whole idea.

In the meanwhile, the debate in a war-crazed Congress ("members rushed up and down the floor like madmen," the correspondent of the London *Times* reported, "exchanging hot words, with clenched fists and set teeth; excitement was at fever heat") largely centered on whether immediate recognition should be given to the Cuban rebels. Only after this proposal had been defeated on the ground that recognition was a Presidential rather than Congressional prerogative, did the two houses get down to the real business of the day: actual wording of the resolution giving the President authority to intervene in Cuba with armed force. There were some differences between the House and Senate, but a final agreement was reached on April 19, and President McKinley signed the resolution the next day.

It declared Cuba to be free and independent, called for Spain's immediate withdrawal from the island, authorized the use of the armed forces of the United States to restore peace, and disclaimed any intention on the part of the United States to annex Cuba.

Popular hysteria had been the culminating factor in persuading Congress to adopt a resolution that was in effect a declaration of war against Spain (the Spanish Government immediately broke off diplomatic relations; the United States declared a blockade of Cuba), but underlying the feverish war spirit of the day there still remained the idealistic belief that the United States had a duty to perform in Cuba. This sense of a dedicated purpose was revealed in the last clause in the Congressional resolution—the so-called Teller Amendment. Adopted without a single dissenting vote in either house, it clearly proclaimed that the United States did not seek possession of Cuba for itself.

"We intervene not for conquest, not for aggrandizement, not because of the Monroe Doctrine," Senator Spooner of Wisconsin emphatically declared; "we intervene for humanity's sake . . . to aid a people who have suffered every form of tyranny and who have made a desperate struggle to be free." Senator Cullom of Illinois, who was no warmonger, emphasized with equal fervor that it was only in the name of liberty that the United States sought to drive Spain out of the New World. And in doing so, he added, it would "earn the praises of every lover of freedom and humanity the world over."

There may have been an element of self-justification in this heavy emphasis on the nobility and selflessness of national policy. Americans have an irresistible propensity to glorify their deeds in romantic, altruistic terms, and on occasion to mask reality behind self-congratulatory phrases summoning up justice and humanity. Nevertheless, the underlying idealism of this first foreign crusade in the name of liberty, so far as the country as a whole and the great masses of the people were concerned, can hardly be gainsaid.

So it was that in April, 1898, the nation embarked, idealistically, enthusiastically, on its war to establish the independence of Cuba. It was to last only ten weeks, cause less than four hundred deaths on the battlefield (those from disease were five times as many), and provide an excited public with a series of spectacular victories for American arms on land and sea. It was all very thrilling—the unexpected, triumphant battle of far-off Manila Bay, Colonel Roosevelt and his Rough Riders gallantly charging San Juan Hill, another American fleet destroying the proud Spanish vessels attempting to escape from Santiago, and the triumphant occupation of Cuba and Puerto Rico. The martial spirit of the American people found exuberant expression in cheering the volunteers as they marched off to the strains of "The Stars and Stripes Forever," and then celebrating the news of these successive victories over a defeated and humiliated Spain. There was nothing (except for the tragic deaths from yellow fever and army scandals over embalmed beef) to mar the glowing picture of America's new-found power. Little wonder that John Hay's pithy phrase has echoed down through the years—"a splendid little war."

But if these ten weeks of fighting appear to be an almost comic opera war in contrast to the massive conflicts of the twentieth century, their consequences nevertheless were on a grand scale. For Spain the war marked the end of her one-time great American empire; for the United States it meant the acquisition of colonies and overseas dominion. The irony of it all has been stressed by almost every historian. A war so eagerly begun to bring freedom to Cuba ended with the forceful imposition of American sovereignty over the Philippines. Idealism gave way to a determined imperialism. The victory over Spain made possible the freedom of Cuba, but its more significant results were the assertion of America's unassailable supremacy in the Caribbean, and, in carrying the flag to the very shores of Asia, the establishment of a new and dominating position in the Pacific.

"This war must in any event effect a profound change in the whole attitude and policy of the United States," the London *Times* wrote in a long analysis. "In the future America will play a part in the general affairs of the world such as she has never played before. When the American people realize this, and they realize novel situations with remarkable promptitude, they will not do things by halves."

The United States had demonstrated that it had indeed become a great power; the nations of Europe could no longer brush aside what they had formerly considered its exaggerated pretensions. Moreover, with such general acceptance of its new status, the United States was constrained to act as a great power. In the circumstances of the time, against the background of Europe's expansionist ambitions, this perhaps inevitably meant an imperialistic policy. The way had been prepared; the idea of overseas possessions had been slowly winning popular support. But, in the aftermath of victory over Spain, it may be even more true to say that the United States simply succumbed to what John Hay had called a "cosmic tendency."

There remains to be considered, very briefly, whether this splendid little war was a needless one in terms of its own objectives, and whether it might or might not have been avoided. The restless, ambitious, jingoist spirit of the American people in the spring of 1898 may make the supposition that the conflict could in any way have been averted seem extremely unlikely. The oppressive policies of Spain, cruelly seeking to suppress the heroic struggle of the Cuban people for freedom, gave a compelling force to the instinctive desire of the American people to come to their rescue. Nevertheless, President McKinley's surrender to the popular clamor, however much it may be excused either as reflecting a sincere doubt of Spain's good will in seeking peace or as a realistic acceptance of political pressures no national leader could have withstood any longer, is still hard to condone.

The war was totally unnecessary in the broader perspectives of history. Spain could not have long maintained her precarious hold over her rebellious colony unless the United States had completely reversed its policy and withdrawn both sympathy and support from the Cuban insurgents. If McKinley had striven more resolutely to keep his power of action sufficiently free, he might well have won the fight along his own lines.

This is admittedly conjecture. It may be argued—as it has been by several American historians—that Spain could never have afforded to free Cuba and was driven by necessity to maintain its position there even if this meant an almost suicidal war with the United States. The implication here is that McKinley was consequently justified in accepting hostilities in order to bring to an end the prolonged agony of Cuban suffering. But in the light of Spain's concessions, however limited and grudging, this is also sheer conjecture.

What remains true is that McKinley exhibited neither the determined leadership nor the moral courage that might possibly have restrained his impatient, war-minded countrymen. In April, 1898, it may have been too late to have kept the situation under control. A much stronger president would probably have been almost equally helpless in the face of the forces which had by then been aroused. But while McKinley had said on first taking office that there was to be no jingo nonsense during his Administration, he had done little, if anything, to combat its dangerous rise while there was still time. His failure did not lie in the field of diplomacy, which found him conducting his negotiations with steady, unrelenting pressure upon a wavering Spanish Government, but in national leadership at home. He cannot be absolved of his share of responsibility in allowing popular hysteria rather than moderation and patience to take command in deciding the issues of war or peace.

CHAPTER XI

Imperialism Triumphant

"The guns of Dewey at Manila have changed the destiny of the United States," the Washington *Post* excitedly proclaimed upon receiving news of that dramatic victory won on May 1, 1898. "We are face to face with a strange destiny and must accept its responsibilities. An imperial policy."

In taking up arms against Spain to secure the freedom of Cuba, the American people had most certainly not envisaged a naval battle in the far-off Philippines, let alone the possible acquisition of these islands as American territory. There is the reputed statement of President McKinley that before the engagement in Manila Bay, he could not have told "where those darned islands were within two thousand miles." But wartime strategy, foreseen by Theodore Roosevelt as Assistant Secretary of the Navy and by Commodore George Dewey himself, made an attack on the Spanish fleet there an obvious and essential naval operation. And once the Philippines had swung within the national orbit, the goals of a latent imperialism naturally embraced these new and beckoning horizons.

The expansionist leaders did not even momentarily hesitate. Anticipating the dramatic news of Dewey's victory, Senator

Beveridge had dazzled an influential audience in Boston with a dream of empire whereby American law, American order, American civilization might be planted on shores hitherto bloody and benighted. "The Philippines," he declared, "are logically our first target." Roosevelt and Lodge moved quickly into line. On June 4 the former was writing Henry White in London that the Philippines "must be ours. . . . We hold the other side of the Pacific, and the value to this country is almost beyond imagination"; and Roosevelt, fretting at an army camp in San Antonio, was admonishing Lodge that, apart from what might happen in the Caribbean, we could not make peace until "the Philippines [are] at any rate taken from the Spaniards."

Newspapers throughout the country—like the Washington *Post*—echoed these patriotic sentiments, and business journals which had originally opposed the war with Spain listened eagerly to the inspiring call of overseas expansion. Where they had heretofore feared foreign adventure as threatening domestic prosperity, they now welcomed the further extension of national boundaries as providing incalculable opportunities for expanding foreign trade. The popular feeling that Commodore Dewey had so unwittingly stimulated was perhaps most succinctly expressed in an editorial in the Philadelphia *Record:* "Our war in Cuba has assumed undreamed of dimensions . . . willy nilly we have entered upon our career as a world power."

A first concrete indication of the country's new temper was the final action on Hawaii. The return of the Republicans to political power after the election of McKinley in 1896 had not automatically assured the success of the expansionist drive that Cleveland had so stubbornly blocked. Even though the Republican party platform called for annexation of Hawaii, a Nicaraguan canal, and purchase of the Virgin Islands, the new President had never given any support to imperialism. In firmly upholding the traditional isolationist foreign policy in his Inaugural Address, he had added: "We want no wars of conquest; we must avoid the temptation of territorial aggression."

Nevertheless, many Republican leaders were anxious to complete the transaction President Harrison had initiated four years earlier, and the pressure upon McKinley for further action mounted rapidly. Within a few weeks Roosevelt felt justified in writing Captain Mahan that, in spite of his earlier misgivings, he was now confident that McKinley was persuaded that the United States could no longer delay in taking Hawaii into the fold. Roosevelt was quite right. One June 16, 1897—only three months after the Inauguration—the President submitted a new annexation treaty which had been quickly concluded with the eager representatives of the Hawaiian Republic.

McKinley was perhaps influenced by a flare-up of excitement over possible Japanese ambitions in the islands. It appeared to have some basis when the Japanese Government protested that annexation by the United States would jeopardize the *status quo* essential to the peace of the Pacific. But the threatened danger was wholly illusory. Japan quickly withdrew its protest when the United States made its position clear. McKinley was nonetheless persuaded that the situation was critical, and he was reported to have told one member of the Senate that if something were not done promptly there would be another revolution in Hawaii "and Japan will get control."

The Senate was again not to be hurried, and indeed such strong opposition developed to annexation that its proponents began to fear they would never be able to muster the necessary two-thirds majority for the treaty's approval. As war over Cuba then grew increasingly imminent, adding new complications to foreign policy, the expansionists consequently turned to a course of action which had been used in the case of Texas. They introduced on March 16, 1898, a joint Congressional resolution for the islands' immediate annexation, and upon the outbreak of hostilities against Spain, the McKinley Administration gave this new move its wholehearted support.

The debates on annexation in 1898 were a rehash of those that had stirred the country five years earlier, and they also foreshadowed the more wide-ranging discussion that would later engross the nation over the disposition of the Philippines. The expansionists urged that the United States needed the Hawaiian Islands for national defense, in the interests of its Far Eastern trade (Hawaii, they reiterated, was "the key to the Pacific"), and because of the islands' value to the American economy. And there were the further assertions of duty and responsibility. The anti-expansionists denied all this. Beyond rejecting the arguments on the strategic and commercial value of Hawaii, they again attacked the whole concept of overseas territorial acquisitions as a denial of the republic's democratic ideals, pouring their scorn on the idea that it was an inevitable development that could not be withstood. "Manifest Destiny," growled Champ Clark, a Missouri Democrat, was "the specious plea of every robber and freebooter since the world began."

The annexationist position was nevertheless immensely strengthened by the wartime atmosphere and by the feeling in some quarters that control of Hawaii was a necessary military measure. It was supported by a number of congressmen, generally opposed to imperialism, who felt that under the circumstances Hawaii was a very special case. One such man was Senator George Frisbie Hoar of Maine who set forth his position very clearly:

If this be the first step in the acquisition of dominion over barbarous archipelagoes in distant seas; if we are to enter into competition with the great powers of Europe in the plundering of China . . . then let us resist this thing in the beginning, and let us resist it to death. . . . But, Mr. President, I am satisfied, after hearing and weighing arguments and much meditation on this thing, that the fear of imperialism is needless alarm.

Senator Hoar, however, as he was later to realize to his infinite regret, was wrong. When Congress passed and President McKinley approved the joint resolution for the annexation of Hawaii—the final step was taken on July 7, 1898—the United States had crossed the Rubicon. The acquisition of these islands was the culmination of a long drawn-out process ("annexation is not change," the President said, "it is consummation"), but it was also as Captain Mahan had predicted the first fruit of a new movement. As early as May, Senator Lodge had happily written Roosevelt that he was convinced that "the Administration is now fully committed to the large policy that we both desire," and a few weeks later he added that the whole annexation program "is growing rapidly under the irresistible pressure of events."

Just as President McKinley had surrendered to the jingoes in asking authority to use armed force in Cuba, so he now appeared to be giving in completely to the imperialists. Any personal opposition to overseas expansion had completely evaporated in the heady atmosphere of a victorious war. For there was not only his spirited support of Hawaiian annexation (he had come to believe, he told his secretary, that "we need Hawaii just as much and a good deal more than we did California"), but a series of concurrent moves, made entirely on Presidential authority, which were serving to link the United States ever closer to the Philippine Islands.

A first step opening the way for the ultimate establishment of American rule was taken on May 4 when the President authorized the dispatch of an expeditionary force of 15,000 men, under the command of General Wesley Merritt, to take and hold the city of Manila. This went far beyond military needs and created a situation which immensely strengthened the hands of those who felt that the United States should retain the islands. There was to be no answering the later argument that where once the American flag had been raised, it would be cowardly and disgraceful to allow it to be lowered.

Nor was this military decision the only sign of the direction in which McKinley was moving. He ordered the troops sent to the Philippines to stop over en route long enough to take over control of the Spanish-held Ladrone—or Marianas—Islands, and on May 25 their convoy ship, after opening fire on the ancient fortress at Guam, accepted the surrender of the Spanish authorities. The imperialists were greatly heartened by this unexpected move and concluded that larger prizes were assuredly in the offing. "Why the President should have taken those islands, unless he expects to hold on to the Philippines," Lodge concluded reasonably, "I cannot conceive."

A little over a week later the President offered a first clue as to his thinking in regard to possible peace terms with Spain in a cable that Secretary of State William R. Day (he had now taken over this post upon the resignation of Secretary Sherman) sent to Ambassador Hay in London. It was proposed that in addition to securing the complete independence of Cuba, the United States should insist on the cession of Puerto Rico, an island in the Ladrones, and a port in the Philippines. Although still thinking in terms of naval bases rather than colonies, the President appeared to have completely adopted the expansionist thesis that in order to play its foreordained role in the world, the United States should be able to deploy its naval forces so as to control those seas considered vital to its national security and to the development of its foreign commerce.

This was not, however, the end of the road that McKinley was now traveling with characteristic caution but steadily increasing zest. By the time that Spain—its forces completely defeated in Cuba as well as in the Philippines—was ready to sue for peace, he was tentatively raising his sights. He was considering the advisability of holding on to more than just a naval station in the Philippines and carefully sounding out opinion in his cabinet. Its members were divided. Day wanted to retain no more than what the President characterized as a "hitching post," and made a motion to this effect. The President did not submit it, and when Day later asked why he had failed to do so, McKinley replied that he was afraid it might have been carried. He did not want his hands in any way tied. The preliminary peace protocol offered Spain late in July consequently provided for the general disposition of Spanish territory already suggested, but included a provision that the United States would continue to hold "the city, bay and harbor of Manila" until a final decision had been reached on the Philippine Islands as a whole.

The Spanish Government protested. "This demand strips us of the very last memory of a glorious past," read its embittered statement, "and expels us . . . from the Western Hemisphere, which became peopled and civilized through the proud deeds of our ancestors." But defeated Spain had no alternative other than submission and reluctantly signed the protocol on August 12.

The appointment of a commission to negotiate the final terms of peace further underscored the President's position on what should be the rewards of victory over Spain. The members of the delegation to be sent to the proposed conference in Paris revealed a clear-cut majority who were already on record as favoring overseas expansion. It is true that Day, who resigned as Secretary of State to head the delegation, remained a very reluctant convert to the need for any territorial acquisitions at all, and that George Gray, Democratic senator from Delaware, was even more firmly in the opposition camp. The other three delegates, however, were avowed imperialists. Senator Cushman Davis of Minnesota had been one of the earliest and most vocal advocates of the annexation of Hawaii; Senator W. P. Frye of Maine was a jingo who had early demanded the complete conquest of Cuba, and Whitelaw Reid, editor of the New York *Tribune,* had long been closely associated with the "imperial party."

The instructions privately given to these delegates on September 16 were imprecise but highly significant. The President told them that while the Philippines were on a somewhat different basis than either Puerto Rico or Guam, upon whose retention they were to insist, the occupation of Manila had opened up entirely unforeseen contingencies. The march of events, he stated, had overruled human action, and then with the sonorous platitudinizing which characterized everything he said, McKinley continued:

Avowing unreservedly the purpose which has animated all our efforts, and still solicitous to adhere to it, we cannot be unmindful that, without any desire or design on our part, the war has brought us new duties and responsibilities which we must meet and discharge as becomes a great nation on whose growth and career from the beginning the Ruler of Nations has plainly written the high command and pledge of civilization.

What this of course meant was that, however idealistic the purposes for which the United States had taken up arms, it could hardly refuse the benefits that might arise from Spain's defeat. Indeed, McKinley candidly added to his platitudes the somewhat more realistic statement that "incidental to our tenure in the Philippines is the commercial opportunity to which American statesmanship cannot be indifferent." Still, he was moving carefully; he was not yet ready to demand surrender of the Philippines out of hand. His more explicit instructions went no further at this time than to state that the United States could not accept less—it was an irreducible minimum—than "the cession in full right and sovereignty of Luzon."

While McKinley was still pondering the question as to whether the United States should go the whole way in taking the Philippines over altogether, the imperialist tide was steadily mounting throughout the country. The popular press continued to lead the way (a *Literary Digest* poll reported that of 182 replies to a nationwide questionnaire, 84 newspapers favored retention of all the islands; 63 proposed at least a naval base), but the organs of the business community had also completely swung into line. They were now ready to accept what the theoretical exponents of mercantile imperialism had been so long arguing and fully agreed with the thesis so eloquently expounded by Senator Beveridge that "the trade of the world must and shall be ours." Looking across the Pacific, they acknowledged the advantage to be gained for the United States if it could obtain a foothold off the Asiatic shore as an entrepôt for Far Eastern trade. The *Journal of Commerce*, the *Wall Street Journal*, and the *American Banker*, formerly so opposed to any overseas commitments, ran both articles and editorials persuasively arguing for retention of the Philippines. The opportunity to expand in the Pacific just as the European powers seemed to be entering upon a division of China, the *American Banker* declared, was "a coincidence which has a providential air."

The religious press took up "the imperialism of righteousness." Stressing the responsibility of the Anglo-Saxon people to extend the area of religious and civil liberty, so vigorously upheld by Josiah Strong and other evangelists in the 1880's, it saw in the acquisition of overseas colonies an important forward step in this inspiring undertaking. It was also agreed that the promotion of trade had a direct relevancy to this whole movement. Robert E. Speer, Secretary of the Board of Foreign Missions of the Presbyterian Church, stated that the missionary welcomed commercial expansion as an ally and necessary part "of the great outward impulse of civilization." Any doubts as to how overseas expansion might affect the principles of democracy within the United States were to be subordinated to the fulfillment of the obligations imposed on the country by its victory over Spain. "Woe to any nation," the *Churchman* warned, "which hesitates for fear its own interests will be entangled."

The value of an expansive overseas policy in quieting the voices of domestic discontent was also advanced in some quarters, as it had been on the eve of the war itself. Republicans with a never-wavering eye on future elections were especially interested in how imperialism could strengthen their own political position, but some Democrats were equally concerned with its role in forging still more closely the bonds of national unity. "We escape the menace and peril of socialism and agrarianism," Henry Watterson wrote in the Louisville *Courier-Journal*, ". . . by a policy of colonization and conquest."

Events in the Philippines during these uncertain days provided still further support for the mounting conviction that, once having become involved in their affairs, the United States had no alternative but to place them under American control. Immediately after Commodore Dewey's victory, the arrival of a squadron of ships from the German Navy, and the somewhat provocative attitude of their commander, gave rise to fears that Germany might have designs on the Philippines. Nothing could have served more convincingly to persuade the American public that the United States needed the islands than any evidence that a commercial rival might also want them.

Soon afterwards a highly complicated situation arose involving the American forces and the Filipino people. A native revolt against Spanish rule had long been simmering beneath the surface, as in Cuba, and Commodore Dewey had from the first been prepared to give it every encouragement. He was largely responsible for bringing the exiled rebel leader, General Emilio Aguinaldo, back to the islands, and in the belief that the Americans would continue to support their cause, the insurgents made ready to set up a Philippine republic. But as the idea that the United States might have other plans gained increasing headway, something had to be done to put the brakes on this movement for independence. Washington instructed Commodore Dewey to try to maintain cooperation with the Filipino leaders, but not to enter into any official negotiations with them.

Whatever they might originally have thought of the insurgents, the American military and naval commanders consequently began to look upon them from a somewhat different point of view. Commodore Dewey now reported that they represented only a relatively small faction of the people and gravely questioned whether the Filipinos could be considered ready for self-government. General F. V. Greene was more emphatic. Should the United States withdraw from the islands, he asserted, "anarchy and civil war will immediately ensue and lead to foreign intervention." Another argument was thus added to the proposition that the United States could not possibly retreat from the position it had assumed.

In these circumstances—the rising popular demand for annexation and the dangerously confused situation in the Philippines themselves—President McKinley undertook early in October (after the peace delegates had sailed for Paris) a political swing around the circle to attend a series of peace jubilees at such cities as Omaha, Chicago, Philadelphia, and intervening points. His talks were all keyed to the forthcoming Congressional elections, but always in the background was the still undecided question as to just how far the United States should go in regard to the Philippines. Should it demand of Spain the cession of a naval base, the island of Luzon, or the entire archipelago? The President referred only indirectly to the peace negotiations in his many speeches, but he played consistently and emphatically on the imperialist theme.

"This war," he declared in one of his major speeches, ". . . will bring to us, I trust, blessings that are beyond calculation. It will bring us also burdens, but the American people will never shirk a responsibility. . . . The currents of destiny flow through the heart of the people. . . . The movements of men, planned and designed by the Master of Men, will never be interrupted by the American people. . . . Seeking only the highest good of the nation . . . pursuing no other path but that of duty . . . we must give the world the full demonstration of our purpose. Duty determines destiny."

While such critical newspapers as the New York *Evening Post* and the New York *World* asked sardonically who determined duty and what did destiny really mean, the press more generally took such ambiguous phrases in its stride and interpreted the President's speeches as a call for the annexation of all the Philippine Islands. The Chicago *Herald,* a friendly paper and one that was believed to reflect very closely the President's views, agreed editorially in discussing the Philippines that "the only humane course is to retain the islands and govern them ourselves." It then pointedly added that, while it would have been inappropriate for the President to have publicly said any more while the peace negotiations were still in progress, "what he might say with propriety has been said and is in harmony with public sentiment."

McKinley returned from his speaking tour fully convinced that his expansionist program commanded widespread popular support. He had not so much been sounding out public opinion as seeking to sway it his way, and he was apparently satisfied with the enthusiastic response that his ponderous orations on duty and destiny had almost universally evoked. Three days after his return to Washington, on October 25, he informed the peace delegates at Paris that on the issue of the Philippine Islands he believed it to be the considered judgment of a majority of the American people that "duty requires we should take the archipelago." When the delegates reached that point in their discussions, he would be ready to give them the final instructions.

They were fast approaching that point at the close of October and in the meantime had themselves engaged in a shifting debate as to whether they should demand the cession of all the islands. There had been no great difficulty in reaching agreement with the Spanish delegation on complete independence for Cuba, or on the cession of Puerto Rico and Guam, but it seemed determined to hold out as strongly as possible against any further concessions. On the very day the President was cabling the conclusions drawn from his speaking tour, the American envoys in turn cabled for definite directions on the stand they should take on the Philippines.

McKinley was now ready. Amplifying the earlier message, his new Secretary of State, John Hay, who had returned from his post as Ambassador to the Court of St. James's to replace Day, cabled that in the President's opinion the question was whether the United States should take over all the Philippines or none of them. Since the latter course was wholly inadmissible, Hay reported in behalf of his chief, "the former must therefore be required."

These final and decisive instructions, embodying one of the most critical decisions on foreign policy any President has ever been called upon to make, were once again based on the ethical concepts that McKinley felt to be so important. "Territorial expansion should be our least concern," he stated; "that we shall not shirk the moral obligation of our victory is the greatest." And he then added that the United States consequently had "one plain path of duty—the acceptance of the archipelago."

In explaining a year later to a group of visiting clergymen how he had reached this critical decision, President McKinley made a statement that has been quoted and requoted because of its possibly unconscious rationalization of the basic considerations that underlie every imperialistic movement—national honor, economic advantage, racial superiority, and moral mission. Gathering together, with undoubted sincerity, these interwoven threads of the expansionist argument, McKinley told the visiting clergymen:

I walked the floor of the White House night after night until midnight; and I am not ashamed to tell you, gentlemen, that I went down on my knees and prayed Almighty God for light and guidance more than one night. And one night late it came to me this way—I don't know how it was, but it came: (1) That we could not give them back to Spain—that would be cowardly and dishonorable; (2) that we could not turn them over to France or Germany—our commercial rivals in the Orient—that would be bad business and discreditable; (3) that we could not leave them to themselves—they were unfit for self-government—and they would soon have anarchy and misrule over there worse than Spain's was; and (4) that there was nothing left for us to do but to take them all, and to educate the Filipinos, and uplift and civilize and Christianize them, and by God's grace do the very best we could by them, as our fellow men for whom Christ also died. And then I went to bed and went to sleep and slept soundly.

In spite of what appeared to be such a clear and humane course to McKinley, the Spanish delegation in Paris for a time resisted surrender of the Philippines so stubbornly that even the imperialist-minded American delegates suggested that some sort of compromise might have to be worked out. McKinley was adamant; he had made his decision. He went no further in softening the American demands than to offer a payment of $20 million for the islands' transfer. Faced with this ultimatum, Spain capitulated. The peace treaty in which it relinquished control over Cuba, surrendered Puerto Rico and Guam, and ceded the Philippine Islands was signed in Paris on December 10, 1898.

While the President may have been justified in his view
that a majority of the American people felt that "duty requires
we should take the archipelago," this did not mean that there
was no opposition to acquisition of the Philippines. Before the
Senate finally gave its approval to the Treaty of Paris, and even
afterwards during the Presidential campaign of 1900, the country
found itself engaged in a great debate as to the ultimate wisdom
of the new imperialistic course on which it was embarking. The
views and opinions that had marked each stage in the process of
Hawaiian annexation were now even more vehemently expressed
on public platforms, in newspapers and magazines, and in the
halls of Congress. In spite of the thunder of applause which had
welcomed him on his swing around the circle in October, approval for McKinley's foreign policy was not necessarily a fore-
gone conclusion as he prepared to submit his treaty to the Senate.

The national debate had its partisan overtones. The Republicans generally supported their President; the Democrats on the
whole opposed him. Nevertheless, there was considerable cross-
ing of party lines on the basic issue of imperialism, and each
side sought to take the high road in urging that the policy it
favored conform not only to the national interest but to the
noblest ideals of liberty and humanitarianism.

In the summer of 1898, opponents of overseas expansion had
taken the first step to form an Anti-Imperialist League, and
while Senator Lodge casually sought to dismiss its establishment
as a "comic incident," it attracted very substantial support
among the most diverse elements in American life. Former President Cleveland remained strongly opposed to what he declared
to be a tragic perversion of the national mission; and for all
their political differences on other issues, William Jennings Bryan
also attacked acquisition of the Philippines as a repudiation of the
fundamental principle that government could only be based on
the consent of the governed. A number of prominent Republican
congressmen, including Speaker Reed, ignored party affiliations
in combatting a policy which they feared would endanger democratic principles at home. Among senators, the most noteworthy

Republican critic was Senator Hoar who had voted for Hawaii's annexation in the belief that it would not involve further expansion. To follow the road advocated by McKinley, he now declared with outraged scorn, would be "descending from the ancient path of republican liberty which the fathers trod, down into the modern swamp and cesspool of imperialism."

In unexpected alliance, Andrew Carnegie, the outstanding industrialist of the day, and Samuel Gompers, head of the American Federation of Labor, were convinced anti-imperialists; a long list of college presidents, including Charles Eliot of Harvard and David Starr Jordan of Leland Stanford, campaigned vigorously against retention of the Philippines, and most of the country's intellectuals and writers refused to be swept along with the expansionist tide. Although in some cases they did not speak out forcefully until later, when Filipino opposition to American rule became more glaringly apparent, William Dean Howells and William Vaughn Moody, Hamlin Garland and Mark Twain, were violently opposed to the whole expansionist program. No one was more bitter against what he called "the Blessings-of-Civilization Trust" than Mark Twain.

"Would it not be prudent," he asked, "to get our Civilization tools together and see how much stock is left on hand in the way of Glass Beads and Theology, and Maxim Guns and Trade Books, and Trade Gin and Torches of Progress and Enlightenment . . . and balance the books and arrive at the profit and loss?" He admitted that, wisely administered, the Blessings-of-Civilization Trust was "a daisy," with more money, more territory, more sovereignty and other rewards than any other game being played, but he thought Christendom was doing rather badly on the whole and was going to suffer for it. "She has been so eager to get every stake that appeared on the green cloth," he wrote sarcastically, "that the People Who Sit in Darkness have noticed it and begun to show alarm. They have become suspicious of the Blessings of Civilization. More—they have begun to examine them. This is not well."

If Mark Twain was suggesting that imperialism might

some day find itself confronted with revolt on the part of the peoples it sought to exploit, another warning voice predicted that in seeking to establish its power off the shores of Asia, the United States was certain to run into grave international difficulties. George S. Boutwell, Secretary of the Treasury under President Grant, pictured China transformed under the directing hand of Russia into a warlike power, giving rise to the danger that the United States might find itself threatened with possible Asiatic war. "For us, independence in policy, peace, and self-assertion will be impossible," Boutwell wrote, "if we enter into the islands of the east."

The anti-imperialists suffered serious disadvantages in their campaign. Their position was a negative one in comparison with the positive, dynamic promise of overseas expansion, and they could hardly make their voice heard over the clamor of the imperialists and jingoes. They were out of step with the spirit of the times. Moreover, they had no real unity, lacked effective leadership, and consequently failed to attract the popular following essential to success.

The imperialists were allied with the dominant party, reflected the ambitious drive for national power that had been gaining momentum throughout the 1890's, and they were also ready, as Lodge once stated, to meet the arguments of their foes on the altruistic grounds to which the anti-imperialists sought to carry them. They repeatedly stressed the obligation of the United States, whatever the risks, to carry the benefits of Anglo-Saxon civilization to the Filipinos. They made the most of the imperialism of righteousness and the historic mission of the United States to spread abroad republican institutions. The imperialists also emphasized more practical arguments. The Filipinos were not capable of self-government, they declared, and echoing the views of General Greene and other military leaders, they vigorously maintained that unless the islands were placed under American control, the consequent political anarchy would lead to their being seized by some other power. The United States also needed and had every right to establish bases for the protection and development of its trade. Only by holding the Philippines, it was argued, could America feel economically or politically secure in the face of the intense commercial rivalry in the Far East.

The most eloquent and impassioned of imperialist orators was Senator Beveridge of Indiana. Taking the position that the principles of self-government applied only to those capable of governing themselves, he said that the United States could not possibly abandon the Filipinos to the wolves of foreign conquest. That the islands were so distant from the United States mattered not at all; the Navy would make them contiguous. But where he placed his greatest emphasis, with all emotional stops pulled out, was on the inevitable forward march of the American flag.

It had advanced across a continent and the folds of glory blazed from ocean to ocean, Beveridge declared, but now carrying the torch handed to him by his forebears, McKinley "plants the flag over the islands of the seas, outposts of commerce, citadels of national defense, and the march of the flag goes on." And the brilliant young orator then sounded the final note in the imperialists' lexicon:

It is God's great purpose made manifest in the instincts of our race, whose present phase is our personal profit, but whose far-off end is the redemption of the world and the Christianization of mankind.

Against this noisy background, the Senate somewhat more prosaically took up in early December the question of whether the treaty providing for the cession of the Philippines should be approved. Resolutions were introduced stating that the United States did not have the constitutional power to acquire overseas dependencies, substituting a protectorate for outright possession, and, more importantly, pledging the future independence of the Philippines. However, administration spokesmen held firm against any limitations on the treaty. They maintained that while there was no intent of enthralling the Filipino people ("we come as ministering angels not as despots," said Senator Knute

Nelson of Minnesota), it would be wholly impractical at this time to make any commitment on their future freedom. Yet there need be no fear of any conflict with democratic principles, they again declared, because American policy "will religiously maintain the best ideals of the Republic, and will be in harmony with justice, generosity, and the highest civilization."

The opposition Democrats and the handful of anti-imperialist Republicans fought a hard but losing battle in combatting administration policy. They argued that possession of the Philippines would not actually benefit the United States, and that in the eyes of the world their occupation would mean a betrayal of the moral principles for which America had always stood. But the lines of division had already hardened. Moreover, the anti-imperialists in the Senate suffered a serious setback when William Jennings Bryan, even though no one was more opposed to overseas expansion, advised his Democratic followers to vote in favor of the treaty in the interests of peace, leaving the annexation question open to further consideration. Whether he was wholly sincere in believing that imperialism could be more effectively combatted in a later public forum or simply wanted to preserve it as a campaign issue in the Presidential election of 1900 may be open to question. The effect of his intervention was nevertheless to weaken the anti-imperialist front.

Still, the outcome of the Senate vote was in some doubt up to the last moment, and on the eve of the day set for the final ballot, startling news from Manila accentuated the existing uncertainties. The Filipino insurgents who had once counted on American support in upholding their independent republic had given up all hope of such aid ever since President McKinley, anticipating the islands' annexation, had extended American military rule over the entire archipelago. They now broke out in open revolt against the occupation forces. As the Senate held its roll call on the treaty on February 6, 1899, the hostilities that belied any idea of the Filipinos' happy acceptance of American rule were already under way.

The revolt heightened the drama and excitement under

which the vote was taken, but there is no evidence that it caused a single shift in existing alignments. The final count was 57 in favor of the treaty, and 27 opposed. The Senate had upheld the annexation of the Philippines, as well, of course, as the less controversial features of the Treaty of Paris, but had done so with only a single vote to spare.

As events were to prove, the ultimate decision had been made but the controversy was not yet brought to a close. By rejecting the peaceful transfer of sovereignty through their uprising against the American occupation forces, the Filipinos added fresh fuel to a revived national debate over the whole imperialist issue. It would become more acrimonious than ever, enter importantly into the Presidential campaign the next year, and subside only after McKinley's triumphant re-election.

The expansionist movement that had now come to its climax did not embrace only the Philippine Islands. The United States had annexed Hawaii, quietly taken over possession of Puerto Rico and Guam, and in this same year 1899 substituted for the tripartite protectorate over the Samoan Islands an exclusive title to American Samoa. The public fully acquiesced in these other extensions of the national domain (the Senate approved the new Samoan treaty without even a record vote), and such opposition to them as had once existed was stilled. But the Philippines, with their 7,500,000 people of varying races and religions, lying 6,000 miles distant from San Francisco and only 600 miles off the Asiatic coast, represented a far more ambitious and dangerous leap into the imperialist sea. Moreover, in seeking to establish its authority over the Filipinos, patriotically fighting for their freedom, the United States was to find itself engaged in a far more protracted, costly, and bloody war than that with Spain. It was not until 1902 that the insurrection in the Philippines was finally suppressed.

As this tragic conflict continued, with American troops resorting to many of the cruelly repressive measures the Spaniards had employed in Cuba, a new dimension was given to the continuing debate over imperialism. There was no change in the basic arguments on either side. The anti-imperialists, however, found all their worst fears confirmed as to the consequences of the United States departing from its democratic and republican principles, while the imperialists were more than ever convinced that duty required them to bring the blessings of civilization to the Filipinos whether they liked it or not.

A sense of moral outrage invigorated the attacks of those who had all along opposed overseas expansion. Their embittered reaction to what was taking place in the Philippines found eloquent expression in William Vaughn Moody's often quoted "Ode in Time of Hesitation:"

> *Tempt not our weakness, our cupidity!*
> *For save we let the island men go free,*
> *Those baffled and dislaureled ghosts*
> *Will curse us from the lamentable coasts*
> *Where walk the frustrate dead.*
> *O ye who lead,*
> *Take heed!*
> *Blindness we may forgive, but baseness we will smite.*

The imperialists would not be stayed. "These Filipinos must be taught obedience," wrote the Washington *Star*, "and must be forced to observe, even if they cannot comprehend, the practice of civilization." President McKinley expressed the same view somewhat more loftily. "Do we need their consent," he asked in rebutting the idea that the United States was forcing its rule on the Filipinos against their will, "to perform a great act for humanity?"

The indefatigable Senator Beveridge visited the islands and returned more than ever convinced that the United States could not renounce the White Man's Burden. "We will not repudiate our duty in the archipelago," he told the Senate on January 9, 1900, as the war there raged on. "We will not abandon our opportunity in the Orient. . . . And we will move forward to our work, not howling regrets like slaves whipped to their burdens, but with gratitude for a task worthy of our strength and thanksgiving to Almighty God that He has marked us as his chosen people."

The election of 1900 did not turn on the issue of imperialism. What the American people felt was really at stake was the continuance of the booming prosperity the country was now enjoying. McKinley promised economic stability; William Jennings Bryan, once again the Democratic standard-bearer, threatened the old dangers of free silver and radical reform. But imperialism was nevertheless in the background. The Republicans stoutly upheld their foreign policy; the Democrats as vigorously opposed it. When the people marched to the polls, they may have voted primarily for prosperity, but they thereby also approved imperialism.

If the smashing victory the Republicans won in 1900 cannot be strictly interpreted as a mandate for overseas expansion, it thus endorsed it by default. The United States would not relinquish the territories it had obtained from Spain, and when the Supreme Court in the famous insular cases favorably resolved the constitutional issue as to whether the nation had the legal right to take over colonies, the final seal of approval was placed on the entire process. "Public opinion expressed at the polls, Congressional action, and now the Supreme Court," stated the *World's Work*, "have established the policy of expansion." The United States was swept along on the universal tide that was carrying every western nation, in mounting rivalry, to establish and maintain overseas colonies or spheres of influence among the world's nonwhite races.

CHAPTER XII

The Open Door in China

The United States' territorial advance to the shores of Asia was a dramatic break with the past, a startling new departure in foreign policy. In many ways even more important for the long future than the actual annexation of the Philippine Islands was the nation's consequent involvement, to a far greater extent than ever before, in the affairs of China.

Interest in trade and commerce with this Far Eastern country had never lapsed; missionary activities kept alive a popular concern with its social progress, and the unhappy immigration controversy was a constant reminder of an awkward diplomatic impasse. But an American territorial possession at the gateway of Asia gave an entirely new aspect to the relationship between the United States and China after approval of the Treaty of Paris. Had the Philippines not become an American colony, providing what was believed to be a base for the further expansion of commercial activity in the Orient, the United States might not have initiated its Open Door policy.

It was this policy, as first set forth by Secretary of State Hay in 1899, and then further elaborated the next year, that directly led to what was to become a mounting rivalry with another emergent world power seeking to expand its influence in the Far East. The United States and Japan, in spite of the close and friendly association they had maintained ever since Commodore Perry's midcentury expedition, were ultimately to find themselves in irreconcilable conflict over China's political status. The Open Door policy was a first step along the fateful road to Pearl Harbor.

The importance of the potential trade with China, as we have seen, was an underlying factor in America's interest in Pacific sea power, in the moves that ultimately led to the annexation of Hawaii and Samoa, and in the decision to hold the Philippine Islands. As a representative spokesman of the country's business interests, Mark Hanna had originally been no friend of overseas expansion, but he was won over to the desirability of retaining the Philippines for the sake of the China trade. He was entirely candid about this—as contrasted with President McKinley's pious exhortations on duty and destiny. "If it is commercialism to want possession of a strategic point giving the American people an opportunity to maintain a foothold in the markets of that great eastern country," he exclaimed, "for God's sake let us have commercialism."

Senator Beveridge touched on every note in the imperialist theme but he never failed to emphasize its economic aspects. "The Philippines are ours forever," he grandiloquently proclaimed in one of his famous orations. ". . . And just beyond the Philippines are China's illimitable markets. We will not retreat from either. . . . Our largest trade must henceforth be with Asia."

In 1900 a spokesman for the Bureau of Foreign Commerce, noting the value of the country's new possessions as gateways for the development of commercial intercourse with the Far East, was to say that they had been acquired only as "an incident of commercial expansion." This was an exaggeration. It ignored the chauvinistic impulses, the instinctive pride in empire, and the sense of national mission that served more effectively than any economic motivation to build up popular support for imperialism. Nevertheless, there was never any question that the lodestone of the China market played an immensely important part in drawing the United States out across the Pacific from Hawaii to the Philippines.

Although the actual trade with China at the close of the century amounted to very little—less than that with Japan and only some 3 per cent of the national total—reality never could compete with the dream. What continued to influence the commercial community, as it had since the opening of the China trade over a century earlier, was great expectations. Here were 400 million potential customers for American goods—agricultural and industrial—and nothing could persuade either farmers or manufacturers that China would not ultimately provide an inexhaustible outlet for their products.

The concern that had developed in the 1890's over this potential market, as already noted, grew out of the apparent design of the European powers, in spite of the most-favored-nation clause in American treaties, to win exclusive control over Chinese commerce for themselves. Great Britain and Russia, Germany and France were jealously establishing their spheres of influence and successively wringing from an impotent Imperial Government special concessions for trade and investment. "The various powers," declared the old Empress Dowager Tzu Hsi, "cast upon us looks of tiger-like voracity."

This process of colonizing China seemed to be approaching a climax in 1898. In retaliation for the murder of two missionaries, Germany demanded and secured the cession of the port of Kiaochow, thereby establishing its virtual control over the rich province of Shantung; Russia exacted leaseholds at Port Arthur and Talienwan in consolidation of a relentless grip on Manchuria, whose railroads it already controlled; Great Britain was further expanding its sphere of influence throughout the Yangtze Valley and obtained a new leasehold on the port of Weihaiwei, and after seizing Kwangchow Bay, France extended its interests in the southern province of Yunnan. And finally, with a significance hardly appreciated in 1898, Japan developed a sphere of influence in the province of Fukien, opposite the island of Formosa which it had annexed after its war with China in 1894. The tottering empire of the Manchus was being so rapidly carved up among the rapacious powers that only their continued rivalry over the spoils allowed the Imperial Government to maintain its shadowy sovereignty over its own territory.

The United States, following the friendly policy which thirty years earlier had been so greatly influenced by the humanitarian ideals of Anson Burlingame, continued to stand wholly apart from this territorial scramble. It insisted on its rights of extraterritoriality in the treaty ports, but it sought no exclusive privileges or concessions. Even as late as March, 1898, it regarded the steps being taken by the European powers with equanimity in the belief that they would not affect American interests. Great Britain, fearful of its rivals' aggressive ambitions, approached the McKinley Administration that month with a proposal for some sort of concerted action in support of the principle of equality of trade throughout all China. President McKinley was not interested. His reply to the British suggestion was that nothing in the situation in China appeared to justify any departure from the United States' well-founded policy of avoiding any "interference or connection with European complications."

Nine months later—even though by that time the decision had been made to hold the Philippine Islands—he reaffirmed his reluctance to become in any way involved in "the China problem." There had been warnings from Charles Denby, the American Minister in Peking, that the empire's threatened partition would destroy American markets. Only vigorous measures to preserve China's autonomy, he stated, could save the day. Secretary of State Day also felt that national interests were threatened. Citing the familiar argument that only new markets could absorb the excess of industrial production "above the demands of home consumption," he urged that advantage be taken of the existing situation to invite more favorable consideration for

American industry and trade in China. Nevertheless, the President continued to believe that the powers would not adopt discriminatory practices within either their spheres of influence or their leased territories. In his annual message to Congress in December, 1898, he stated that the assurances he had received that American rights in China would be respected "obviated the need of our country becoming an actor on the scene."

Such complacency over European commercial policies seemed hardly warranted in American trade and investment circles. They saw the doors swinging shut in China just as acquisition of the Philippines provided a base for further commercial expansion. American trade there was not growing as they had hoped; American investors had only a tiny stake in railroad, mining, and other investments. Unless the United States promptly did something to protect its interests, they felt—as did Minister Denby—that it might well find itself almost completely excluded from the China market.

Although anything but a matter of serious concern to the American people as a whole, the pressure from commercial quarters had indeed been progressively mounting throughout 1898. Early in the year a lead article in the *Literary Digest,* analyzing current newspaper opinion on events in China, found that there was general agreement that the territorial scramble was "a conscious or an instinctive move of all Europe against all America, in competition for the markets of the world." Soon afterwards a series of articles in the *North American Review* expounded on the importance of America's future in Asia and asked whether the United States could continue to stand aside while the European powers sought to pre-empt the field with monopolistic controls. And about this same time Charles A. Conant, the Washington correspondent of the *Journal of Commerce,* wrote a highly influential article on such matters in the *Forum.* He again emphasized the widely held view that the only great undeveloped market capable of absorbing the excess production of American industry was the Chinese Empire. Here was an unexampled commercial opportunity, Conant declared, but it would be lost if the United States hesitated to safeguard its interests.

As 1898 gave way to 1899, such general expressions of opinion took on a more concrete form. A group of important cotton textile exporters, railroad promoters, and mining entrepreneurs who had organized the American Asiatic Association forwarded a series of petitions to Washington urging adoption of a more vigorous Far Eastern policy. At the annual meeting of the National Association of Manufacturers, speaker after speaker called for government support in expanding trade throughout the Pacific, and the New York Chamber of Commerce submitted a memorial to President McKinley asking for immediate action. "The administration at Washington," it stated, "seems to be supine about the menace to these important interests of our citizens in China."

Supplementing this aroused concern over the economic aspects of the China question, missionary groups were also seeking encouragement and support for their activities. They had long felt that China represented the most promising field for their program of evangelization, more significant than Japan. "There is a great Niagara of souls passing into the dark in China," lamented one strong-minded missionary. "Every day, every week, every month, they are passing away! A million a month in China all dying without God!" Looking back on these days, the well-known leader of the Student Volunteers for Foreign Missions, Sherwood Eddy, was to recall that "China was the goal, the lodestar, the great magnet that drew us all."

One and all, the missionaries believed that full advantage should be taken of the new opportunities for their work that had been opened up by the results of the Spanish-American War. Moreover, China not only constituted in their eyes a challenging field for the extension of Christianity, but also for the further promotion of democratic ideals and social progress as interpreted by the West. On the thesis that trade was an ally of the missionary movement, as Robert E. Speer attested, they were ready to back any move that might more effectively safe-guard America's over-all position in eastern Asia.

This broad interest in China led to some popular support for a program of cooperation with Great Britain, as first proposed by the British Foreign Office, in seeking to uphold what was already being generally called "the open door" to trade. It was strengthened when in the early spring of 1899 Lord Charles Beresford, a Member of Parliament and representative of the British Associated Chambers of Commerce, toured the United States urging adoption of such a policy. The New York *Sun* called for recognition of the solidarity of American and British interests in dealing with the China problem, and the Philadel-phia *Record* urged the fullest possible cooperation in developing additional opportunities for foreign trade. Among other political leaders, Senator Lodge expressed emphatic approval for taking a stand alongside Great Britain in a joint declaration that the ports of China should be "opened to all nations equally or none."

John Hay had assumed his post as Secretary of State just as this demand for a more energetic China policy began to gather momentum. While American ambassador in London he had favored a more cordial response to British overtures for coopera-tive action than President McKinley had been willing to make. His attitude, however, was based on a compelling desire to strengthen Anglo-American relations rather than any great in-terest in China. In his new post he realized the practical diffi-culty of acting in concert with Great Britain (even though it might win Lodge's support), and consequently did not at first do anything whatsoever to invigorate Far Eastern policy. He apparently did not believe any more than did McKinley that the new concessions that the Chinese Government had granted the European powers threatened American commercial interests.

Hay could not, however, remain indifferent to the mounting pressure for action. More and more memorials were flowing into Washington from cotton exporters and other firms doing busi-ness in China. *The New York Times* flatly stated that American interests had "not been intelligently represented or adequately appreciated by the State Department." Finally, in the summer of 1899, Hay felt compelled to canvass the possibilities of an independent move by the United States.

In the light of the subsequent evolution and ultimate consequences of the Open Door policy, its immediate origins provide a curious and fascinating chapter in the annals of American diplomacy. This policy was not the inspiration of John Hay, let alone that of President McKinley, but rather the fruition of the ideas of two otherwise rather obscure men—William W. Rockhill and Alfred E. Hippisley. Hay had brought Rockhill, an American diplomat with former experience in Asia, to Washington as head of the Department of Latin American Affairs, but his more important function was to serve as an adviser on the Far East. Hippisley, an English friend of Rockhill's who had been in China in the employment of the Imperial Customs Inspectorate, was a happenchance visitor that summer in Baltimore. In their mutual discussions about China, these two men elaborated the principles that until 1941 provided the basis for America's continuing Far Eastern policy.

Acting entirely in his private capacity—he was not a representative of the British Government—Hippisley suggested that the United States undertake to resolve the problem of China by seeking from the powers some sort of international guarantee that there would be no interference with foreign trade, or any other foreign interests, in their respective spheres of interest. Rockhill immediately endorsed this idea. He would have liked to go further, as indeed Hippisley would have also. Highly sympathetic toward China, both men would have preferred a statement of policy by the United States that "would be understood by China as a pledge on our part to assist in maintaining the integrity of the Empire." They realized, however, that such a proposition would be politically unrealistic, and they limited their aims to the more modest proposal which they thought might prove acceptable to the McKinley Administration.

Rockhill took the matter up with Secretary Hay. The latter was at first very hesitant. "I am fully awake to the great impor-

tance of what you say and am more than ready to act," he wrote
Rockhill on August 7, 1899. "But the senseless prejudices in
certain sections of the 'Senate and people' compel us to move
with great caution." What Hay obviously feared was that in
adopting a course which the general public might associate too
closely with British policy in China, even though the United
States acted independently, the Administration would be charged
with being pro-British.

Rockhill and Hippisley nevertheless continued to press their
idea, and to combat Hay's fears of any adverse popular reaction
to their plan, they shrewdly played up its possible political rewards. "The public need know nothing of the steps taken by the
Sec. of State," Hippisley suggested, "till the negotiations have
been consummated, and the announcement then that the U.S.
had secured China's independence and so served the cause of
peace and civilization would be a trump card for the admin.
and crush all the life out of the anti-imperialism agitation of
Bryan, Croker & Co." Whatever the weight of such an argument (and events were to prove its validity), Hay soon swung
into line. Some two weeks after his first demurrer, while vaca-
tioning in New Hampshire, he somewhat casually dropped
another note to Rockhill:

If you have time between now and next Wednesday to set down your
views on this question—in the form of a draft instruction to Mr.
Choate, Mr. White, Mr. Tower and General Porter [the American
ambassadors to the major powers]—I would be greatly obliged. . . .
I am taking a good deal for granted—your presence in Washington,
your leisure, and your willingness to give us a *coup d'épaule*. But
if it should not be convenient, all right.

It was convenient. Rockhill and Hippisley promptly drew up
the draft instruction embodying the proposal they had already
discussed with the Secretary of State. It remained highly limited
in its scope. The powers were merely asked to subscribe to an
understanding that within their respective spheres of influence or
leased territories there would be no interference with any treaty

port or vested interest; the Chinese treaty tariff would apply to all foreign merchandise imports, and harbor dues and railway rates would be the same for the nationals of all countries. There would be, that is, full equality for all foreign trade.

Secretary Hay accepted the Rockhill-Hippisley memorandum in its entirety, and after President McKinley's approval had been secured, it was embodied virtually word for word in official instructions to the American ambassadors abroad. What became known as the Open Door notes were dispatched to London, St. Petersburg, and Berlin on September 6, 1899, and then a month later to Paris, Rome, and Tokyo.

The public was not informed. A first hint that something was brewing in Far Eastern diplomacy was contained in an article in the *Literary Digest* which referred to a "widely credited report" that a move was under way to assure the Open Door in China. On December 17 *The New York Times* noted rather obscurely that it had learned from "an authentic source" that Germany had been asked to cooperate in such a program, and at the end of the year it gave front-page prominence to a further story saying that Secretary Hay had reached a common understanding with the powers for "a continued open-door policy." These rumors then gained substantial authority by an announcement on January 3, 1900, that the Secretary of State had said at a cabinet meeting that his negotiations to secure the Open Door in China were proving to be "eminently successful."

The replies of the powers were not, however, quite as receptive to Hay's proposal as this optimistic statement suggested. They were one and all somewhat evasive, insisted on reservations, and even then made their consent provisional upon that of the other powers. The reply of Russia was in fact more nearly a blunt refusal than an acceptance. What Secretary Hay had decided to do was to interpret their replies as unqualified acceptance of an Open Door policy, thereby placing them on record in a way which it would be extremely difficult for any one of them to repudiate. On March 20 he consequently took the bold step of formally announcing, as a means to assure the moral sanction of the world for his policy, that in each case the assent to his proposals had been "final and definitive."

The popular reaction within the United States was an immediate and universal paean of praise for what Secretary Hay had achieved (or said he had achieved) in resolving the China problem. *The New York Times* enthusiastically declared that he had succeeded "in repairing the huge blunder of his predecessor" in rejecting the British Open Door proposals. The *Review of Reviews* characterized his coup as "one of the greatest achievements ever won by diplomacy." The Philadelphia *Press* said that securing adherence of the powers to the Open Door policy was "a larger achievement and more brilliant triumph" than the victory over Spain. Overnight John Hay had become a national hero whose skill in singlehandedly guaranteeing the commercial position of the United States in eastern Asia, and carrying to successful completion so noble a work of peace, was universally hailed as deserving the nation's highest praise.

Standing out almost by itself in this overwhelming chorus of approval was the note of skepticism voiced by the Springfield *Republican*. It found something "rather funny," as its editorial writer expressed it, in believing that the powers' bland acceptance of Hay's proposal really amounted to very much. It soberly warned that the United States had placed itself in a position where, if it were to be consistent, "it must guarantee by military force the political integrity of China, or share in its possible partition." There was no hint or suggestion that the ultimate protagonist in determining the fate of China might be Japan rather than any one of the European powers, but otherwise the Springfield *Republican*'s lonely dissent from Secretary Hay's extravagant claims showed remarkable prescience.

The more general reception given to announcement of the Open Door policy was a perhaps natural consequence of several interwoven factors—political, economic, and emotional. An international agreement on China was a happy diplomatic triumph for the McKinley Administration, whose successful prosecution of the war against Spain was countered by the slow progress being made in subduing insurgent revolt against American rule in the Philippines. It held out the promise of a further expansion of trade and commerce in eastern Asia. And it constituted an apparent victory for world peace in allaying the threatening rivalry of the European powers over China's possible dismemberment. But what perhaps appealed even more to the American public, its conscience somewhat troubled by the consequences of the nation's imperialistic course, was that this memorable stroke of diplomacy could be interpreted as safeguarding the independence of a nation that had become the helpless victim of European despoilers. It was a reaffirmation of the idealism that the American people always liked to believe was the real force behind their country's foreign policy.

The Open Door notes hardly went so far as any such interpretation of their significance suggested. They accepted the existing spheres of foreign influence within China and said nothing whatsoever about the Empire's political or territorial integrity. They applied only to equality of trade (nothing about investments or other aspect of economic policy) within very marked limitations. Nonetheless, it was the popular verdict that the United States had performed an immense service for the liberty of the Chinese people.

The possible gap between promise and performance was to be revealed within a few months. During the summer of 1900 the always latent antiforeign feeling in China gave rise to a dangerous popular uprising, the Boxer Rebellion, and the foreign powers—including the United States—found themselves constrained to intervene with military force in defense of their nationals in China. The possibility that this situation might lead to the final breakup of China seemed highly likely. The United States thereupon took a further and even more significant step along the road on which it had started with the original Hay notes.

It did not this time seek to win any other nation's specific adherence to its policy. Acting solely on his own responsibility,

Secretary Hay set forth in a new circular note forwarded to the powers on July 3, 1900, the course the United States intended to follow in any final settlement of the new China crisis. Its policy would be designed, Hay declared,

> to seek a solution which may bring about permanent peace and safety to China, preserve Chinese territorial and administrative entity, protect all rights guaranteed to friendly powers by treaty and international law, and safeguard for all the world the principle of equal and impartial trade with all parts of the Chinese Empire.

Here was the logical projection (which Rockhill and Hippisley originally favored) of the concepts underlying the first Open Door notes. Whether or not such a policy conformed to the national interest—and this was to be repeatedly questioned in later years—it appeared to constitute a firm commitment for America's defense of China's independence.

The circumstances that had given rise to this new declaration of American policy were highly dramatic. As the antiforeign revolt gathered momentum early in the spring of 1900, armed bands of Boxers roamed the countryside throughout northern China, first attacking the "secondary devils," or Chinese converts to Christianity, and then moving with fire and sword against the foreigners themselves. One contemporary report stated:

> Peking, Tientsin, and Paotingfu are encircled by bands of maddened and fanatical people whose numbers are swollen by an excited crowd of vagabonds, and who, being maintained by leaders in high position, rob, pillage, burn and kill as they pass. For the moment their activity is directed against Chinese converts, Catholic and Protestant. . . . They do not conceal their object to get rid of all foreigners . . . by means of a destruction of religious missions and a general insurrection against European and American residents . . . and on their flags they now assert they act by imperial command.

In June the Boxer forces invested Peking and after massacring over two thousand Chinese Christian converts, surrounded the legation quarter where the foreigners in the capital (after the assassination of the German Minister and the chancellor of the Japanese legation) had taken hasty refuge. For over a month no word was received in the outside world of their fate, and it became widely believed they had been killed. Then on July 17 a message at last reached Washington from the new American Minister in Peking, E. H. Conger, that told of the frightening siege of the legations and concluded: "Quick relief only can prevent general massacre."

An allied rescue expedition, to which the United States contributed 2,500 troops (Japan had the largest contingent of some 8,000 men), had already been organized, and after a number of false starts it advanced on Peking in early August for the relief of the legations. As the whole world waited anxiously and fearfully for news, word finally came through that it had been in time. The Boxer forces melted away, the Empress Dowager Tzu Hsi fled the capital, and on August 14 the allies lifted the legations' eight weeks' siege. Seventy-six foreigners had been killed and 179 wounded, but the rest of the total of 900—civilians and foreign guards—had been almost miraculously saved.

Secretary Hay had agreed with utmost caution to American participation in the allied relief expedition. His instructions to Conger were that the only concern of the United States was the protection of American interests and American citizens—"there must be no alliances." And his sole purpose in dispatching his memorable circular note outlining American policy was to set an example and try to exert moral pressure that would restrain the other powers from seeking to take advantage of China's chaotic situation.

For a time it appeared to be highly unlikely that anything could be done to keep them in check. "There is not a single power we can rely upon," Hay exclaimed bitterly on one occasion, "for our policy of abstention from plunder and the Open Door." By November he was so disillusioned that he seemed ready to abandon his whole policy. Under pressure from the War and Navy departments, he went so far as to instruct the American Minister to sound out the Peking Government on the cession to the United States of a naval base at Samsah Bay, in the province of Fukien. This project did not get very far, however. Ironically enough it was the Japanese Government, within whose sphere of influence such a concession would lie, which pointed out the contradiction between any such move and the principles underlying America's professed program. Hay thereupon reverted to his original position and once more sought to exert his influence to bring about a solution of the problems raised by the Boxer Rebellion without any territorial exactions. The danger of China's possible partition was ultimately averted, though more from the European powers' mutual jealousy than any American action, and Hay finally had the satisfaction of seeing the objectives of his circular note of July 3 at least temporarily realized.

The final Boxer settlement was not concluded until September, 1901. The powers insisted on very heavy indemnities for the destruction wrought by the rebel bands (the United States was later to return its share to China for educational purposes), and on the right to maintain troops in both Tientsin and Peking as a protection against any future threats to foreign lives and property. The agreement, however, constituted continued recognition of the Imperial Government and made no direct infringements on its political or territorial sovereignty. It also sustained, at least in theory, the principle of equality of trade for all foreign nations.

The further evolution of the Open Door policy is a topic beyond the confines of this narrative. So far as its origins are concerned, however, it may be said that John Hay acted in what he believed to be the best interests of the United States in seeking to safeguard the country's commercial interests in China at a time when they appeared to be seriously endangered by the rival ambitions of the European powers. There was also the consideration that his policy, especially as amplified in the summer of 1900, sought to ensure the independence of China, not only in the American interest but in that of the Chinese people. In its broadest sense, the Open Door policy grew naturally out of the whole history of American relations with the Orient; it was the

culmination of forces which had been at work since the close of
the eighteenth century.

What Hay hardly realized at the time—although he was
soon to do so—was that his policy deeply involved the United
States in a highly complicated situation which was a projection on
the Far Eastern stage of the mounting rivalries of the European
powers in their own power struggle at home. William Rockhill
was sent to Peking as a special commissioner in July, 1900, and
soon after his arrival he was writing Alfred Hippisley of his
growing discouragement over the efficacy of a policy which he
had himself done so much to promote. He was "sick and tired of
the whole business," Rockhill told his old friend, and finding it
increasingly difficult to sustain the American position in the face
of European political intrigue, could only hope that it would be
"a long time before the United States gets into another muddle
of this description."

While Hay apparently felt very much the same way, as some
of his later actions were so clearly to demonstrate, he never contemplated any withdrawal from eastern Asia. He accepted the
consequences of both overseas expansion and the further involvement in China. He recognized, and was himself fully prepared to implement, the larger role that the country had been
called upon to play in international affairs. "The United States of
today cannot go back to where the country was fifty or a hundred
years ago," he declared. "Whether we will or not, whether for
better or worse, we must go forward."

The public had applauded Secretary Hay's further development of the Open Door. Among other newspapers *The New York
Times* declared that the Administration had won renewed title to
the confidence of the entire country by its wise and statesmanlike
policy. "Nothing so meteoric had even been done in American
diplomacy," was Henry Adams' later comment. The American
people were most certainly not fully aware of all the possible
implications of what was happening, but in the summer of 1900
they unreservedly accepted the stand the United States had taken
in defense of China's political and territorial integrity. Moreover,

in spite of all the successive advances and retreats during the next forty-odd years, the Open Door policy continued to maintain an almost mystic hold on the popular imagination somewhat comparable to that exerted by the Monroe Doctrine.

CHAPTER XIII

Turn of the Century

At the turn of the century the United States had experienced a remarkable advance from the circumstances and conditions prevailing forty years earlier when it stood on the threshold of the Civil War. With the preservation of the Union it had dramatically demonstrated the inherent strength of democracy to a skeptical world, and in succeeding years it had so effectively developed its incalculably rich natural resources as to give the nation a measure of economic and industrial power surpassing that of any other country. It had built up a new, modern navy and acquired the overseas bases and colonial possessions that enabled the Government as never before to speak with a voice of authority in international affairs.

While the United States may in fact have been a great power before the war with Spain, it was its territorial expansion into the Caribbean and the Pacific that led to its being fully accepted as one both at home and abroad—a peer of the European powers which had heretofore seemed to hold all the major stakes in the great game of international politics. Indeed, Theodore Roosevelt, so soon to become President, was prophetically to say that the United States would itself hold the balance of power on the world stage of the new century.

While most Americans rejoiced in these dramatic developments, there were also those who looked back nostalgically to a day when the country had been able to go its own way almost entirely oblivious of the outside world. William Allen White, the brilliant editor of the Emporia (Kansas) *Gazette* and friend of presidents, accepted the implications of imperialism—"this is what fate holds for the chosen people"—but he noted also that many thousands of his countrymen could not "help longing for the old order." It was their conviction that on embarking on this new and ambitious course, something simple and fine in American life had been irretrievably lost. Finley Peter Dunne reflected this same feeling in more homely terms when his barkeeper sage, "Mr. Dooley," looked back to "th' good old days befur we became . . . a wurrld power." Remembering how "our favrite sport was playin' solytare," he sadly commented that now that we had cut in on the big game, "be Hivens we have no peace iv mind."

The European powers accepted the entry of the United States into their exclusive club, in some cases hopefully and in others fearfully. There had been little sympathy for America, except that shown by Great Britain, in its war with Spain, and not too much enthusiasm for its determined advance across the Pacific. In the aftermath of war, discussion in the European press dwelt upon the possible emergence of an "American peril," and true to the traditions of Old World diplomacy, foreign writers speculated over the various combinations into which the European powers might now be drawn, either with or against the United States, to safeguard their national interests in the twentieth century. The old concept of America against Europe, born of the clash of principles a century and more earlier, had a possible new significance now that the United States had itself become a world power.

The sometimes fearful views of the European chancelleries in respect to the United States' future role were underscored by the extent of the empire it had acquired after the war with Spain. Much to the surprise of a cynical Europe, this country had, it is true, made good its pledge to grant Cuba its freedom, but it had nevertheless clearly established American paramountcy in the Caribbean. The retention of a naval base at Guantanamo Bay, together with Cuba's acknowledgment of the United States' right to intervene in its affairs should the stability of the new republic be threatened, the annexation of Puerto Rico as an "unincorporated territory" in the Union, and the unequivocal reassertion that any future canal linking the Atlantic and the Pacific would have to be wholly under American control, left no doubt that the United States would never tolerate any foreign interference in this whole strategic area. Henceforth the Caribbean would in effect be an American lake, fulfilling the goal which the early expansionists had so hopefully envisaged when they first sought to obtain naval bases in the Virgin Islands, Santo Domingo, and Haiti.

The acquisition of territory in the western Pacific was even more significant, going as it did so far beyond the imperialists' early ambitions. The United States had not only acquired Hawaii and Samoa, as had so long been urged, but in taking over the Philippines accepted a wholly unanticipated responsibility. It might still be extravagant to assume, as Senator Beveridge did with such expansive confidence, that America held full control of the Pacific, but its naval power had been extended to the Asiatic mainland. Even though the bloody war to suppress the revolt of the Filipinos was to continue well into the new century, there could be no real doubt of its outcome. On July 4, 1900, the first step was taken to transfer authority in the islands from the military command to a civilian commission, and the Filipinos themselves well knew that the independence for which they had hoped had given way to American rule.

The United States had established an empire; it held dominion in far-off seas. Nevertheless, neither the bright hopes of the more aggressive imperialists nor the dark forebodings of the anti-imperialists were to be realized in future years. Even as the century ended, enthusiasm for "the march of the flag" was beginning to subside, and there was no popular support for any further acquisition of territory. With the imperialist fever that had swept over the country losing its virulence, foreign affairs were once again to be pushed into the background. The nation became more and more absorbed in domestic problems with its energies firmly directed to promoting the growing movement for progressive reform.

There remained the involvement in eastern Asia growing out of the Open Door policy. If this was to have even more important consequences for the future, as already suggested, than overseas expansion itself, they were hardly foreseen at the opening of the new century. While the American people had enthusiastically hailed Secretary Hay's first exercise of the United States' new influence in the field of world diplomacy, they soon came to feel that the national interest was not sufficiently engaged to encourage any further intervention in the Far East. For the sake of trade and commerce, and also in support of the political and social progress of the Chinese people, they continued to approve the principles underlying the Open Door, but they were not prepared to make any binding commitments for its support or to back up any effort to uphold it by a show of force.

The close accord that characterized Japanese-American relations still prevailed. Japan had raised no objections to American acquisition of the Philippines; it had cooperated loyally with the western powers in the relief expedition sent to Peking at the time of the Boxer Rebellion. If there were already ominous stirrings beneath the surface of Japanese life, they were again not generally apparent to the American people. As already noted, the acute controversies over Japanese immigration and the mounting political rivalry on the Asiatic mainland had not yet materialized at the turn of the century.

Among other aspects of the position of the United States in 1900, by far the most significant was the new accord that characterized Anglo-American relations. Great Britain had not only stood alone among the European powers in showing any sympathy for the United States at the time of the war with Spain. It continued to manifest friendly feelings in succeeding years. The British Government let it be known that it had no intention of challenging the new position the United States had established in the Caribbean, welcomed the American advance across the Pacific, and remained generally ready to cooperate in Far Eastern policy. On either side of the Atlantic it was now felt, even more keenly than in the aftermath of the Venezuela controversy, that the two great Anglo-Saxon nations had so much in common in their basic ideals and fundamental purposes, as well as in their common heritage and common language, that there was no longer any place for the acrimonious disputes of the past.

Although the arbitration treaty which Secretary Olney and Lord Pauncefote sought to conclude in 1897 had proved to be impossible of realization, the idea of closer ties kept being revived. Something like an alliance appealed greatly to American imperialists as a means of furthering the mutual interests of the two countries. Captain Mahan called for what he described as "accordant relations," and Senator Beveridge, with his usual oratorical flourishes, spoke of "an English-speaking people's league of God for the permanent peace of this war-torn world."

During the Spanish-American War a number of highly significant statements had been made on Anglo-American solidarity. While still Ambassador in London, John Hay told a distinguished gathering that there was "a sanction like that of religion which binds us in a sort of partnership in the beneficent work of mankind." Replying to such overtures, Colonial Secretary Joseph Chamberlain declared that even war would be cheaply purchased "if in a great and noble cause the Stars and Stripes and the Union Jack could wave together over an Anglo-Saxon alliance."

These cordial relations were severely tried during the Boer War. The United States was to adopt a policy of strict neutrality, but the instinctive American feeling for the underdog led to widespread sympathy for the Boers (after all the war was unpopular in England itself), and to a revival of earlier mistrust of

British imperialism. *The New York Times* sought to take a more realistic attitude. "England stood by us," it declared, "let us stand by her." In spite of what the United States was itself doing in the Philippines, popular sentiment could nevertheless not be wholly reconciled to a colonial war fought against a people struggling for their freedom and independence.

As Secretary of State, Hay exerted all his influence in seeking to allay such anti-British feeling and made known his own determination that nothing should be allowed to disturb the new Anglo-American *rapprochement*. Knowing very well (as his actions in regard to the Open Door policy revealed) that anything in the nature of a formal Anglo-American alliance was "an unattainable dream," he nevertheless strove constantly to bring the two countries closer together. "As long as I stay here," he wrote Henry White soon after becoming Secretary of State, "no action shall be taken contrary to my conviction that the one indispensable feature of our foreign policy should be a firm understanding with England."

One factor helping to strengthen the accord he sought was a dimly-felt sense of danger, shared by the peoples of Great Britain and the United States, arising from the ambitious policies of the new Germany. England saw a direct threat to its age-old command of the seas in the rising German Navy; having confronted Germany in Samoa and the Philippines, the United States wondered about possible colonial threats in Latin America. Looking toward an uncertain future, both Great Britain and the United States accepted a community of interests in any challenge to the existing balance of world power.

Whatever else may be said of the manifold changes wrought in American policy at the turn of the century, this policy nevertheless still remained firmly based on the fundamental principles that had been bequeathed the republic by its founders. It has been noted that in one sense Cleveland's annual message to Congress in 1885 was a final tribute to the country's traditional aloofness from world affairs. The subsequent course of events that witnessed the United States breaking through the ramparts of its continentalism to extend its influence and power over an ever wider sphere would certainly seem to bear out this interpretation of Cleveland's conservative stand on first assuming the Presidency. Nonetheless, the United States steadfastly adhered throughout these days of overseas expansion to the basic proposition, implicit in the heritage of Washington and Adams, Jefferson and Monroe, that it should always maintain complete freedom of action.

No one of the moves made in acquiring overseas territories or intervening in the affairs of eastern Asia involved a direct political commitment to any other power. The nation continued to steer clear, as every President throughout its history had insisted that it should, of anything that could be construed as an entangling alliance. If the United States was ready to participate more extensively than ever before in international affairs, it still maintained what was in a traditional sense an *isolationist* policy, as distinct from a physical *isolation* marked by continental borders.

This somewhat ambiguous approach to its new world role was conspicuously illustrated by participation in the peace conference which, on the summons of the Russian Czar, met at The Hague in 1899. The attendance of an American delegation, a distinguished group headed by Andrew D. White, the president of Cornell, and including Alfred Thayer Mahan, was itself a sign of the new times, but the hand of the past was also seen in the cautious approach of the delegates in signing the resolutions adopted at the conference.

The proceedings at The Hague, attended by representatives of twenty-six nations, actually came to very little. The four conventions finally concluded dealt largely with the rules of warfare rather than the maintenance of peace. The only agreement of any real significance was one seeking to provide the means for the pacific settlement of international disputes by setting up a Permanent Court of Arbitration. In signing this relatively innocuous convention, as they did, the American delegates took great pains to show that their action did not represent any change in basic

American policy. They attached to their acceptance of the Permanent Court of Arbitration a reservation that nothing in the convention should be construed as requiring the United States "to depart from the traditional policy of not intruding upon, interfering with, or entangling itself in the political questions or internal administration of any foreign state." The language was cumbersome but the intent was crystal clear. The United States remained as strongly committed to a policy of no entangling alliances as it had been throughout the nineteenth century.

The spell of the Washington legend, as former Secretary of State Olney wrote, remained all-powerful in spite of everything that had happened to broaden American interest in world affairs. He himself would have liked to see the United States accept a greater responsibility—even foreign entanglements—in cooperating with other nations in the furtherance of world peace. But he realized that the time for any such change in a historic attitude had not yet come. Analyzing the continuing hold of isolationist doctrine on the public mind, Olney wrote:

A rule of policy originating with Washington, preeminently wise for his epoch, ever since taught in schools, lauded on the platform, preached in the pulpit, and displayed in capitals and italics in innumerable political manuals and popular histories, almost becomes part of the mental constitution of the generations to which it descends. They accept it without knowing why and they act upon it without the least regard to their wholly new environment.

In these circumstances the American people faced at the opening of the new century a future of steadily expanding national power in whose exercise they still remained strongly bound by the precepts of the past. The expansionist forces that had been slowly evolving ever since the Civil War, though sometimes far beneath the surface of domestic tranquillity, had finally led to overseas empire and intervention in eastern Asia. The old restraints nevertheless remained on further commitment. The American people, not entirely clear as to where their country actually stood in the confusing complex of international politics, were as yet unwilling to accept the full implications of the new position the United States had attained. They remained very reluctant to shoulder the responsibilities and obligations inescapably thrust upon them in facing the challenges to the peace of the world that were so soon to arise in the new century.

Further Reading

The period in the history of American foreign policy treated in this narrative—that is, the years from 1860 to 1900—is broadly covered in several books dealing with foreign policy as a whole. The most useful are Samuel F. Bemis, *A Diplomatic History of the United States* (rev. ed., 1955); Thomas A. Bailey, *A Diplomatic History of the American People* (rev. ed., 1958); Alexander de Conde, *A History of American Foreign Policy* (1963), and Richard W. Leopold, *The Growth of American Foreign Policy* (1963). The appropriate sections in Samuel F. Bemis, *The American Secretaries of State and Their Diplomacy* (10 vols., 1927–1929), may also be read with profit, while four collections of documents and other contemporary material (again for the entire period of American foreign policy but with important sections for the years 1860–1900) are Dorothy B. Goebel, ed., *American Foreign Policy, a Documentary Survey, 1776–1960* (1961), William A. Williams, ed., *The Shaping of American Diplomacy* (1956), Ruhl Bartlett, ed., *The Record of American Diplomacy* (rev. ed., 1964), and Norman A. Graebner, ed., *Ideas and Diplomacy* (1964).

There has been also recently published (after the completion of the present book) a volume dealing specifically with the latter half of the nineteenth century which heavily emphasizes economic causation: Walter LaFeber, *The New Empire: An Interpretation of American Expansion, 1860–1898* (1963).

The diplomacy of the Civil War is recorded from different approaches by three historians: Ephraim D. Adams, *Great Britain and the Civil War* (2 vols., 1925); Jay Monaghan, *Diplomat in Carpet Slippers: Abraham Lincoln Deals with Foreign Affairs* (1945), and Frank Owsley, *King Cotton Diplomacy, Foreign Relations of the Confederate States* (rev. ed., 1959). No one of these books really treats the topic as a whole or is completely satisfactory. A very perceptive and more general article is Norman A. Graebner's, "Northern Diplomacy and European Neutrality" in David Donald, ed., *Why the North Won the Civil War* (1960).

For the more immediate post-Civil War years there is as yet no adequate study of William H. Seward's foreign policies, but those of his successor are very well covered in Allan Nevins, *Hamilton Fish* (2 vols., rev. ed., 1957), and general developments in succeeding years are treated in Alice F. Tyler, *The Foreign Policy of James G. Blaine* (1927) and Charles C. Tansill, *The Foreign Policy of Thomas F. Bayard, 1885–1897* (1940). A new and interesting attempt to give a greater significance to foreign policies under Presidents Garfield and Arthur is David M. Pletcher, *The Awkward Years* (1963), while a recent article suggesting the continuity of expansionism over the entire period is Milton Plesur, "Rumblings Beneath the Surface—America's Outward Thrust, 1865–1890" in H. Wayne Morgan, ed., *The Gilded Age* (1963).

The dramatic story of Maximilian in Mexico is best told in H. Montgomery Hyde, *Mexican Empire* (1946), and the most satisfactory account of American policy is Dexter Perkins, *The Monroe Doctrine, 1826–1867* (1933). For the further development of the Monroe Doctrine see also the latter author's *The Monroe Doctrine, 1867–1907* (1937), or in briefer compass his excellent one-volume study, *A History of the Monroe Doctrine* (rev. ed., 1963). A good account of the canal question is Gerstle Mack, *The Land Divided: A History of the Panama Canal and Other Isthmian Canal Projects* (1944). A more general treatment of these various topics is found in Samuel F. Bemis, *The Latin American Policy of the United States* (1943).

Among books dealing with American relations with Canada and Great Britain are Robin Winks, *Canada and the United States: The Civil War Years* (1960), John B. Brebner, *North Atlantic Triangle: The Interplay of Canada, the United States and Great Britain* (1945); Charles C. Tansill, *Canadian-American Relations, 1875–1911* (1943), and for the later Anglo-American *rapprochement*, Lionel M. Gelber, *The Rise of Anglo-American Friendship* (1938).

The most useful over-all account of American policy in the Far East remains Tyler Dennett, *Americans in Eastern Asia* (1922). It may be supplemented by material dealing with the years 1860 to 1900 found in Foster Rhea Dulles, *China and America, The Story of Their Relations Since 1784* (1946); Payson J. Treat, *Diplomatic Relations Between the United States and Japan, 1853–1905* (3 vols., 1922–1928); and, more recent and very brief, William L. Neumann's *America Encounters Japan: From Perry to MacArthur* (1963). For Korea there is Fred H. Harrington, *God, Mammon and the Japanese: Dr. Horace N. Allen and Korean-American Relations, 1884–1905* (1944). On immigration see Mary R. Coolidge, *Chinese Immigration* (1909).

For the thrust into the Pacific, the Hawaiian story is related in Sylvester K. Stevens, *American Expansion in Hawaii, 1842–1898* (1945) and with even more detail in two books by William A. Russ, Jr.—*The Hawaiian Revolution, 1893–1894* (1959) and *The Hawaiian Republic and Its Struggle to Win Annexation* (1961). On Samoa there is most importantly George H. Ryden, *The Foreign Policy of the United States in Relation to Samoa* (1933).

Naval developments are treated in William E. Livezley, *Mahan on Sea Power* (1947) and Harold and Margaret Sprout, *The Rise of American Naval Power: 1776–1918* (1946).

The period embracing the outbreak of the war with Spain and subsequent overseas expansion is both more fully and more interestingly covered than the years before 1890. Three rather general books are Julius W. Pratt, *Expansionists of 1898* (1936); Foster Rhea Dulles, *The Imperial Years* (1956), and Ernest R. May, *Imperial Democracy: The Emergence of America as a Great Power* (1961). The latter book is based on a wide investigation of European as well as American source materials. Provocative articles presenting somewhat different approaches to the controversial aspects of this period, as suggested by their titles, are Thomas A. Bailey, "America's Emergence as a World Power: The Myth and the Verity," *Pacific Historical Review*, XXX (1961), 1–16; Thomas McCormick, "Insular Imperialism and the Open Door: The China Market and the Spanish-American War," *Pacific Historical Review*, XXXII (1963), 155–169; and

Richard Hofstadter, "Manifest Destiny and the Philippines" in Daniel Aaron, ed., *America in Crisis* (1952).

The part that President Cleveland played in stimulating the nationalist spirit prior to the events of 1898 is discussed in Allan Nevins, *Grover Cleveland* (1933) and more particularly in three more specialized articles: Nelson M. Blake, "Background of Cleveland's Venezuela Policy," *American Historical Review*, XLVII (1942); Walter LaFeber, "The Background of Cleveland's Venezuela Policy: A Reinterpretation," *American Historical Review*, LXVI (1961); and Joseph J. Mathews, "Informal Diplomacy in the Venezuela Crisis," *Mississippi Valley Historical Review*, L (1963).

There is very interesting material dealing with President McKinley's role during the events of 1897–1900 in Margaret Leech, *In the Days of McKinley* (1959), and also in the more recent and well-researched study by H. Wayne Morgan, *William McKinley and His America* (1963).

No entirely satisfactory account of the war with Spain itself is available. The most readable, with its rather satirical approach, is Walter Millis, *The Martial Spirit* (1931), while Frank Friedel's *Splendid Little War* (1958) is most notable for its illustrations. Another recent volume is David F. Healy, *The United States in Cuba, 1898–1902* (1963).

On the origins of the Open Door policy the best accounts are found in A. Whitney Griswold, *The Far Eastern Policy of the United States* (1938); Tyler Dennett, *John Hay* (1933); Paul A. Varg, *Open Door Diplomat: The Life of W. W. Rockhill* (1952), and Charles S. Campbell, Jr., *Special Business Interests and the Open Door Policy* (1951).

Among other books apart from those already cited which help to portray the scene at the turn of the century are Charles S. Campbell, Jr., *Anglo-American Understanding, 1898–1903* (1957); Allan Nevins, *Henry White: Thirty Years of Diplomacy* (1930); Julius W. Pratt, *America's Colonial Experiment* (1950); Calvin D. Davis, *The United States and the First Hague Conference* (1962), and, provocatively pointing toward the twentieth century, George F. Kennan, *American Diplomacy, 1900–1950* (1951) and Robert E. Osgood, *Ideals and Self-Interest in America's Foreign Relations* (1953).

Index

Adams, Brooks, 159

Adams, Charles Francis, as ambassador, 4–5 6, 8, 11, 19–22; at Geneva Tribunal, 66

Adams, Henry, 10, 18, 22, 159, 218

Aguinaldo, General Emilio, 191

Alabama, 20–22, 63, 65; *see also Alabama* claims

Alabama claims, 62–7, 74

Alaska, 45, 59, 72; negotiations for purchase, 48–57

Albert, Prince, of England, 10

Allen, Dr. Horace N., 87

Angell, James B., 82

Antietam, battle of, 16, 18

Anti-imperialism, 195–7, 201–2

Anti-Imperialist League, 195

Apia (Samoa), 105–6

Appleton, John, 48

Arthur, Chester A., 41, 82–3, 125

Babcock, General Orville E., 57–8

Banks, Nathaniel P., 56

Bayard, Thomas F., as senator, 59;

Bayard, Thomas F. (*cont.*)
Secretary of State, 68, 69, 103, 109; ambassador, 139

Bazaine, Marshall, 28, 34

Belknap, Admiral George E., 117

Bemis, Samuel F., *quoted*, 72

Beresford, Lord Charles, 209

Berlin General Act (Samoa), 106–7; (Congo), 123

Beveridge, Albert, 160, 222; on imperialism, 183, 189, 198, 201–2, 204; relations with Great Britain, 224

Bigelow, John, 32, 34

Bismarck, Chancellor, 103, 105

Blaine, James G., on canal issue, 38–9; Latin American policy, 40–43, 122–3, 137; sealing dispute, 72—3; Korea, 86; Chilean affair, 128, 130–31

Blockade, in Civil War, 7, 12, 13, 19

Blount, James H., 114–15

Boer War, 144, 224–5

Bolivia, 40